Ef·
Pricing for
Accountants

A practical guide to pricing your accountancy services for maximum profit

Mark Wickersham

Special thanks to Steve Pipe

Copyright © 2011 Mark Wickersham

ISBN: 978-0-9551007-1-0

Cover design and page layout by Steven Levers, Sheffield

Printed in Great Britain by Berforts Information Press Ltd.

4P Marketing – *proven, practical, professional and painless marketing solutions for accountants*
www.4p-marketing.co.uk

Contents

About Steve Pipe

Steve is my inspiration, my mentor and friend. I first met Steve in November 1998 when I was running my own Accountancy Practice. And, as so many other accountants have found since, Steve completely changed my life. He helped me to think about running an accountancy practice in a completely different way... his passion for this great profession gave me the hunger to learn about business, about best practice and about the skills necessary to truly make a difference to the clients accountants work with.

For over 10 years we have worked together to help make a difference to the accountancy profession. Throughout those years it has been an honour to work with Steve; I have learned so much and continue to be inspired by his thinking.

Over the years Steve and I have created thousands of resources for accountants. Over those years we have learned from each other and worked together on ideas and resources. This book borrows from some of those resources, many of which were written by Steve. So this book would not have been possible without the massive input from my friend, Steve.

Other people to thank

Susan Clegg: Susan is a gifted writer who co-authored the 2005 book "Everlasting Phone Impressions" with Paul Shrimpling. She regularly writes newsletters and articles for the accountancy profession and has been simply brilliant in proof reading this book.

Tom Holdsworth: Tom is a recent graduate in English who joined the AVN team in late 2010. And in the short space of time that Tom has been part of our great team he has proved that he has a gift for writing. Tom has a great career ahead of him (hopefully as part of the AVN team) and, like Susan, has been a huge help in proof reading this book.

The AVN Team: AVN has a wonderful team of people who are passionate about making a difference to the accountancy profession. At the time of writing this team consists of; Andy Bond, Andy Wells, Claire Glossop, David Williams, Debra Lowndes, Elaine Horrey, Emma Slack,

Ian Patterson, James Miller, Jane Donoghue, Jean Bray, Jenny Lukas, Joanne Law, Jonathan Holroyd, Julie Twigg, Kate Wickersham, Laura Newby, Luke Jackson, Lynsey Ayling, Michael Pipe, Paul Herrett, Paul Bradley, Paul Flynn, Philippa Jennings, Rachel Clark, Ryan Sample, Sarah Cross, Shane Lukas, Steve Pipe, Steven Baldwin, Stuart Finlayson, Sue Davenport, Susan Clegg, Suzy Gunning, Tom Holdsworth, Tom Scott, Tracy Bettley, Trevor Hinds and Vicky Martin.

Ron Baker: Back in 1999 I came across "Value Pricing" by Ron Baker. This book had a massive impact on the way I thought about pricing. Shortly afterwards Ron was the keynote speaker at an AVN conference. Ron's thinking made me realise that accountants in general know very little about pricing, and yet the opportunities from getting it right are un-limited. It was Ron's first book that inspired me to help the UK accounting profession make better pricing decisions. And it was Ron's first book that was the inspiration for creating "Time's Up", the UK's first and leading software for helping accountants price compliance services.

Foreword

The quickest way
to improve your profits

The easiest way to make more money is simple… get the price right.

It's also the fastest way of transforming your profits. If you put your prices up by 10% the impact is immediate.

As you'll see when you read this book, the evidence is clear:

- The market does not set prices; firms do.
- In other words, prices are a choice made by practitioners.
- Some firms are much better at making pricing choices than others.
- The way firms make those pricing choices has a fundamental impact on their profitability and success.
- By studying how the most successful firms price other practices can transform their results.

Time and time again we see firms that fully understand value pricing (and that doesn't mean simply giving a fixed price in advance of doing the work) get superior results.

There are many great books on pricing theory. What I wanted to do in this book is focus on making everything relevant to accountants and as practical as possible. I wanted to make it as easy as possible for you to take the ideas and do something with them.

I hope you enjoy reading this book, and most importantly I hope you take some action. And when you get great results please, please tell me all about your successes. You never know, you might appear in the next edition of this book.

Mark Wickersham FCA
The UK's leading thinker on pricing for the accountancy profession
www.4P-marketing.co.uk

P.S. Although there are some amazing real-life stories contained within this book, my personal favourite is the one in chapter 14. This is a must read.

Preface

A horrible mistake

I started my accountancy practice on 31 May 1996 at the age of 29.

I thought I knew everything.

That was my first big mistake in business... you can never know every-thing. Learning is a continual process and if we want to get better results, we need to keep learning to find a better way. Steve Pipe opened my eyes to this in 1998.

I qualified as a Chartered Accountant in 1991 and worked for three dif-ferent accountancy practices before setting up my own practices. It was a big leap of faith to leave full time employment and start a practice from scratch. And this may not have happened if – two weeks earlier – I hadn't travelled to London one Saturday to hear Chris Frederiksen's "How to set up your own CA practice." This seminar gave me the confidence and suf-ficient knowledge to realise that it was possible to build an accountancy practice from scratch.

Over the next 2½ years I built my practice to just over £200,000 of recur-ring fees with about 200 clients and somewhere around that time had a team of 13 people. The practice grew very quickly, largely from sending out mailshots and following them up using telesales.

From a growth point of view it appeared successful. Unfortunately I never made a profit in that first 2½ years and cash flow was a constant battle. Quite simply I was over-trading... I was growing far too quickly (had moved office premises twice in those early years), my fixed costs were spiraling out of control and my bank debt was getting unsustainable.

Fortunately, in November 1998, I met Steve Pipe at his 3-day Masterclass in Exeter (this was Steve's third Masterclass – AVN having started two months earlier in September).

Steve helped me realise that I actually knew very, very little about running an accountancy practice. And that many of the things I had learned on more conventional 'practice development' courses were actually wrong. In the couple of years following that Masterclass, my practice and my life changed considerably. I focused on getting the right clients and the right team and ended up generating the same level of fees with considerably less clients and considerably less people, started to make money and clear the bank debt. A few years later I sold the practice to the client managers through a management buyout.

I made lots of mistakes in those early years... too many to list here. However, there were two mistakes that nearly crippled my practice:

1. *Hiring the wrong people* – I now realise that I knew absolutely nothing about how to find, interview, recruit, motivate and keep great people. I made the mistake that many small practices make of trying to keep costs down... I didn't use recruitment agencies so that I could save their costs and this meant I never had a very big pool of candidates to choose from (I often recruited someone because they were the only option!). I recruited lots of school leavers and graduates and trained them up because they were cheap. But I realised that they needed so much hand-holding that I wasn't getting much work done myself. Most of them were never going to make good accountants, and the few that showed potential left as soon as someone was prepared to pay them more. Hiring the wrong people cost me a fortune. Today – at AVN – we use a completely different process to recruit great people, and I'm proud to say that we have one of the very best (if not the best) team of people that any business could wish for. A team of passionate and enthusiastic people – every one of whom is making a real difference to the lives of so many UK accountants. And this comes from a unique recruitment process we have developed over the last 5 or 6 years (if you want to know how that works I would be delighted to tell you sometime).

2. *Getting the pricing horribly wrong.* This was my number one mistake and it cost me many, many thousands of pounds in lost profit.

When I started my practice I was very focused on growing my 'gross recurring fees' as quickly as possible, rather than on profitability. This error is common amongst accountants I talk to, and probably stems from the fact that traditionally accountancy practices are valued based upon a multiple of fees (a formula that I predict will change in the not-too-distant future). And so as accountants in practice we become obsessed by building capital value at the expense of building a profitable practice... we look to get as many clients as possible, even when many of those clients are the wrong type of clients and working with them drains our energy.

My ill-thought through strategy at the outset was – when seeing a prospect for the first time – to find out what they were currently paying their existing accountant. This often involved some feeble excuse for needing to see a copy of their last set of accounts... the first thing I would look for is the line in the profit and loss that said "accountant's fees." Of course, some clients were wise to this, so gave me a doctored set of accounts where they had applied Tippex to that number. Being a typical accountant I would then pull out my calculator and pretend to do some tax planning calculations, when really I was taking fixed costs and deducting all the itemised amounts, knowing that "accountant's fees" would be the balancing figure.

Having found this number I would prepare a fee quote with my proposal magically coming in at about 10% less than the current accountant. In those early days I used to kid myself that my ability to win new clients was outstanding... after all, I was signing up at least half of all prospects that I saw. In reality – and in hindsight – I was being incredibly stupid. I was positioning myself (without really realising it) as a *cheap* accountant.

It was little surprise that I wasn't making much money.

In fact what has become apparent to me over the years is that the vast majority of accountants know incredibly little about pricing strategy, pricing psychology, pricing tactics and pricing best practice. Most accountants charge prices that are far too cheap and do not reflect the value they give to their clients or the years of training, learning and experience we have undergone. So given that most accountants don't know how to price and price too low, why on earth would anybody have a pricing strategy based upon what the previous accountant charged? And yet that's exactly what I did. And that's what most accountants do... we base our fees on what our competitors are charging. It's mad.

I learned many things from the pricing mistakes I made. For example...

I often advised unincorporated clients and prospects to transfer their sole trader business or partnership into a limited company where they would save many thousands of pounds in tax. After I went through my internal script for explaining the advantages and disadvantages of incorporating and the tax benefits, they would always ask "How much will it cost?"

That was easy to answer. You see, I spent my first 6 years in the profession working at (and qualified at) the largest independent firm in Sheffield. A firm in Sheffield that many other practices in the area aspired to be like. And I knew that they typically charged £300 for forming a limited company.

So with my wonderful strategy of basing price on the competition, and even worse, going in cheaper, I always responded to the "How much will it cost?" questions with, "Between £200 and £250."

What staggered me is how often (and certainly over half the time) the response I would hear was "Ouch! That's a bit expensive." I'd heard that people from Yorkshire were said to be tight, but surely they appreciated all the work that incorporating a business entailed. Surely they knew that the price I was quoting was a good price. How an earth can they say, "That's a bit expensive." It made me really angry. Until some years later I realised that the fault was all mine. I knew absolutely nothing about pricing strategy. I hadn't learned any pricing tactics. I didn't know pricing psychology existed. I hadn't considered the importance of having pricing systems and tools. I just assumed I knew how to run a successful accountancy practice.

Here is just one of the many things I learned from the mistakes I made...

Never ever quote a vague range of prices. When I used to answer the "How much will it cost?" question with, "Between £200 and £250" I left the meeting thinking the client would be happy with a bill for £250. The client left the meeting thinking the bill would be £200. And so more often than not, it would end in a fee dispute, ill-will created with the client and sometimes a bad debt that needed writing off. When you give your clients a price, tell them exactly what it will cost at the outset… giving a vague range of prices is simply the wimp's way of pricing. This is what people do when they are not confident about their ability, not confident about the value they offer to their clients, and would rather avoid any conflict (i.e. the process of agreeing a fee) than make a profit on a piece of work.

Throughout this book I will explain everything I have learned over the last 10 years. And everything I talk about works. It worked for me whilst I was in practice. And it's worked for dozens and dozens of firms I have had the pleasure to work with over the last 10 years (some of whom have kindly allowed me to include their success stories within this book).

The strategies, tactics, psychology, systems and more that I cover are extremely powerful. For example, once I realised what I was doing wrong with my proposals for incorporation work I put in place some systems. Overnight my pricing increased more than threefold. And because I had a system for answering the questions, "How much will it cost?" – a system that demonstrated the value – no one ever said "That's a bit expensive" again… even though I was charging over three times the fee (and you'll read case studies in this book where firms using these same ideas are charging in the region of **fifty times** what they and I used to charge for this sort of work).

Chapter 1
Your Pricing Strategy

"Prices are the single most important element in your profit equation. Get them right and you make a profit. Get them wrong and you make a loss."

(Pipe and Wilson, 2010)

It's as simple as that.

So the trick – of course – is to make sure you get them right rather than wrong.

Clients care about prices. But they are certainly not the only thing they care about - and your entire business and marketing strategy should reflect that fact.

In other words, you should never compete on price alone. Instead you should start by making sure that what you are offering exactly meets the needs of your ideal clients. And then you should make sure that you compete on the basis of giving those clients "maximum value" rather than the "lowest price".

Later on we'll look at what is meant by "maximum value".

In 2008 AVN carried out a benchmarking survey of 209 UK accounting firms. Some of the results of this survey appeared in the July 2008 edition of Accountancy Magazine in an article written by Steve Pipe. The survey showed that firms in the bottom quartile were generating less than £52,000 in profit per partner, i.e. the bottom 25% of firms were making less than this (and some were making losses). By way of contrast, the top quartile firms were making from £110,000 in profit per partner (and the very top performing firms were achieving more than £300,000).

That is a vast difference in performance.

That same survey identified a huge difference in pricing strategy between the top performing firms and the worst performing firms.

More recently, in September 2010 I co-authored the Tax Club's Research Report called, "Your blueprint for a better tax practice." The Research Report looks into best practice across 180 UK accounting firms and demonstrates a huge gulf in the way firms think about pricing and their pricing strategy. I have included some extracts from this Research Report within this book.

The amounts of money at stake are simply too huge to ignore the lessons we can learn from these top performing firms.

But before we look at your strategic options let's look at some more numbers.

What-if analysis

In AVN's 2008 benchmarking survey of 209 independent practices referred to above it showed that the average UK firm of accountants has fees per partner of £247,008 and an average profit per partner of £78,000.

Think about this for a minute… if you are an average firm and you increase your prices by 20%, then assuming that you do not lose any clients and that your salary costs are fixed in the short term*, your profits will increase to £127,402 per partner. Based upon the 2008 AVN survey that would move your practice from being an average firm to firmly inside the top quartile.

So increasing your pricing can be the quickest way to transform your results.

Of course you may lose some clients by doing this. So let's factor that in. Let's assume that you lose 10% of your clients by doing this. If that happens your profit per partner will still increase to £97,761.

And that's only one of the benefits. Which clients do you think you will lose? Will you lose your best clients that really value what you do? Or will you lose those clients that only want the cheapest possible accountant, that continually complain and are slowest to pay your bills?

* Although it is possible to hire more people (or to make people redundant) in the very short term your salary costs are fixed. And so for most accountancy firms variable or direct costs are negligible. Of course it may be that you outsource work and therefore have a more significant variable/direct cost. If this is the case, then the negative impact of losing clients from increasing prices is lessened because, with less clients, you will reduce your direct costs.

Suggested action: Have a look at the numbers for your practice. Investigate the impact of changing prices globally and the impact of losing clients.

Your strategic options

You really only have two strategic choices.

CHOICE 1: to pursue a strategy often referred to as "low-cost leadership". This is a strategy where you make a conscious choice to be cheap and undercut the competition. However, it is very, very rare for this to be a sensible choice. To do this you must have something unique in your cost structure that means that you have lower costs preventing your competition copying your strategy. A UK business that pulls this off spectacularly well is Richer Sounds. But it is arguably very difficult for an accountancy practice to do this.

CHOICE 2: to have a highly differentiated service that adds value, so that you can charge a premium price.

Everything else is – at best – going to make you average. And looking at the state of the UK accountancy profession, average is not a nice place to be.

A word of warning… if you are a solo practitioner currently working from home with no employees it is tempting to conclude that you have a low-cost advantage and can therefore price cheaply. That is not a sustainable strategy for this reason; if you price cheaply and grow your practice, sooner or later you will need premises and some help, and this new fixed cost will kill your profits. Trust me… I once did exactly that and paid a heavy price.

In all the research I have carried out, the top performing firms of accountants all pursue option 2, i.e. focusing on being different, adding value and charging premium prices.

But my clients only choose me on price

If your clients choose you on price, it's because you haven't given them any other reason to choose you. You haven't made your products or services sufficiently different or better. So clients see you as the same as the other practices, with the only thing that differs being the price – so they'll choose the cheapest price. And that's your fault! Because you haven't given them any reason to do anything other than choose the cheapest.

What's more, if clients CHOOSE you on price, then they'll probably also LEAVE you on price. In other words, if they choose you solely because you are the cheapest, then as soon as another accountancy firm offering an even cheaper price comes along you'll lose them as clients.

So there's a double whammy from competing on price. You make lower margins. And you have less client loyalty. So the lifetime value of your clients is lower too.

So what strategic decision are you going to make?

2

Chapter 2
Your "Magic Price"

"You will never get paid more than you think you are worth"

Paul Dunn and Ron Baker

To illustrate the concept of your "Magic Price" let's start with a few questions.

How much profit would you make by giving your products or services away for free? Well, your sales would be zero – and you wouldn't make a profit, would you?

How much profit would you make if you sold your product or services at, say, 1000 times their current price? Well, the chances are that nobody would buy them. So again your sales would be zero – and again you wouldn't make a profit.

So at those two extremes – a ridiculously low price and a ridiculously high price – you don't make profits. But at some of the prices in between those two extremes you will make a profit. And at ONE price somewhere on that spectrum – let's call it the MAGIC PRICE – you'll make the most profits.

It's that magic price that you are looking for – the magic price that will earn you the most profits.

So, here's the really important question for you… is the price you currently charge exactly that magic price?

And if your answer is "Yes", how do you know that you are charging the magic price? How can you be sure, absolutely sure? What proof do you have? How strong and how up to date is your evidence? How many other prices have you tested? What is the precise impact on your short term and long term sales, and on your short term and long term profits, of your current price and all the other possible prices?

So what we are going to look at together now is how to FIND your magic price and how to increase the profits you make when you start USING that magic price.

Let's start with how to find your magic price.

Well, in one sense it's really easy. For every possible price, work out the quantity you will sell at that price. This will give you what economists call your "demand curve"; and it will look something like this:

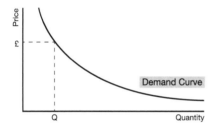

You have a demand curve for every product or service that you sell. The next step for every possible price is to multiply it by the demand to calculate your sales, deduct the variable costs associated with those sales and deduct your fixed costs. This gives you a profit for each price point.

The resulting graph will look something like this:

Finally, simply pick the price that gives you the highest profit.

Simple? In theory, yes, but not in practice. Once you know how many you are going to sell at each price, calculating your sales costs and profits should be fairly straightforward arithmetic.

But the big problem, of course, is in estimating how many units of a particular product or service you can sell at each price.

Most text books on pricing will cover up to four ways to come up with such an estimate. The first three are:

- Expert judgment
- Historical market data, and
- Customer surveys

Unfortunately they all have major weaknesses. There is probably nobody "expert" enough to give you reliable estimates – so usually it just ends up being guesswork. The historical market data you would need probably doesn't exist – and if it does it is probably out of date or relates to the prices of other companies' products, and isn't absolutely accurate (or perhaps even indeed relevant) for your situation today. And customer surveys sound like a good idea – but all too often your clients will say one thing in surveys and do something entirely different when it comes to actually parting with their hard earned cash.

You may have to rely on those three methods to some extent. But wherever possible you should try to include at least some TESTING in your estimation process. After all, the only thing that really counts is not what experts think, or what happened in the past, or even what your clients say they will do. The only thing that matters is what happens when clients are asked to part with money. The only thing that actually matters is how much they actually spend at different prices.

So you need to find ways of testing different prices.

But don't "bet your business" by doing anything reckless or irreversible. Be creative. And find ways to test different prices safely.

But however you decide to test, always remember the two golden rules of testing.

- Only change one thing at a time – since if you change more than one thing, for example the price and the packaging, you won't know whether it is the price change or the packaging change that causes clients to change how many they buy, will you?
- Always measure the results before and after the change very carefully indeed.

So changing your current price to something closer to your magic price is a great thing to do... and it's the easiest way to increase your profits… since nothing else needs to change in your business. You get more profits without changing your product, service, marketing, packaging or overheads. Everything stays exactly the same… except your prices and profits.

This is where pricing systems really help. When you have pricing systems in place within your practice it becomes much, much easier to test. In later chapters, we'll look at some of those pricing systems, such as "menu pricing" systems.

However, here is an idea to consider:

Consider increasing your fees by 20% for one month. For all clients who have a year end at the end of this month write to them all and tell them how much their fees will be for preparing their accounts this year. Quote a fee that is 20% more than the previous year.

At the end of the month see how many of those clients agree to the fee and how many choose to leave for a cheaper accountant. Then measure the results, i.e. calculate the turnover you will generate from those clients and compare that with what it would have been had you not changed the price and assuming all those clients would have stayed. Then look at the implications on your cost base and from those, estimate what your profit would have been had you left the changes unchanged against the actual profit.

If the profit increases, then repeat it in month 2. If after 3 months you are making more money, then from month 4 test the same process with a 25%

increase in fees. And even if the profit doesn't change you will be making the same amount of money but with less clients, i.e. with less effort.

By testing it one month at a time you are not "betting the business"... you are only testing it with $1/12^{th}$ of your client base. In other words, the absolute worst that can happen – and this almost certainly won't happen – is you lose approximately $1/12^{th}$ of your clients.

Note:

Before you implement this idea, I recommend you read the rest of this book first. There are lots of other things you can do (for example, the way you create those fixed fee proposal letters) that will help the client to see the value and be less sensitive to the price.

Finally, if you think you are stuck with low prices and low profits, don't complain about it... do something about it. You make those choices. The choices you made in the past have determined the profits you are making today. And the choices you make today will determine the profits you make in the future.

3

Chapter 3 - Time's up...
an end to time-based billing?

"The value of anything in this world is solely determined by the person who pays for it."

Austrian School of Economists

Ten years ago when I first started helping accountants with their pricing over 90% of accountants used time sheets as the basis for billing.

In those 10 years I have seen a sea-change in attitudes. In fact a survey carried out by the Tax Club in 2010 (more on that later) shows that for tax compliance work 15.2% of the 180 firms surveyed use time-based billing, 55.6% use fixed fees and 29.2% use value pricing. Arguably the 180 firms surveyed are not representative of the profession as a whole because almost all of those 180 firms are either AVN members or Tax Club members, and therefore think differently and get better results. Nevertheless, it shows clearly that attitudes are changing within the profession.

So where did time-based billing come from?

Well, I think you'll be surprised by the answer... because a large part of it seems to come from the father of COMMUNISM, Karl Marx.

You see, it was Karl Marx, in his labour theory of value, who first said that the value of a commodity (i.e. a product or service) is solely determined by the labour inputs that go into it. But if Marx was right, then a rock dug out of a mine next to a diamond would have the same value as the diamond because it takes just as many man hours to dig out the rock as it did to take out the diamond… and yet you don't see many rocks in a jewellery store, do you? And if Marx was right, a junior footballer would be paid the same salary as his club's top-scoring star player - because they are both on the pitch for the same length of time, 90 minutes.

But clearly that's not the way the world works.

It's not the time spent, or any other element of its cost that determines the price… it's the value to the client that determines the price. This is why a beautiful diamond is more expensive than an ugly lump of rock, and why a top scoring footballer earns much more than a junior player.

Under cost plus pricing you start with how much your product costs – in other words, the direct cost of the materials and the labour time involved, PLUS some allowance for your fixed costs or overheads. And then you add a mark up to reflect your target profits… as if there was something magical or God given about those target profits. And, hey presto, you have a price calculated without ever having to worry about what your clients think, without ever having to worry about what your stuff is worth to your clients, or without ever having to worry about what anyone else is charging.

It is expressed as:

Price = Cost + Mark-up

In the accounting profession where '*time is being sold*' this formula is better expressed as:

Price = Hourly rate x Hours

where "Hourly rate" is expressed as:

Hourly rate = Overhead + Desired Net Income
Expected hours

This is a cost-plus formula. Desired net income is the mark up, so hourly rate multiplied by hours is our way of calculating our costs inclusive of our mark up.

You may have spotted that I used the phrase *where time is being sold*. You see many accountants believe that is what they are selling... and so they see time-based billing as an acceptable way of pricing. But that is completely wrong.

Accountants are NOT SELLING TIME.

Just ask your clients what they are buying from you. Your clients will tell you lots of things, such as, "I am buying tax savings", "I am buying peace of mind knowing that my returns are correctly filed", "I am buying solutions to my financial problems". They won't say, "I am buying your time."

Clients do not buy time, they are buying a result. They are buying value.

Despite the fact that pricing experts in the last century concluded that the labour theory of value has no validity – and many industries moved away from cost-plus pricing – the accounting and legal professions have clung onto it.

And this is probably out of habit and a lack of understanding. Time sheets are common in the profession and arguably are an adequate measurement system and means of cost control, but mistakenly are also used for pricing decisions.

This practice of so-called "time-based billing" turns pricing from a marketing activity to an administrative task of simply adding up hours and multiplying them by an hourly rate. And it can have disastrous results... as you will see later.

But wherever it is used, in essence Cost Plus pricing calculates prices in SPLENDID ISOLATION by looking inwards and focusing entirely on your internal costs and your internal profit mark-up. And it effectively assumes that nothing else – including clients and competitors – actually matter.

And when described like that, COST PLUS pricing sounds bizarre, perhaps even stupid, doesn't it? And there's a very good reason for that.

It IS bizarre! And it is often also pretty stupid!

Now I say that because the very first lesson that basic economics teaches us is that prices should be set according to supply and demand. But

Cost Plus pricing completely ignores the demand side of the equation – because it completely ignores what clients want and what they are willing to pay.

In Ron Baker's book, "Value Pricing for Professionals" he lists 13 disadvantages of time-based billing. Here are some of them:

- Clients don't feel that cost plus pricing is fair – because it gives you no incentive to be efficient - and can even reward you for being slow or inefficient.
- It focuses you on time and costs - rather than on delivering benefits, results and value to your clients – and so, by encouraging you to take your eye off the ball, gives your competitors an opportunity to meet your clients' needs more fully.
- It puts all the risk on the client – since they have to foot the bill for overruns, inefficiencies, cost increases, mistakes and the time it takes you to learn how to do something new – and the more risk clients have to take, the less keen they are to buy from you.
- Cost plus pricing also discourages technological and productivity advances – since there is little incentive to find ways of cutting costs if they merely lead to lower prices with no change in profits.
- It can also makes you lazy about exploring and testing new ways of pricing – since the way you currently set prices seems so easy that you might not be inclined to change it.
- And often it prevents you from giving clients what they really want - fixed prices up front – because until you know how long a job takes and what your other costs actually are, you have no idea what the cost plus price should be.

Ultimately you will get less new business compared with firms that adopt a better approach.

Let me illustrate this...

At a recent seminar I described the following situation.

Imagine you need a solicitor to help you solve a problem with a supplier that has caused you a loss of £20,000. After asking around you identify 3 firms of solicitors that may be able to help.

You visit the first one which is the biggest and longest established firm in your region; they have been around for 100 years. When you describe your problem they tell you that they specialise in this type of work, and whilst they can't promise you that they will get you a successful award for damages they demonstrate a good track record. When it comes to the subject of price they tell you that they will charge you £200 per hour for partner time and £100 for associate time. They are unable to give you an accurate idea of the total cost because at the outset it is impossible to know how long it will take. For example, it may or may not go to court. However, they reassure you by telling you they will invoice you on a monthly basis for all time spent and on their invoice they will itemise exactly what they have done.

You thank them for their time and visit the second firm.

This firm has been around for 20 years and is an average sized firm of lawyers for your region. Once again, they tell you that they have a great track record with this sort of work and think they **might** be able to help you receive damages of £20,000. When it turns to the question of price they tell you that they normally charge out £200 for partner time and £100 for associate time, but to make it easier for you to budget they provide you with a fixed price of £4,000.

Finally, you visit the third firm. This is a smaller firm that was set up just 5 years ago. Once again they demonstrate that they have a great track record with this type of work. And when the subject turns to price they say, "It's impossible to say how long this work will take us and it's impossible to tell you whether or not we will be successful in achieving a successful claim. However, we appreciate that you do not want surprise bills and we also appreciate that if we are unsuccessful you will not want to pay a big bill. So what we can offer you is a fixed price of £6,000 in the event that we are successful. And if we are unsuccessful we will not charge you a single penny."

Which of these 3 firms of lawyers would you appoint?

When I asked this question in the seminar not a single delegate in the room chose the firm that offered a time-based billing approach. Some of the delegates chose firm two, and the vast majority chose the third firm.

The reason why nobody chose the first firm is because **clients hate time-based billing**. They want to know what the costs are going to be *in advance*.

Firm number two used a technique called "Fixed Pricing". This is something rapidly gathering momentum within the accounting profession.

And that's a good thing. Because in November 2005 Sage carried out a survey of over 2,000 business owners. One of the findings was this: Surprise fees top the list of frustrations for businesses. Again, more evidence that clients hate time-based billing.

Here's an interesting thing about Fixed Pricing... it takes the risk of cost-overruns away from the client's shoulders and places it on yours. Think about it for a moment; under time-based billing if you are slow, inefficient or make mistakes the job takes longer. If the job takes longer the client gets a bigger bill. So the risk of these cost-overruns resulting from you taking longer are borne by the client. In contrast, by giving a fixed price you now take all the risk if the job takes longer. Now at first glance this might be thought of as a bad thing for you. But actually, it's fairer on the client. It means you have to focus on being more efficient. And it's a fact that by removing the risk from the client they will pay a premium price. After all, that's why people take out insurance... they pay a premium to remove risk. So when you switch from time-based billing to fixed prices you can – and absolutely should – increase your prices to reflect the shift of risk from the client to you.

Of course it does mean that sometimes you will give a fixed price that results in a loss. But provided you do increase your prices, then as you get better at fixed prices more often than not you will set prices that result in additional margin. You will make extra profit much more often than the occasional losses.

Here's a popular misconception within the accountancy profession.

Fixed pricing is **not** the same thing as value pricing.

Whilst many firms of accountants are now implementing fixed prices, very few really understand value pricing.

Let's go back to the 3 lawyers.

And remember that most of the delegates in the survey would have chosen firm 3, not firm 2.

Firm 2 used Fixed Pricing. Think about the value to the client for a minute. If the firm is successful in getting an award for damages of £20,000 then the value to the client is the £20,000 in their bank account. However, if the firm fails in the claim then the client gets nothing. And so the value is nothing. And with a fixed price of £4,000 for doing the work the client is out of pocket. This is **not** value pricing because the price can be greater than the value.

On the other hand firm 3 recognises that they have not delivered any value if they do not succeed and so they promise not to charge a single penny. As a result the price is linked to the value; if the value is zero the price is zero; if the value is £20,000 the price is £6,000.

Of course, this brings in a further level of risk to you, i.e. the risk that if you do not add any value to the client you don't get paid. But isn't that how it should be? Our focus should **always** be on adding as much value to the client. And as you'll see from the case studies throughout this book, when you do this the rewards can be massive; far outweighing the losses you suffer from not being able to bill in those cases where you are unable to achieve a result for your client.

Remember that I said, "Cost Plus pricing calculates prices in SPLENDID ISOLATION by looking inwards and focusing entirely on your internal costs and your internal profit mark-up."

Value pricing, on the other hand, gets it right by considering both supply AND demand. It considers demand by starting with what clients are willing to pay. And it considers supply by hygiene checking costs to make sure that it is worth supplying (i.e. is sufficiently profitable) at the price that clients are willing to pay.

So value pricing gets it RIGHT, and cost plus pricing gets it WRONG.

Value pricing wins the theoretical argument – because it follows the one piece of advice that every single economist agrees on… prices should be set according to supply AND demand.

And value pricing also wins the common sense argument…

As I said earlier, clients are NOT buying time. They are buying a result. And so this means that as accountants we are not selling time. Instead we are really selling knowledge.

So when we help the client save £10,000 in tax from some planning that took two hours to do, the client is buying from you the result, i.e. your knowledge that helps them to save £10,000. And this is what we should base our price upon and not the two hours. The two hours spent is irrelevant to the client and from your perspective, if you bill based upon those hours then you are massively under-selling yourself.

This is because it took you much longer than two hours to get that result for your client. It took you years to obtain the knowledge to know how to achieve the result… all your past training, the time spent going on CPD courses, reading books, experience gained from helping other clients. All this has put you in a position to enable you to help your client save £10,000 in tax.

So the sensible way to set your prices is to use VALUE PRICING and to base your prices on what your clients are willing to pay… which will depend on how valuable what you do is to them and what their other options are. You should then of course check that those client driven prices are sufficiently greater than your costs to make sure that they give you an acceptable profit.

There are three keys to making that kind of value pricing a success and we will look at them after the next chapter.

But first, here is a case study from a firm that has only recently started the transition from time-based billing to fixed fees and value-based pricing…

Case study – Marcus & Co

Marcus & Co is a one-partner practice based in Birmingham, with 12 team members and around 420 clients. The Practice Manager, Paul Matthews, gave us the following account of how fixed fee pricing has improved their business:

"We have been working hard recently to move away from time sheet billing and to get all of our clients on to fixed fees for the compliance and tax returns. Although we are moving away from time sheet billing, we do still use this process on certain clients where we have problems, though the partner in question will decide depending on the circumstances. We do not have any plan in place to move completely away from it.

We have been seeing great improvements from this new system as clients seem to be receptive to fixed fee pricing. In terms of fees, we estimate that there has been around a 30% increase on average per client and very few clients have left us as a result of the pricing changes. Indeed the fixed fee pricing has, pro-rata, increased our turnover by around 30%.

Our system incorporates two areas. For compliance work we charge companies with up to £500,000 turnover a set fixed fee as we are aware of what the job entails. We therefore understand the nature of their business. For non-compliance work we tend to give a fee based on value. As a hypothetical example, a £60,000 saving as a result of tax work would generate a charge of around 10%.

We have introduced a fixed fee pricing system, which differentiates between businesses of differing sizes. To introduce clients to the new system we send out a letter with the various benefits of the fixed fee process and especially outline how it provides excellent value for money. We also stress the fact that the price change incorporates a number of other, extra services. This change has allowed us to charge more for those clients with poor records and provide a higher level of service for those who wish to pay us more for a higher level of service and attention. This has also meant that we have been able to concentrate more on services that add value to the client's business".

4

Chapter 4
Research findings: A shift away from time-based billing

In the summer of 2010 the Tax Club carried out a survey of 180 firms of accountants. Here are a couple of extracts from the research report.

Tax compliance services

In that survey it asked firms how they usually price their tax compliance services and it's interesting to see that over the last 10 years or so there has been a significant change in the profession away from time-based billing (only 15% of firms in the survey price their compliance services at the end of the service based on how much time is recorded on the time sheets).

However, although the majority of firms now give fixed prices up front, those fixed prices are based on how long they think the work will take, rather than based solely on value. This is still a positive shift away from time-recording for pricing purposes, but for many firms there remains a huge opportunity from moving towards a true value-pricing approach.

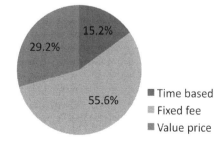

Figure 2 – How tax compliance work is priced

Tax planning services

The survey also asked firms how they usually price their tax planning services. What's really interesting here is that tax planning presents the perfect opportunity for value pricing, and yet many firms resort to traditional time-based billing.

In fact, as you can see from figure 4 below, more firms resort to time-based billing for planning services (36%) than for compliance work (15%).

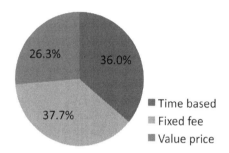

Figure 4 – How tax planning work is priced

This suggests that, faced with the uncertainties over planning work (i.e. how long the work will take and whether the planning will yield the desired results), many firms simply go back to the comfort of their time sheets.

And that is a very big missed opportunity.

One of the things we have seen at the Tax Club is case study after case study of firms using value pricing for their tax planning services and getting significantly better results.

So the evidence is clear; accountancy practices are waking up to the realisation that time-based billing is not an acceptable way to price. So let's now look in the next few chapters at how to price on value.

5

Chapter 5
The art of value pricing

*"Cost-plus pricing is not an acceptable method... as it ignores the central factor of the **client's perceived value**"*

Robert J Dolan and Hermann Simon

In this chapter we will look at two areas; firstly the value equation so that we can build up an understanding of how to add value, and secondly the 3 keys to value pricing.

The value equation

A thorough understanding of the value equation is essential for mastering the art of value pricing. The value equation is expressed as:

VALUE = PERCEIVED TANGIBLE BENEFITS
+ PERCEIVED EMOTIONAL ASSOCIATIONS – PERCEIVED PRICE

The key to charging higher prices is to increase the value to the client. And there are 6 elements of the equation that you can work on:

1. **Improve the tangible benefits** – this means improving the product or service so that it gives a better result for the client. These are often quantitative things and could include, *increasing* sales, profit, cash flow or efficiency, *reducing* costs, time or complaints, *improving* service, quality or skills, *creating* systems or products.

2. **Improve the perception of the benefits** – perceptions are critical. The way that you describe your offerings or the way you package them can give the impression that they are a better offering. For example, if you created a document that explained all of the checks and balances that you carry out when preparing a set of accounts (such as reconciling the bank, sales ledger control accounts, VAT reconciliations) it will help the client understand the care that you go to in ensuring that the accounts you produce are as accurate as possible. I have never come across a firm of accountants that has done this. The reality is that all accountants do this when preparing a set of accounts, but they don't tell their clients. The first firm that does explain with crystal clarity the process of preparing a set of accounts will give the perception that their product is better than the competition. So don't just focus on improving the benefits... look at what you already do and become better at educating your clients about what you do.

3. **Improve the emotional associations** – clients aren't only buying a product. They are also buying the feelings that go with that, sometimes referred to as the 'qualitative' value. For example, the speed of delivery can be really important to the client, the way the product is presented, and their perceptions of your knowledge and brand. Also the interactions you have with the client; we are in a people business and so you should ensure that the whole process of dealing with your practice is a great experience. This could include the way your clients are greeted in the reception area and the way you answer the telephone.

4. **Improve the perceptions of the emotional associations** – as with 2 above this simply means be better at explaining the things that you do to provide a better service. For example, tell your clients about how they can pick up the phone and talk with you whenever they want without it costing them a penny... that shows them you care.

5. **Reduce the price** – whilst reducing the price means that the value will increase, this is the only one of these 6 elements that I recommend you DO NOT do.

6. **Reduce the perception of price** – there are several tactics for making the price seem smaller. For example, rather than quoting the price for a year's work, why not express it as a monthly amount? Whilst the total amount the client will pay during the year remains the same, a monthly amount makes the annual cost appear less. Another tactic is to express the price after tax relief (assuming that your fees will be tax deductible).

The three keys

There are three key things you need to work on to master value pricing:

- Increase the value
- Explain the value so that your clients understand and appreciate the value
- Link your price to the value so that as your clients get more value from what you do, they gladly pay you a higher price

Increase the value

Although we have already explored this when we looked at the value equation here are a number of practical examples of how you can do this:

- Use colourful graphs, charts, ratios and commentary that show trends and ratios to make their accounts more useful and understandable.
- Carry out a diagnostic review and report to identify the key options for strengthening their cashflow and putting more money in their bank account.
- Provide a performance measurement and improvement system. Help your client summarise all the numbers that really matter on a Balanced Scorecard or One Page Plan to give them all the information they need to make better decisions and get better results.
- Help your clients understand and manage their breakeven point so they are more able to survive falls in demand.
- Benchmark your clients against others in their industry to identify the areas where they can most easily improve their sales, profits and cash balances.

- Attend regular meetings with your clients, and help them continually update their action plan in the light of new issues, information and opportunities as they arise.
- Produce regular cashflow forecasts to ensure your client's plans can be funded and they do not get into financial difficulties.
- Identify which of the 8 key profit drivers has the greatest potential for each of your clients. For example, for an accountancy firm these may include recovery rates, average charge out rate, conversion rates from meetings with prospects, productivity and so on.
- Review the 23 profit strategies that lie behind the 8 profit drivers and help your client prioritise and action them. Of course it doesn't have to be 23, but you should be able to identify a number of strategies that will improve the key profit drivers you have identified. For your accountancy practice, many of the pricing ideas in this book will help you to improve some or even all the key profit drivers for your practice. And many of the ideas in this book will be ideas that you could adapt to help your clients improve their own key profit drivers.
- Help your clients to identify and manage their profitability by customer and/or product line, so that they can build on their higher profit areas and deal with their lower profit areas.
- Help your clients to analyse their sales pipeline. You could then use sales improvement software (such as that available to AVN members) to identify how to drive sales up.
- You could take the ideas from this book and help your clients to evaluate alternative pricing strategies – since getting pricing right is usually the fastest and easiest way to increase the profitability of sales.
- Consider the Tax Credits implications of any planning so that you maximise the impact on your clients' bank account. Many accountants neglect Tax Credits planning and yet this is an area where you can add massive value to your clients and charge premium prices.

Of course, you need to make sure that your products and services are exactly what your clients, especially your ideal clients, need and want - i.e. they offer the best and most appropriate combination of benefits.

Explain the value

Make sure that your clients fully understand those benefits - i.e. because unless they understand that what you have to offer is special, they will assume it is average, and that means that you'll only be able to charge an average price. So managing their perceptions is vital.

We will look at the key issue of explaining the value in later chapters.

Link your price to the value

The price you charge should be based upon the value to the client and not the amount of time the work will take. There are many different ways of linking price to value, some of which include:

- The 'no win no fee' policy of some lawyers
- The contingency fees charged by many corporate finance advisers when helping clients do big deals – so that client only pays if and when the deal goes through (when they usually pay a very big fee by the way)
- The cost reduction consultants who charge a percentage of the money they save you
- The percentage commissions that estate agents charge you to sell your house – which are higher if the estate agent gets you a higher price, and are not payable at all if they don't sell it for you

Of course, all of the above examples relate to linking the price to 'tangible benefits'. But do not forget the emotional associations (qualitative benefits). This is something I will discuss further in chapter 11 on iterative digital pricing.

The following case study describes the experiences and results of a firm that is a relative new-comer to value pricing, but as you will see, in a short space of time has started to see big results.

Case study – two partner firm

The following success story was provided by an accountancy practice with 2 directors and a team of 4, based in Exeter, Devon. It details their application of a value pricing system.

"After attending a Tax Club meeting in 2010, and specifically off the back of the sleeping partner class 4 NIC app, we introduced a system for using value based billing for any one-off work that we carry out as a practice. As a firm, it became clear that we were undervaluing the work that we were performing and that we were losing fees as a result. On the whole, prior to the change, we were billing based more on time sheets for most things.

We had started to keep a record of our charges for particular work, such as CGT/IHT planning and compliance, and have calculated the fees based on the value of the assets and/or tax savings available to our clients. As a result of this, we plan work with less emphasis on the time spent working on the client as the fee is calculated using this new method.

We are now being paid more for the work we are doing than we were before, though fees vary from job to job, and are based on the advice that we can give to save tax. However, we can now say that where 3 or 4 hours work would show below £250 of time on the timesheet, we have been able to charge upwards from £1,000, or by reference to the value. At the moment we essentially only offer value based billing for one-off work. It is hard to add value to basic compliance work in such a way that is quantifiable to a client.

The reaction from clients has been encouraging. We've had no complaints. Quite the opposite, in fact, since we have taken great care to explain it all very carefully: the key point being the guarantee that the fee will not exceed a certain amount and that if we cannot achieve a saving there is no charge. The focus of our explanation is now on the net amount that will end up in the client's pocket rather than what is paid to us, since that is what they really care about. And as good accountants we are able to put a lot of extra money in their pockets, so our clients are very happy.

Our biggest success to date was in calculating the optimum way for a client to gift a property to his son using a trust and we were able to illustrate the IHT and CGT savings achieved and charge a percentage of the saving rather than the time spent. This resulted in a fee of £1,700 plus VAT, rather than hundreds as we would have had before. The repayment itself came to approximately £8,500".

And to close this chapter here is another case study from an AVN member that is a master of value pricing. Gavin Taylor of Mayes Business Partnership fully understands the art of value pricing as demonstrated by the following case study…

Case study – Mayes Business Partnership

On 25 November 2009 Gavin Taylor of Mayes Business Partnership received a Tax Club pricing system, and when we interviewed him 20 days later on 15 December he had already generated £3,500 of additional fees by using one of the systems, and was very confident that another £7,500 would follow shortly.

The system in question gives you everything you need to reclaim Class 4 NI Contributions in respect of sleeping partners. And here is how Gavin and the team at Mayes used it:

STEP 1 – They used the data mining facility in IRIS to identify all their partnership clients. The Directors then reviewed this list to identify those where there were sleeping partners. This resulted in a list of 15 clients where a reclaim may be possible.

STEP 2 – They identified how much Class 4 NIC had been paid by each of the sleeping partners over the last six years. As a result they were left with five clients where the potential reclaim was large enough to justify the fee.

STEP 3 – Gavin, the Tax Director, rang these five clients and explained that a new opportunity had arisen to get them a refund. He also explained that now that HMRC had lost the Arctic Systems case it was now safe to make this kind of claim – and this explanation in turn meant that none of his clients turned round and said accusingly "why haven't you done this for me before?" He also explained that the fee would be 25% of the refund they actually obtained – so they had nothing to lose.

STEP 4 – Not a single client has said no. In fact two of them said yes immediately, and Gavin has already used the documents and processes in the system to submit their refund claims. The other three are taking a little longer to confirm, due to holidays etc. But Gavin is confident that they will also say yes, and that given that there is a further £30,000 refund at stake between them, then his additional fees at 25% will be a further £7,500.

Commenting on what he had done Gavin said:

"In total I expect that we will earn an extra £11,000 by using this system. And I expect that we will have spent a total of around 10-15 hours to earn those fees. So at the equivalent of close to £1,000 per hour it is very rewarding work. But clients see that as fair because we have been proactive, we are doing all the work and taking all the risk, and they are banking a very sizeable amount of cash they wouldn't otherwise have got and without having to do anything to get it. So everyone wins."

6

Chapter 6
Practical application: Adding value with Tax Credits

"At the 2009 National Tax Conference a show of hands showed that over 98% of accounting practices did not offer clients a tax credits service, despite the significant profit generating opportunities it presented."

"Your blueprint for a better tax practice", the Tax Club

The 2010 Tax Club research report, "Your blueprint for a better tax practice" goes on to explain the huge opportunity Tax Credits presents to accountants to add value. And when you find ways to add more value to your clients the opportunity to charge higher prices presents itself.

What we found out from that research last year is that many, many firms of accountants are finding ways to charge much higher prices for dealing with Tax Credits compliance work compared with Income Tax Return compliance work... even though there is less work to do and much of the work is already done as part of preparing the tax return.

The following case study is a great example of the opportunities that may result from offering a Tax Credits service:

Case study – McGregors Business Services

This is the story of how Ian Rodgers, a sole practitioner trading as McGregors Business Services in Leicestershire, has earned over £6,000 in extra fees in the first month since launching a new proactive Tax Credits service.

In late July 2009 Ian went on a Tax Credits course and realised how much scope there was to provide a better service to clients in this area. Previously, like most other firms, they had specifically excluded Tax Credits from the scope of their engagements. But now he realised there was a better way. So in early August Ian launched a new four step service.

STEP 1   As his tax team work on a client's tax return they systematically and automatically also run the client's numbers through their Tax Credits software provided one or more "triggers" are present. The triggers include, of course, having income below £58,000. It is important to note that this is not just done some of the time, when they think about it. It is part of the checklist and is done every single time. Ian estimates that in the first month of doing this with the random selection of tax returns that they have worked on, they have identified potential claims in about 15% of cases.

STEP 2   If they need more information, they get it. Then they tell the client what they have done, and what they have found. If no Tax Credits are available, they tell the client so and get the brownie points for at least having tried. And if they are available, they tell the client the net amount of extra cash (i.e. net of their fees) that appears to be at stake so the client can make an informed decision as to whether they want to go ahead.

STEP 3   If the client is interested, they then agree the pricing structure for the service before the work starts (so there are no surprise bills later). In the first year that involves a £395 set up fee and 10% of any extra tax credits obtained over and above what the client was receiving already. And if the client optionally wants ongoing help extending or repeating the claim in future years then the additional charge is £195 to £295 a year. To date every single client they have offered this to has been happy with his fee structure - so their conversion rate from opportunity to sale has been 100%.

STEP 4   They do the work using a standard system. As a result it can be done very professionally and very profitably by relatively junior team members.

The morals from this story are crystal clear:

- There is a huge untapped market for Tax Credits support
- It can generate very significant fees (remember, Ian's firm has earned £6,000 in the first month alone, and for them as a small firm that is just the tip of the iceberg)
- If priced and delivered properly – using value pricing and systems - it can be extremely profitable work
- The key is to be proactive – i.e. not to wait until a client asks you for Tax Credits advice (since most never will because they have no idea of the possibilities), but to systematically identify every case where Tax Credits are available

If you haven't read this research report I suggest that it is essential reading if you want to improve the way that you price and improve the profitability of your practice.

I listed in the previous chapter that considering your clients' Tax Credits position is one way of increasing the value. You could do this by adding a line to your fee proposals and quotes for compliance work that says something like...

"As part of this fixed fee we will also review your Tax Credits position in detail to see if you might be entitled to Tax Credits. If you are we will consider ways to increase your entitlement. And if you are not, we will explore tax planning ideas that might enable you to become entitled to Tax Credits. In other words, we will look at this area in detail to see if we can find ways of putting extra money into your personal bank account. Please note that if we can help put extra money into your bank account in this way there will be an additional fee for dealing with the planning and completion of the paperwork, but in the spirit of our *no surprises* fixed fee policy we will not carry out any further work until you are happy with the price."

You can find out how to get a *free* copy of the report mentioned in this chapter in the "**Further Help**" section at the end of this book.

7

Chapter 7
Price discussions

Remember, the secret to getting the right price – a price that truly reflects the VALUE – is to EDUCATE the client.

Remember, you will have a **price discussion** with your client…

… the question is, "**When will it take place?**"

As accountants we are often a little uncomfortable about discussing and agreeing price with clients. The easy option is to avoid the issue of price with the client and just do the work. But at some point you are going to want to send out a bill for the work that you have done.

The COWARDLY option is to say nothing, agree nothing and simply do the work. Then at the end of the job, once the accounts and tax returns are filed, we produce our wonderful work-in-progress reports which add up the time costs on the ledger, produce a bill and send it to the client.

And the trouble with that approach – yet another problem with time-based billing – is that very often the quantum of the bill is a surprise to the client (remember, the 2005 Sage survey shows that "surprise billing" is the thing that business owners hate the most about accountants). And at that point you're going to have that price discussion.

The trouble is, when you have the price discussion after you have done the work the client has the leverage. You have already performed the service. The client is in the driving seat and can decide whether to pay the bill, whether to argue with you over the amount, or whether to simply not pay you. Short of threatening legal action there is very little you can do.

So given that you are going to have a price discussion, let's get used to the fact that the very best time to have that discussion is BEFORE you carry out the service. At that point <u>you have the leverage</u>.

In other words, the client has a need for your service. And if you are unable to agree a fee, then at least you haven't incurred any work.

So however much you don't like having price discussions, you will have them. They are a fact of professional life so deal with them right up front.

Pricing emotions

Before we look at how to discuss price in your fee proposals and quotes you should consider the three emotions related to pricing:

- Price resistance
- Price anxiety
- Payment resistance

Ouch! That's a bit expensive

Price resistance is when the client says, "Ouch! That's a bit expensive." It's a natural reaction – and particularly common when you have not adequately explained the value of what you do.

As accountants we hate it when clients say, "Ouch! That's a bit expensive." And because we hate it we try to avoid it by keeping our prices low.

However, if you never experience price resistance from your clients, guess what? That's right... your prices are too low.

So you need to change your mind set. You should welcome price resistance. Only when you get some price resistance do you know that you are on the right track with your prices.

Buyer's remorse

The second pricing emotion is price anxiety, often referred to as "buyer's remorse."

This is the feeling you get when you buy something and then afterwards worry whether or not you did the right thing. This tends to happen when we buy luxury items like an expensive new car. We are unlikely to experience "buyer's remorse" when we buy a loaf of bread. Similarly, our clients are unlikely to experience this when buying compliance services from us, since they need those things. However, it may arise if they buy some consulting services from you.

There are a number of ways of dealing with this pricing emotion. One of the ways of doing this is using a fixed price agreement that contains a commitment for both you and the client to regularly review the scope of the agreement with a view to changing it if needs change. This will ease any worry the client may have that they are locked into an agreement which they later regret.

Another great way, and arguably the best way, is to offer guarantees, which we cover later on in this book. A well worded guarantee will reassure the client by removing any risk that they have made a bad buying decision.

I don't want to pay

Payment resistance is simply the customer's unwillingness to write the cheque.

And we know from the amount of lock-up (i.e. debtors and work in progress) amongst firms of accountants that this is a major problem. In fact, the 2008 AVN benchmarking survey mentioned in an earlier chapter shows that the average lock-up is 108.5 days and for the bottom quartile of firms this is 147.3 days and more.

There are a number of things you could implement to reduce debtors and bad debts, and these include:

- Switch to monthly billing. By billing every month it minimises work in progress and ensures you get paid more regularly (and if not you have the option of ceasing any further work).
- Allow clients to pay you by standing order (preferably in advance than in arrears). This makes your cash flow much easier to manage.
- Standing orders are a great way to get paid but they do have a number of drawbacks, including not being notified if a standing order has been cancelled and the inability to change the amounts (if you change your fees you have to ask the client to cancel the standing order and then set up a brand new one). Getting paid by direct debit is becoming increasingly popular amongst accountancy firms and solves many of the problems associated with standing orders.
- Offer the client finance. There are finance companies that will offer this facility to accountancy firms. Essentially it means that the client signs a simple finance agreement and pays your fee by monthly installment to the finance company. The finance company pays you the full fee within a month. So you get paid in advance and the client gets to spread the payments. This facility can also be used to allow clients to clear any existing debtor balances they have with you.
- The number one idea though is really simple… ensure you get paid BEFORE you commence the work. This is something that many accountancy firms I work with are doing and are getting very little, if any, resistance from their clients. After all, accountancy is a service industry and most people are used to paying in advance for services. For example, you don't get to take your car home from the local garage after it has been serviced until you have been paid; if you are buying a new house and need a valuation doing in order to secure the mortgage most valuers will ask for payment up front before they carry out the valuation; and payment in advance is how the oldest profession works.

So when you have price discussions with your clients – whether verbal or in writing – bear in mind the 3 pricing emotions and factor them into your discussions. So I'll finish this chapter with a few tips relating to the sue of fee proposals and quotes in your price discussions.

Fee proposals and quotes

There are two ways to do a fee quote. The wrong way. And the right way.

Most quotes you will ever see do it the wrong way... not just accountants; trades people, landscape gardeners, architects.

This is how most people lay out their fee quotes.

They start with the scope of the work; which is usually a list of the features of the work they will carry out. And then right at the end – usually the very last thing you read – is the price.

So guess what is on the reader's mind when they have finished reading a quote?

That's right... the price. So by setting out our fee quotes in this way we focus the customer on the price and encourage them to be price shoppers.

Let's now do things a different way... the RIGHT way.

This time start with the price up front. After all, you will have a price discussion, so get it out of the way first.

Then tell your client what you will do for them; the scope of the work. And don't just list the features. Talk in terms of benefits. Include your Unique Selling Points (USPs), the things that make you different. And list the optional extras.

When your reader has finished reading the fee quote the lasting thoughts are all the benefits of using your services and the things that make you different. You've turned their focus away from price and onto value.

Explaining the value is one of the 3 keys to value pricing. I have introduced you to this area in this chapter and in the chapters that follow you will find even more ideas, tips and techniques for getting better at explain value to your clients.

8

Chapter 8 - Charging clients what they are willing to pay

"Customers don't want to be treated equally. They want to be treated individually... any company that treats a customer the same as 'everybody' is treating that customer like nobody."

Peppers and Rogers

Let's start by reminding you of one of the most profound principles in the field of pricing. And that principle is this...

... **different clients value things differently**.

We all value things differently. We all have a different perception of the value of any product or service. So we all have a different maximum amount we are willing to pay for a particular product or service.

It's our personal judgement call – and it's entirely subjective.

"So what?" you might be thinking.

Well, this seemingly tiny observation has a profound implication. You see, it means that whatever price you are currently charging, that price is WRONG!

Is that a big enough implication for you?

Actually, I probably need to clarify that statement that your price is wrong. Let me be more precise.

If you have a single price for your product, then that single price is WRONG... no matter what that single price actually is.

You see, having only a single price causes you to lose out in two different ways....

For some clients that price is too high – so they don't buy, and you lose them as a client.

And for other clients that price is too low – so you end up charging them less (and earning less profit) than they are willing to pay. Which means you lose again.

Economists call the amount by which you lose in this second scenario the "Consumer surplus" – and it is shown by the shaded area on the supply and demand diagram you can see below.

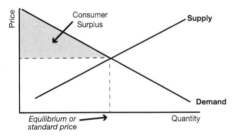

So one of the keys to dramatically improving your profits is to claw back some of this consumer surplus by charging different clients different prices.

But how?

Well, the good news is that there are lots of ways of charging different clients different prices.

So let's look at some numbers to illustrate the power of this concept.

EXAMPLE

Imagine that for a basic tax return the cost to you is £50 (chargeable salary costs, printing, postage etc) and that for your basic tax return service there are three potential clients: A, B and C.

- Client A is willing to pay £200
- Client B is willing to pay £150 and
- Client C is willing to pay £100.

If you set a single price at £100, then all three clients will gladly pay you that amount. So you'll make total sales of £300 and total profits of £150.

Single price of £100	Quantity sold	Revenue	Cost @ £50 each	Profit
Client A	1	£100	£50	£50
Client B	1	£100	£50	£50
Client C	1	£100	£50	£50
			Total Profit =	£150

If you set a single price at £150, then Client C won't buy. But the other two will gladly pay you £150 each. So you'll make total sales of £300 and total profits of £200.

Single price of £150	Quantity sold	Revenue	Cost @ £50 each	Profit
Client A	1	£150	£50	£100
Client B	1	£150	£50	£100
Client C	-	-	-	-
			Total Profit =	£200

If you set a single price at £200, then only Client A will buy. So your total sales will be £200 and your total profits will be £150.

Single price £200	Quantity sold	Revenue	Cost @ £50 each	Profit
Client A	1	£200	£50	£150
Client B	-	-	-	-
Client C	-	-	-	-
			Total Profit =	**£150**

The MAGIC PRICE is the price at which you make the most profits. So in this example the MAGIC PRICE is £150 – since at that price you make £200 in profits – which is **33% higher than at any other price**.

Now £150 is the MAGIC PRICE… because there is no other single price at which you can make higher profits.

We can illustrate this graphically as follows:

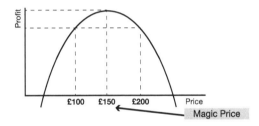

But we also know that: Client A is willing to pay £200, Client B is willing to pay £150 and Client C is willing to pay £100.

So, if instead of charging those three clients all the SAME prices, we charge them the full price they are willing to pay, then our total profits will be £300. **Which is half as much again as the £200 profits we made at the magic price.**

Different prices	Quantity sold	Revenue	Cost @ £50 each	Profit
Client A pays £200	1	£200	£50	£150
Client B pays £150	1	£150	£50	£100
Client C pays £100	1	£100	£50	£50
			Total Profit =	**£300**

Now it's vital to recognise that there is nothing fishy or special about the numbers in our example.

YES, we've kept the numbers as simple as possible. And YES, the real world is much more complicated.

But those complications do nothing to alter the fact that if you can find a way to charge different clients different prices – so that they each pay what they are willing to pay – then you will ALWAYS make more profits than you do by using any single price... even if that single price is your magic price.

In our example we made 50% more profits by switching from the magic price to charging each client the full price they were willing to pay. In your business the impact could be more or less than 50%. But there WILL be an impact. Charging different clients different prices WILL increase your profits... and probably by a lot!

Economists call this "price discrimination" – but we prefer the Plain English description of charging different clients different prices, since that's what it actually involves.

But how do you actually do it?

Well, the key is being much more creative about pricing. Here are some possible ways

- Timing (e.g. Peak v Standby) – this is a common technique used by many different industries including rail travel and telecommunications. It is an idea that accountants can also use. For example, some firms charge higher prices when clients drop off their tax return information in the busy season for tax returns (typically December and January). There are two ways of doing this; some firms charge a penalty for bringing the records in late, whilst others offer a discount for bringing the records in early (by a pre-agreed date). Those firms that offer a discount will typically inflate the fixed fee so that the discount simply reduces the fee to what it would have been, in other words, the net effect of either the "penalty" or "discount" tactic are the same. However, offering clients a discount is likely to be much better received than by penalising them. So think carefully about the way you implement ideas and the language that you use... small things can make a massive difference.

- Creating different versions (e.g. Premium v Economy) – if you want to avoid competing on price consider creating premium versions of your products and services, for example, AVN Accountants use the Performance Measurement and Improvement system (PMI system) which is a premium accounts preparation service. In fact, you could take any of your products or services and create a premium version.

First you will need to come up with the premium version by making it more valuable (you could build in some of the ideas we discussed earlier on for increasing the value). Once you have a premium product you will need to come up with a brand name – 'The PMI system' is the brand name that AVN Accountants use for their premium accounts compliance service. And you will then need to package the product or service. The PMI system is an 8-step process that is packaged in a folder that the client uses to keep track of all the numbers that are important to them and their business.

In "Power Pricing" by Dolan and Simon they explain the concept of *'asymmetry in price tiers.'* It has been proven that whilst premium products might compete with each other, and economy products might compete with each other, there is little price competition between premium products and economy products. This is illustrated by the following diagram.

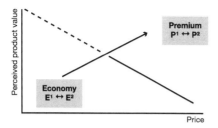

- For example, whilst there may be price competition amongst premium beers, because there is a perception that a premium beer is a better product than an economy beer, consumers will not take into consideration the price of economy beers when buying a premium beer. So one way to avoid competing with your competitors on price is to create premium versions of your products and services.

- Bundling (e.g. A La Carte v Table d'Hote) – Bundling is a simple idea; you simply take a number of individual products and services and package them into one bundle. So in the restaurant industry the Table d'Hote is simply a bundle that may consist of a starter, a main course, a dessert and coffee. Very often the price of the bundle is less than the sum of the individual elements within the bundle, which is usually the case in the restaurant industry… in this case, more price sensitive customers will sacrifice choice in order to benefit from the better value of the set menu.

  However, it is important to note that you DO NOT have to make the bundle cheaper than the sum of its parts. Sometimes you can make the bundle more **expensive** than the sum of its parts. This is much easier to do if the bundle is carefully designed to create a better solution for the customer. If the customer's perception of the bundle is that it does better solve their problem then they will perceive it to have a higher value and so you are able to charge a premium price. One incredibly powerful technique that accountancy firms can use is to create bundles and offer a range of bundles. We call this "menu pricing".

So let's now look at menu pricing.

9

Chapter 9
Menu pricing in practice

There are 4 important steps to making menu pricing work for you.

STEP 1 – Make sure that you have a range of packages for different budgets.

The first thing you need to do is create a range of different service offerings – in other words, by bolting added value extras onto the same core product to make different packages.

And having created your range of packages, one of the best ways of presenting them to your clients is in the form of a menu. In other words a detailed Plain English list of the different options available to your clients – spelling out what is special about each of them.

For example, many AVN Accountants have menus like this for each of their core services:

- There's a Plain English menu for their 3, 4 and 5 star self assessment tax return service (see the next chapter for a practical discussion of exactly how to do this).
- There's a another Plain English menu listing their 3, 4 and 5 star company incorporation services (see chapter 14 for more details of how to do this).

- And yet another for their 3, 4 and 5 star end of year accounts service (see chapter 11 on iterative digital pricing for practical example of how to do this).

And all of those menus spell out exactly what you get, give prices, and have a series of tick boxes that make it easier for their clients to choose which of the three packages best meets their needs and budget.

They also include a separate set of tick boxes for all the additional optional extra services that clients might want to buy on top of one of the standard bundles.

The Magic of Three

You may have noticed that all of the examples above have involved giving the client a choice of THREE options, i.e. a 3, 4 and 5 star service offering. There is a very good reason for that.

And that reason is what has been called THE MAGIC OF THREE.

You see, there is a kind of magic in offering clients a choice of three options. Research suggests that if there are more than three options people tend to get confused. And if there are less than three options you don't give people enough choice. So three options seems to be the magic number.

STEP 2 – How you price those different versions

In his book "Full Price", pricing guru Thomas Winninger says that you get the best results if the price difference between the most expensive and the middle option is smaller than the price difference between the middle and the cheapest option.

So, for example, if the 5 star package is £200, and the 3 star package is £100, then the 4 star package shouldn't be set in the middle at £150. It should be set above the middle at, say, £170.

And there are two reasons for that:

- Firstly, the most popular package will normally be the middle one – so you are leaving money on the table if you pitch it so that it is worth only £150. Why not make more money by making it worth £170 so that you can price it at £170?
- And secondly, if the gap in price between the middle option and the most expensive option is smaller, more people will upgrade to the top option because they perceive that it gives them the best value for money by offering a lot of extra benefits for a little extra money.

So always price your middle option at higher than the mid-way point between your two other options. It will help you to make more money!

STEP 3 – How you describe them to your client

The language you use to describe the three options is also very important. What you want clients to appreciate is that your three options represent GOOD, BETTER and BEST…. and categorically not Bad, OK and Good.

So while 'Economy, Standard and Premium' and 'Bronze, Silver and Gold' are better than nothing, they do give slightly the wrong impression. After all, economy does sound a bit cheap and nasty, while in sport, anything less than a gold medal is seen by many people as a failure.

I know they are only words, but they do matter.

So it is often better to describe your packages as 3, 4 and 5 Star – since that implies that the cheapest service is still better than a one and two star alternative. And some clients will even take it to imply that your competitors actually offer a one and two star service that is not as good as the 3-5 star service that you offer!

STEP 4 – How you present and explain the benefits to your client

Once you have created, priced and named each package you then need to explain the benefits to the client. How you present and explain them to your clients is vitally important,

For each package you should create a "service information sheet" which sets out in precise detail exactly what you will do for the client. And this should be worded in terms of the benefit to the client and not simply the feature.

For example, as part of your incorporation service you might provide a tax planning review where you explain the difference between taking money out as a salary versus a dividend and how these compare with how they are currently taxed as an unincorporated business. If this is what you do, tell the client that.

So your service information sheet might say, "We will provide you with an overview of tax planning."

But don't stop there, because that is a feature. What is the benefit to the client? The benefit to the client is that it will help ensure that they get cash out of their new limited company in the most tax efficient way. Great. That's better. But so what? What does that mean to the client? It means they have more cash in their personal bank account. So say that.

So your service information sheet might say this:

We will provide you with an overview of tax planning to ensure that you understand the most tax efficient ways of withdrawing money from your company. This means that you will have more money in your personal bank account.

Do not take for granted that your client will know or understand what you can do... list absolutely everything that you do and every single benefit to the client.

STEP 5 - Show the client the most expensive option first

One of the best ways to use prices to help you sell more is what is called TOP DOWN PRICING.

It sounds a bit weird, doesn't it? But actually it's very simple because it just means showing clients your most expensive items first.

In other words, starting with your top of the range items and then working down to the progressively cheaper items. Hence the name top down pricing - because it involves working from the top down.

But don't let its apparent simplicity fool you… it is phenomenally powerful.

And it's phenomenally powerful because it's been PROVEN to increase the average amount that clients spend, by encouraging more clients to buy your more expensive options.

The Macy's experiment

Now you might be thinking that you already do everything possible to persuade clients to choose your most expensive options… but a fascinating experiment at Macy's Department store in New York suggests that you might need to think again.

What they did was give ten professional shoppers $1000 each to go into Macy's and buy whatever the salespeople offered – without ever asking about or mentioning price. So these were clients who were willing and able to spend $1000 – but only if the salespeople gave them the chance to do so by showing them the more expensive options!

But what actually happened was that not one of the shoppers was able to spend more than $350. For example, the hat salesperson brought out a $75 hat (that was probably in her price range) rather than the $200 top of the range hat that the client would gladly have bought. So, in effect, the salespeople were GUESSING how much clients were willing to spend – and were then only suggesting options that matched their guesses. But in most cases their guesses were wrong!

So Macy's could have trebled its sales from those 10 clients, from $350 to $1000, if it had trained its team not to guess how much clients were willing to spend – and had trained them instead to show clients the most expensive items first… to use top down pricing.

But WHY does top down pricing work?

Quite simply it works because if you show your most expensive stuff first, people tend to buy more expensive things than if you show them the cheaper stuff first.

And to prove that, imagine that you sell three versions of a business plan preparation service – priced at £500, £680 and £800.

Imagine that you show your client the cheapest service first – working from bottom up as you go along. Your client might not like the £500 version you show him first because it doesn't quite have all the bells and whistles he is looking for (perhaps it doesn't include a cash flow forecast). But as soon as you reach the £680 version, and he sees that it gives him everything he wants, he will want to buy it. And he probably won't want to waste his time looking at even more options, because the £680 one has everything he wants. So you probably won't get a chance to show him the £800 top of the range version.

Now imagine that you had started at the expensive end first – and had worked from the top down.

The worst that can happen is that you show him the £800 version first, he's not interested and instead settles for the £680 version you show him second - the same £680 version as before.

But there is also a chance that when he sees the £800 version he will be so impressed that he decides to buy that. After all, it gives him everything he wants… and a little bit more. So if it is within his budget he will probably buy it. And having made up his mind to buy the £800 version, again he probably won't want to waste his time looking at even more options. So you won't have to show him the £680 and £500 versions – and he won't buy them.

So under top down pricing the WORST that can happen is that you end up selling the same £680 version as you would have done if you had started at the bottom. So you're no worse off.

And the best that can happen is that you end up selling the £800 version. So you're better off.

Case study

Back in 1999 when I was running my own accountancy practice in Sheffield I launched a range of business consulting services. The entry level was a 2-3 hour programme called the Business Builder priced at £750. The next level was a 2–3 day programme called the Business Edge priced at £3,000. And the top level was a 12-month programme called Making It Happen priced at £30,000.

I had just come across the concept of Top Down Pricing at that time.

One day a one-man band self-employed photographer came into my practice to do some work for me. He wasn't a client at the time. When I asked him how business was he explained that it was OK and he needed to grow his business. So I invited him back for a consultation to go through a few ideas and to explain how I could perhaps help him.

At that consultation I found out that his turnover was only £12,000 and he was not making any profit; he was being supported financially by his girl-friend. It would have been very easy to pre-judge the client and presume that he would not be willing to buy my business consulting services.

Nevertheless, I went through my sales process because it had been proven to work before and is based on solid research.

So I told the photographer all about the Making It Happen programme. I did precede my explanation by telling him that I would not let him buy this service and that I was only describing it so that he had a better idea of what I could do for him. And I told him right up front that it was £30,000 and not appropriate for him.

I then described the Business Edge programme and that it was £3,000 and to my amazement, as soon as I had finished describing it, he said, "That's exactly what I need." I never did tell him anything about my £750 service. But had I have started with that, I'm pretty sure that is what he would have bought. So Top Down Pricing earned me an extra £2,250.

In his book "Influence: Science and Practice" Robert Cialdini describes the 'contrast principle' where the same thing can be made to seem very different depending on the nature of the event that precedes it. In this case, after presenting a £30,000 service offering by contrast a £3,000 service offering appears cheap. If on the other hand you explain a £500 service offering first, then by contrast the £3,000 service offering appears expensive.

Note: Back in 1999 I had not come across the research by Tom Winninger. Had I have done so I would have probably earned higher fees for my middle level service offering.

So top down pricing can't possibly make you worse off – but it can very easily make you better off.

I was an extra 300% better off. An extra 25% better off in the Business Plan example above. And an extra 300% better off in the shopping test they did at Macy's.

But that isn't the only advantage that top down pricing has over the bottom up approach.

If you show clients your cheapest options first and then try and persuade them that they need the more expensive one... they may well end up thinking that you are trying to rip them off. And that's certainly not good for business either.

So top down pricing wins hands down!

Pulling it all together

When working with AVN Accountants I have found that using this combination of menus and top down pricing has two big benefits:

- Firstly it makes it easier for clients to get exactly the service they are looking for, and
- Secondly the service clients are looking for is often a more comprehensive (and therefore more expensive) one than they would have chosen without a menu. Since without a menu they wouldn't have known what their options were – and so often end up going for something that almost, but doesn't quite meet their needs.

The combination of menu pricing and top down pricing helps AVN Accountants to make more money from clients who willingly and gladly upgrade to a level of service that more closely meets their needs - and for which they are happy to pay more because it gives them more.

In the next chapter I set out a practical example of how you can use everything from this chapter to create a range of different tax return services. This includes a great case study from Nino Pucacco of P&A Accountancy Services where he shares with us how he changed the way he prices tax returns… by creating different versions of his products and services at different prices. Nino fully understands the concept of charging different clients different prices. This is a simple but powerful concept, that when implemented correctly is guaranteed to increase the profitability of your practice.

To end this chapter, the following case study is a great story of how another practice has taken this idea and made it work.

Case study – Gemini Accountancy

Sian Kelly is the sole founder of Gemini Accountancy, which is based in Sutton Coldfield and has around 12 PLCs as clients. They started just 6 months ago and yet Sian is able to report the following pricing strategy success:

"I recently started up a new Accountancy business and we have been offering packages to our clients at different prices for different service levels. We have introduced service levels which incorporate quarterly, bi annual or monthly reviews and a tax planning meeting in the third quarter of the accounting period. This has meant that preparing the year end accounts has been much quicker.

We offer 3 levels of service for our standard compliance work. They are:

Classic   This is our basic accounts package, which includes, amongst other things, corporation tax, online accounts and a biannual review. It costs £175 per month.

Premium   On top of the Classic level, this also incorporates a quarterly review and unlimited phone support. It costs £295 per month.

Premium Plus   This is our highest service package and comes with a monthly review and management strategy meetings. It costs £595 per month.

I have also been able to encourage my clients to use online accounting software, saving me time and allowing me to review management accounts monthly if they wish. This benefits me greatly in that our clients are able to input their figures on a monthly basis, which allows me to generate their monthly management accounts. Also, at the end of the year it is much easier for me to use the monthly figures to compile the clients' annual review. On top of the figures that the online service provides, I provide a commentary and review. This massively decreases my workload and I am therefore able to generate fees without having to do as much work. As a result, I do not charge for access to the online accounting software.

I have been trying to explain how the different service levels add value to their business and how the client can make better strategic use from the management accounts that we prepare. We have had a very high take up rate of the increased service levels resulting in higher fees. As yet, we haven't 'failed' with the pricing structure and only one person has so far taken up the classic package. We tend to find that clients generally go for the middle (Premium) package. To date my biggest success is to increase a fee from £1,500 to £3,500 annually".

10

Chapter 10
Practical application: pricing your tax return service

In "Your blueprint for a better tax practice" the survey looks at how firms of accountants charge for pricing self-assessment tax returns. Below is an extract from that research report.

In the survey we asked firms how much they would charge for doing self assessment tax returns. The question was broken down into three parts, with each being a very specific service. These were:

- **Employee** - How much do you typically charge to do the simplest tax return where the only additional pages are for employment income (e.g. a director)?
- **Rental income** - How much do you typically charge for a simple tax return with additional pages for just rental income, including producing an income and expenses schedule for the net income from property (e.g. a buy-to-let investor)?
- **Self employed** - How much do you typically charge for the simplest of self-employed income where you produce a very simple set of income and expenditure accounts (e.g. a sub-contract labourer or dental associate)?

The results are shown in figure 3 below:

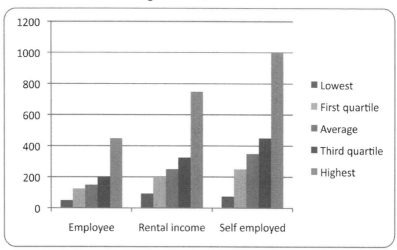

Figure 3 – Typical prices for self assessment returns

The numbers behind figure 3 are shown in the table below:

	Employee	Rental income	Self employed
The bottom practice charged	£50	£94	£75
The worst 25% of firms charged	£50 - £125	£94 – £200	£75 - £250
The below average 25% of firms charged	£125 - £150	£200 - £250	£250 - £350
The average firm charged	£150	£250	£350
The above average 25% of firms charged	£150 - £200	£250 - £325	£350 - £450
The best 25% of firms charged	£200 - £450	£325 - £750	£450 - £1,000
The top firm charged	£450	£750	£1,000

These results show that there is a very significant range of prices. The bottom firms are only charging about a third of what the average firm charges and yet the top firms are charging about **three times** what the average firm charges.

So clearly there is no such thing as "the market price" for tax return work (or as you will see later, for any other area of tax work). Instead the reality is that firms and not the market set their own prices. And some do it very much better than others!

The case study below is an extract from an article written by sole practitioner Nino Pucacco, which appeared on both AccountingWEB and in the Tax Club Bulletin in 2009. It is a perfect illustration of how to charge higher prices for self assessment tax return work.

Case study – P&A Accountancy Services

"To me the two most important principles for the long term success of the profession are simple. Firstly, we must be truly proactive. And secondly we must price properly so that our clients get a really good deal and we earn a good profit for the contribution we make to their success.

We changed the way we price tax returns, basing it on how many different sources and types of income a client has, and what level of service they want. We also use pricing software to instantly show the client exactly what their investment will be for each of our 3, 4 and 5 star service packages, and how much discount they can claim if they give us all the information we need by a set date. This approach is generating excellent results: for example, the other day we signed up a new tax return only client on our 4 star service for just over £500.

I should stress that our 3 and 4 star packages are not in any way "worse" than our 5 star service. It is the breadth of what they cover that differs, not the quality of the work done. For example, our 4 star service might bundle in an income tax planning review while our 5 star service might also include tax investigation insurance and a preliminary IHT estimate."

The following case study is another great example of how some firms are thinking about the pricing of tax services.

Case study – Ad Valorem

Here is how one sole practitioner turned a £125 tax return only client into £53,000 of fees in the last 18 months.

At a recent AVN seminar Nigel Adams, a sole practitioner from Buckinghamshire, stood up and told the group how he had used an AVN inspired idea to earn him £53,000 from a single client.

STEP 1 - He wrote to all his tax return clients offering them the chance to upgrade to a £500 a year "Premiere Tax Return" service. And a very pleasing number took him up on the offer.

STEP 2 - As part of the Premiere service, the higher fee meant that he could be much more proactive in searching for tax planning possibilities for participating clients.

RESULT 1 = One of his tax return only clients who upgraded was a high net worth individual who had previously paid £125 a year for a basic tax return. By spending a bit more time on this client's affairs Nigel was able to identify some sophisticated tax planning that generated very sizeable savings for the clients. What's more, because the client paid a value based fee, the planning also generated £53,000 of extra fees for Nigel.

RESULT 2 = The tax planning was not actually carried out by Nigel – it was done by a tax boutique that Nigel introduced his client to. So much of the extra fee that Nigel earned was in the form of a "payaway" from the boutique. Nigel still had to hold his client's hand through the process. But he didn't have to do the really hard work, since the boutique did all the technical work (and took all the engagement risk), and as a result Nigel's role was extremely enjoyable and lucrative.

The 3 morals of this story
1. Offer your clients the chance to opt into a more expensive Premiere service.

2. Link up with specialist tax boutiques that can bring (a) the most so-phisticated tax planning solutions to the table, and (b) will also share a significant portion of the value-based fees they charge to the client in the form of a payaway. Full details of how to do this are given in the section "Better service: Advanced tax planning" below.
3. Be much more proactive in identifying tax planning opportunities - and don't just stop at the obvious, but also explore the more so-phisticated options since that is where the big savings can often be found (and hence the big fees earned).

Why is there such a vast range of prices being charged for a very clearly defined standard service that probably does not vary much from firm to firm? And how do some firms charge up to 3 times more than the average?

The case study from Nino Pucacco above provides some clues to the last question. You see, Nino is a master of pricing. He understands pricing and uses menu pricing very effectively.

Remember, the first step to effective menu pricing is to **make sure that you have a range of packages for different budgets**.

A good place to start is to think of what you currently do and treat this as your basic – or 3-star – service offering. This might include completing the tax return, calculating the tax liability or repayment, filing the tax return, some level of support and a subscription to your tax newsletter.

Then think about what additional things you could do to create more value. Here are some ideas for what you could include within your next level of service offering:

- Tax investigations support (professional fee protection insurance)
- Advice and consultations for their immediate family
- A greater level of support
- Provision of a general tax health check
- Provision of a business tax health check

And here are some ideas for your highest level of service offering:

- Calculating an estimate of their IHT position
- An IHT health check
- Creating a personal balance sheet showing their personal assets and liabilities and their net worth

Step 2 is to work out **how you price those different versions**.

The key here is to create a pricing structure and test it. Since your entry level of service is likely to be based on what you currently do then perhaps a price similar – although I would recommend 10% higher – to what you currently charge. When pricing your middle and highest service offerings remember the research from Tom Wenninger (you may want to re-read the previous chapter to remind yourself).

Research suggests that if you get the price structure correct about 50% of clients will select the middle option and twice as many clients will choose the top option over the bottom option. You might find this a useful benchmark for testing.

If you find that most of your clients are choosing the cheapest option then either there is too big a price jump to the next service offering or there is not enough perceived benefit in the next service offering (either because the bundle of benefits is not sufficiently attractive or, as we'll discuss below, you have not communicated the benefits sufficiently well).

If this is the case, make some changes and test again.

Just to illustrate the power of this concept, if you currently have 300 clients that pay an average price of £150 for your tax return service then your recurring income is £45,000.

If you successfully create a silver and gold service with, say, £250 for your silver service and £325 for your gold service and you find that 50% of clients choose the silver service and of the rest twice as many go for the gold service than those that go for the bronze service then you have the following:

No. of clients	Service	Price	Total income
50	Bronze	£150	£ 7,500
150	Silver	£250	£37,500
100	Gold	£325	£32,500
		Total	**£77,500**

Note: For the purpose of this illustration I have used the terms 'bronze', 'silver' and 'gold'. Whilst there is nothing wrong with these 3 labels, I personally prefer to use '3-star', '4-star' and '5-star' simply because to me the term 'bronze' suggests poor quality. In contrast offering a '3-star' suggests that your firm does not offer a '1 and 2-star service'

The above table shows a possible increase in gross recurring fee income of over 72%.

Steps 3 and 4 are how you describe, present and explain the benefits to your client. In general, as accountants, we are not very good at communicating the value of what we do. We must get better.

The way to do that is to create a service information sheet that tells the client exactly what they get. And there are two key things to be aware of:

1. You should include **everything** you do for the client, regardless of how insignificant that is to you (it probably isn't insignificant to the client).
2. You should describe those things in terms of the benefit to the client and not simply a list of features.

For example, if you calculate your clients' tax liabilities then tell them that is what you do. But don't just say, "We will also calculate your tax liability and payments on account," tell them what the **benefit** is to them. So you might say something like:

"We will also calculate your tax liability and payments on account, so that you know exactly how much to pay and when to pay it."

11

Chapter 11
Iterative Digital Pricing

We have seen how powerful menu pricing can be for accountants. Iterative digital pricing takes things a step further and puts the customer in complete control of designing their own bespoke package and the price. It works particularly well for compliance-based services where calculating the value is more subjective than, say, tax planning.

I refer to it as 'iterative digital pricing' for two reasons; firstly it allows the customer to iteratively go through a menu of prices and secondly it is digital because it makes use of technology.

So as to make this chapter as practical as possible I will describe the process using Time's Up as an illustration. This is a piece of software I wrote along with my close friend Shane Lukas back in 1999. Since then it has been used by hundreds and hundreds of accountants and transformed their results from pricing compliance services. For more than a decade this process has been proven to work time and time again in helping accountants significantly increase their prices and capture more of the value they create.

The software is designed to be used in front of the client or prospective client, i.e. they are involved in the process. And because the client sees the price build up within the software it is reported that clients do not query the price... unlike when a client asks "How much will that cost?" and the accountant seemingly picks a random number out of the air, which evokes the "That's a bit expensive" response. It's a little bit like menus in

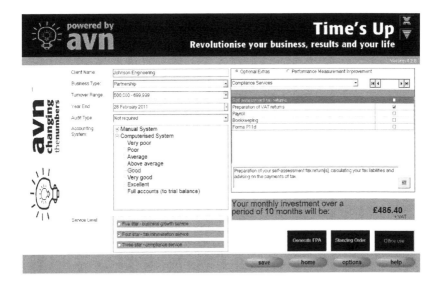

restaurants... when the price is printed on a menu the customer doesn't think to question the price with the waiter because it is there in writing.

What Time's Up does is capture some basic details about the client's circumstances (and since it is used primarily for pricing annual accounts preparation and audit work it asks about the type of trading entity, the size of the business and the quality of the books and records). Based upon this information it presents the client with three possible bundles (using the menu pricing principles we talked about earlier).

It also allows the client to tailor the service to their precise needs by offering dozens of options. For example, if the client is looking for a full compliance service and does not want to deal with any compliance issues themselves, it will offer VAT return preparation, bookkeeping services, payroll and so on. The client chooses all the things they would prefer the accountant to deal with.

As you work through Time's Up with the client it shows the price at the bottom (which can be expressed in a number of ways, e.g. an annual amount). The screen shot below is an extract from the software and in this case shows the price as a monthly investment. This price continually changes as the client builds up their own bespoke package.

One of the really powerful things about this approach is in cross-selling. It provides a systematic way of telling the client about all the other things you do. Not just the additional compliance services but also additional tax planning services, management information services, business development services and so on. In fact, this software tool allows the accountant to add as many optional extra services as they like. It makes it very easy to tell the client about everything you offer and consequently it makes it very easy for the client to buy much, much more from you.

Another really powerful aspect of the Time's Up approach is when you get to the end of the package-building process and the client sees the final price. If the price is more than they are willing to pay or can afford then there is no need to lose the business or crash and burn on your price. Instead you simply work through the software with the client to amend the package until you have a package that is priced at an amount that the client is both willing to pay and able to pay. This process could involve removing some of the optional extras. It could involve changing the bundle, e.g. from 5-star to 4-star. Or it could involve suggesting to the client that you provide some bookkeeping training to help them improve the quality of their record keeping (which will make a dramatic difference to the price and is shown very visibly by the software*).

You may have noticed that Time's Up uses many of the techniques and ideas mentioned in this book, including obvious ones such as menu pricing, top down pricing and changing the perception of price by expressing it as a monthly amount. Others include the language used (it describes the price as an 'investment' and not a 'cost', which may seem insignificant yet these little things can make all the difference) and also the layout of the fixed price agreement produced by the software.

* Another big benefit of the Time's Up approach is the process used to identify the quality of the client's books and records – which turns an objective assessment into something very subjective. This process works brilliantly well in educating the client or prospective client in the amount of work that is involved in preparing a set of accounts. It really helps the client to see the amount of meticulous work carried out by the accountant and helps them to see why your prices are high.

Is it value pricing?

Remember that in the chapter "The art of value pricing" I talked about the value equation. Value is made up of both tangible benefits (which are the quantitative elements) and emotional associations (which are the qualitative elements).

For some services that accountants offer the tangible benefits are very easily quantified, for example, with tax planning work it could be the amount of tax saved, with consultancy work it could be the amount of additional profit and with Tax Credits compliance the amount of money claimed. In these cases value pricing is much easier... it is much easier to link the price to the value.

But just because you cannot quantify the benefits easily does not mean that you cannot value price.

Iterative digital pricing is a form of value pricing. As the client builds up their bundle with those services that are valuable to them so the price goes up. And if any particular element of the package does not represent value they will remove it from the package.

Whilst services like preparing VAT returns might not put money into their bank account (like tax planning does) it will save them time... and reducing time and effort is something that clients value. This is a tangible benefit and one that could be quantified (all you would need to do is estimate the amount of time the client would save and then agree with the client what their time is worth to them).

And remember that value pricing is not just about the tangible benefits but also the qualitative emotional associations. For example, payroll and VAT services not only save the client time when done by you, they also reduce the risk of errors and penalties.

So hopefully in this chapter I have been able to show – using a practical application – that value pricing is not restricted to those services, like tax planning, where the benefits can be precisely quantified. You can apply the principles in this book to every service offering you have... it just means that for some services you have to think a little more creatively in linking the price to the value. But the rewards from successfully capturing the value in terms of much higher margins (and also happier clients from a fairer way of pricing) are worth the extra effort.

This is what three practitioners have told me about their experiences with using this way of pricing...

Sole practitioner **Alan Cowperthwaite** started using Time's Up in 2010 and recently said this about its impact:

"Even though we're in the jaws of a recession, pretty much the only clients we lost were the smaller ones where we had never priced properly. All our good clients stayed. And some of the fee increases were pretty big. For example, I had one client where the fee went up from £2,000 to £4,000 and he said to me afterwards that it was still 'very reasonable', and another where due to their growth the fee went up from £1,500 to £7,000 and he settled it the very next day. So our experience is that when you serve clients properly, and explain the situation carefully, fee resistance melts away."

Note: *Alan is doing some incredible things and you can read his full success story at the end of chapter 16.*

Guy Fallowes of Fallowes & Co in Surrey wrote to us in 2010 and said,

"Our Client Managers having been using Time's Up for over a year with good results, giving us bigger fixed fees and improved cash flow. However, we only began consistently using this in front of clients a few months ago and are now experiencing significantly increased fees with clients' appreciating the transparency and opting for higher service levels."

Steve Bentley of Bentley Financial Management Services who only started in practice in 2009 wrote,

> "As a new business, without AVN I know I would have seriously undervalued my work. By using the AVN resources and Time's Up I have been able to sell additional services to my clients and charge them far more than I would have otherwise dared. In fact my first 3 clients will be paying me an average fee of £5,250 this year."

If you are interested in finding out more about Time's Up and how it helped Alan, Guy and Steve to achieve these sort of results you will find a special offer to attend free Proactivity training in the Further Help section at the back of this book.

12

Chapter 12 - When your competitors are cheaper

"It may be illegal to be crooked, but it isn't illegal to be stupid. Fundamentally it isn't the crooks we should fear in business (since they never sell below cost) but rather it is the honest idiots... because they are the ones who foul up the works... by giving away their products and services by cutting their prices."

Steinmetz and Brooks

If your competitors are cheaper than you there are two things you can do. One of the two is smart and the other is usually stupid.

The STUPID thing is to try to compete with them on price – by cutting your prices and perhaps even starting a price war. Unless of course, this is your pricing strategy. But as discussed in Chapter 1 it is very rare that this is an appropriate strategy for an accountancy practice.

The SMART thing to do is not to even try to compete on price and pursue a pricing strategy of having a highly differentiated service that adds value, so that you can charge a premium price.

If you choose the smart route – not to compete on price - then you will need to master one of two key skills... and preferably both of them:

- You will need to prevent your clients worrying about your higher prices
- And you need to become much better at justifying your higher prices – in other words, much better at handling price objections

We'll be looking at the second of those two skills – handling price objections - in the next chapter.

So in this chapter we'll be focussing on the first of those two skills – preventing your clients from worrying about the fact that your prices are higher.

But before we look in detail at how to do that… let's go back a step and look at why it's not usually smart to compete on price. Why it's not usually smart to cut your prices. And why it's certainly not smart to join a price war.

When competitors undercut your prices the temptation is, of course, to cut your prices too.

And even if it ends there, and doesn't turn into a price war, you're still probably going to be worse off… because lower prices often lead to lower profits.

But very often price cutting like that turns into a price war. After all, if your competitor's intention was to be cheaper than you, then if you cut your prices, they'll have to cut theirs again in order to stay cheaper than you. And so it will go on, with everybody cutting their prices… and in the end, everybody cutting their own throats too!

And while lower prices might be good news for clients in the short run, unless you actually want to throw away your profits, it certainly won't be good news for you.

Usually everybody loses from price wars. But if there are going to be winners, those winners will be the low cost leaders like Richer Sounds that have designed their businesses so that they will always have lower costs than anybody else.

But how can you stay out?

The guiding principle behind all of them is simple… if two competing products are the SAME then clients will choose the cheapest. But if one of the products is DIFFERENT and BETTER, then clients will pay more for it.

As we said in the close to the chapter "Your pricing strategy" if clients choose you on price, it's because you haven't given them any other reason to choose you. So you need to differentiate what you do.

Always remember that...

The right clients will gladly pay more when they understand that they are getting more

The general rule is:

- Most people don't really buy on price
- They <u>say</u> they do... but that is only a ploy to get you to reduce your prices
- Don't fall for it!

Of course there are some people who are genuine price buyers. You may even have some amongst your client base. Here are some of the characteristics of genuine price buyers; they:

- Do all the complaining
- Take up lots of your time
- Tell others how little they have paid
- Leave when they get a cheaper offer
- Forget to pay you

So the key advice is: <u>avoid them at all costs</u>.

Seven strategies for when your competitors are trying to undercut your prices:

1. Link a price cut to something else, for example, ask for three referrals.
2. Create a lower priced alternative, for example, a 2-star service.
3. Cut the price of a few services, for example, offer self-assessment returns as a loss leader.
4. Make it difficult to compare prices, for example, express your prices as monthly amounts and highlight things that your competitors might charge extra for (such as unlimited telephone support).
5. Bundle in extras that most clients don't already buy, for example, an annual inheritance tax review and healthcheck.

6. Alert clients to the risks of going for the cheaper option, after all, they wouldn't trust the health of their family in an unqualified doctor, so why trust the health of their business in an unqualified accountant?
7. Focus on quality and service by better communicating the benefits and value of what you do.

Of course, from time-to-time you will get price objections. The next Chapter contains some ideas for dealing with those objections.

13

Chapter 13
Dealing with price objections

Let's face it... however good your products or services are, sooner or later somebody is going to say they are too expensive. They might be serious, or they might just be "trying it on". But, either way, you can be absolutely certain that it is going to happen some of the time.

Remember what we said earlier about *Price Resistance:* if nobody ever objects to your price, then you must be too cheap!

You also know that the better your reply to those objections, the fewer sales you'll lose, and the less you'll give away in discounts.

So, like all successful businesses, you must make sure that your replies are as good as they can possibly be. And that means creating a script.... continually testing it.... and continually improving it.

What we're going to look at here are the other seven steps you must also take in order to become really good at handling objections. And those seven steps are:

Step 1 Understanding what objections really are... you see, objections are actually opportunities in disguise. After all, if the client wasn't interested he wouldn't bother to object, would he?

So the fact that the client IS objecting tells you that he IS interested. And therefore you should welcome his objection – because it means that you are one step closer to making the sale. So the first step is to replace your "*oh no, an objection*" mindset, with an "*oh great, an objection*" one!

Step 2   Identifying every possible objection, for example, "*That's too expensive*", "*We can't afford it*", or "*Your competitors are cheaper*". Draw up a list. And add to the list every time you or your team get a new kind of price objection.

Step 3   Seeing those objections from your client's point of view... recognise that objections are really just a request for more information. Don't get defensive. And don't get confrontational.

For example, "That's too expensive" is really a request for more information; it actually means "Why should I pay that much?" So treat the objection for what it is – a question. And help your client by giving them the best answer you possibly can. Work with them so that they get the answers and the information they need to make a fully informed decision.

Step 4   Scripting your replies to each and every possible objection. If it's not written down it's not a SYSTEM. And if it's not written down you won't be able to test or improve it. You won't be able to train your team in how to use it. And they won't be able to practice using it.

So you MUST write your scripts down.

Step 5   Continually testing and improving your scripts. It's vital to try out different scripts with clients. Measure how well each of the scripts works. And use the script that gives you the best results... until your tests uncover a script that gives you even better results, of course!

Step 6   Training yourself and your team in how to use them.

Step 7   Practice, practice, practice. After all, nobody is born knowing exactly how to handle objections. They have to be shown how – and they have to be given an opportunity to practice in a safe environment.

Your objection-handling scripts

Here are some thoughts to get you started with your scripts.

If your client says, **"It's a bit expensive!"** you need to find out more information. You need to find out what you are up against. So say something like, "Expensive compared with what?"

What if they say, **"I'm not paying that!"** You need to uncover the real issues and get something more specific. So why not ask, "Why not?" Or perhaps even better, "Can I ask why you say that?"

Or they might say, **"I can get the same thing down the road for half the price."** If that was really the case then it begs the question why aren't they? Also, what they can get down the road is almost certainly <u>not</u> the same thing and not for half the cost either. What they really want is your superior service at the other firm's cheaper price… don't fall for it.

Instead respond with something like…

"That's probably because they, and their clients, know what their service is really worth. Just as we and our clients know what our service is really worth.

After all, you can buy a Skoda for a lot less than an Audi or a BMW, can't you?

And I expect that's why they're cheap and we aren't."

And how will you respond when they say, "**I'm only paying £X now!**" Here's a possible script for you to use…

"I imagine that you're only thinking of changing accountants because you aren't happy with the service you're currently getting. So something about your £X arrangement is wrong, isn't it?"

Then continue with…

"The simple truth is that, as someone once said 'nothing has ever been invented that can't be made cheaper if it is made worse.' In life you generally get what you pay for. So if you aren't happy with

what you are getting from your current accountant, you'll probably have to invest more in order to get a better service.

Those ARE our prices. And they are the prices that all our other clients are very happy to pay. Like you, though, at first some of them thought that those prices were a little high. But what they found was...."

Then explain all of the benefits you offer.

Whatever you do:

* Do not apologise
* Do not give in... don't crash and burn your prices

Instead you should:

* Believe in yourself
* Stay firm
* Acknowledge that you aren't the cheapest
* Explain why... using the scripts you have prepared
  and practiced in advance

If necessary change the package... take out some of the elements of the service. If your 3-star service is too expensive, offer them a 2-star service instead.

And if all else fails, here is an optional "Power Strategy"...

* Write to all other accountants in your town
* Ask them if they want you to pass them leads where you are too expensive?
* Add those that say "yes" to your list of cheap accountants
* Charge them a commission for introductions

So when you then meet one of these "Genuine Price Buyers" introduce them to one of the cheap accountants on your list and charge the other firm a **commission**.

14

Chapter 14
Practical application:
Incorporation services

In "Your blueprint for a better tax practice" the survey looks at how firms of accountants charge for helping their unincorporated clients incorporate. Below is an extract from that research report.

How much do firms charge for their incorporation service?

This is the question that was asked in the survey:

Survey question

How much do you <u>typically</u> price for incorporation (i.e. incorporating an existing sole trader or partnership business, including advice, and related paperwork such as registering for VAT and setting up a PAYE scheme)?

Note: this excludes any fees for goodwill planning which is the subject of the next question.

Some firms in the survey have a minimum price which they will never go below (which is what the first part of the graph shows) and the second part of the graph shows the typical prices that firms charge:

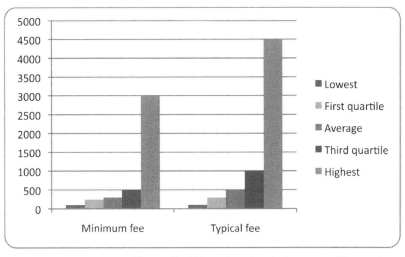

Figure 5 – Prices for simple incorporations where there is no goodwill capitalisation

The numbers behind figure 5 are:

Incorporation	Minimum fee	Average fee
The bottom practice charged	£100	£100
The worst 25% of firms charged	£100 - £250	£100 - £300
The below average 25% of firms charged	£250 - £300	£300 - £500
The average firm charged	£300	£500
The above average 25% of firms charged	£300 - £500	£500 - £1,000
The best 25% of firms charged	£500 - £3,000	£1,000 - £4,500
The top firm charged	£3,000	£4,500

For those firms that use value pricing we also asked those firms the highest prices they had been able to charge. Surprisingly 63 firms in the survey had charged £1,000 or more. In fact, breaking this data down it is as follows:

24 of these had successfully charged between £1,000 and £1,500

11 of these had successfully charged between £1,501 and £2,500

17 of these had successfully charged between £2,501 and £5,000

10 of these had successfully charged between £5,001 and £10,000

And 1 firm had successfully charged £18,000

There is clearly something to be learned from these 63 firms.

And, equally clearly, there is no such thing as "the market price" for this type of tax work. Once again, it is firms and not the market that set their own prices. And some firms do it very much better than others!

For example…

Case study – P&A Accountancy Services

Here is a case study from 2009 in which Nino Pucacco explained how he successfully improved the way he prices incorporation work:

"I would not have believed this possible at any time, let alone in the jaws of a recession… but in the last three months we have proactively and systematically talked to four of our smallish clients and as a result they have agreed to pay us an extra £28,250 in fees to help them incorporate. Those are quite big fees for us since we are a small two partner firm with 3 staff.

In all four cases they were unincorporated businesses that are all paying us £1200-£1,800 pa for their annual accounting service, and one of them was also buying management accounts from us. So they are very typical clients, and yet the extra fees we have earned amount to more than 4 times our core GRF from these clients.

In all four cases we had previously talked to them about incorporation, but they had never really been interested. So this time we decided to tackle the whole process differently. Here is a step by step summary of exactly what we did that worked so well:

Step 1 – A three meeting plan

We mapped out a three meeting approach – since clearly the issues were too big for the client take in properly at just one meeting. The first meeting was to sow the seed. The second meeting was to add the detail and obtain a cheque from the client for £299 + VAT to cover the cost of an independent business valuation. And the third meeting was for the client and, crucially, their significant other, to come in to discuss the valuation and have all their remaining questions answered.

Clearly all of this involved proactively investing time with our clients that we had no certainty of ever being paid for – since the fee was only agreed after the third meeting. But it was unquestionably the right thing to do for our clients, and because profits are a consequence of doing right things for clients, it was clearly also the right thing to do for our practice.

Step 2 – Seeing clients in the right order

We identified the first four clients we were going to talk to, and the order in which we would approach them. Getting the order right was essential, since we wanted to fine tune our process and our skills with the simpler cases before moving on to the more demanding ones. This was also reflected in the fees we were able to earn, which were (in chronological order) £750, £2500, £4000 and £21,000.

Note: *Nino did not participate in the survey, so none of his fees mentioned here are included in the table of results given earlier.*

Step 3 – Making the benefits crystal clear

Across our three meetings we diligently went through all the pros and cons of incorporation, as of course you must. But once we got to the tax issue we found it invaluable to use Incorporation Tax Planner software to be able to instantly show the client the tax position with and without incorporation, and to do "what if" calculations to see how robust the tax savings were.

In most cases, however, the clincher was the tax saving from capitalising goodwill and creating a loan account balance that the client could subsequently draw down on free of tax. The software we used allowed us to both instantly quantify the tax savings, and also to show them how big their resulting tax free loan account balance would be. And it was this latter number that proved decisive for most of our clients.

Step 4 – Pricing properly

As we went into this process we were acutely aware of two pieces of research. Firstly, most accountants grossly under-price incorporation services, and as a result are forced to cut corners and not provide the comprehensive service that clients really need. Secondly, despite what their accounts show, most accountants actually make a loss. In my opinion those two facts are inextricably linked: when you charge too little you let your clients down by not being able to do a proper job, and you let yourself down by making losses.

We didn't want to let anybody down, so we decided to use value pricing by linking the fee to the amount of tax saved. This was made easier for us because our incorporation software automatically calculates a value based fee on the screen. What is more, because the fee is calculated by the computer you tend to meet much less price resistance than you would if the client felt you had just conjured it up out of thin air yourself.

As a result we have significantly enriched our clients' financial affairs. To our clients, therefore, our fees represent only a tiny fraction of the extra tax they are saving, so from their point of view they are getting a really good deal. And from our point of view we are being paid properly and profitably for our contribution. So everybody wins.

Final thoughts

The extra £28,250 we have earned from the above is just the start for us. Obviously we have other unincorporated clients to talk to as well. But we are finding that, across the board, being more systematically proactive than ever before is creating a mountain of extra work (and profitable extra fees) for us in 2009. So much for the recession!"

How much do firms charge for their goodwill planning service?

This is the question that was asked in the survey:

Survey question

How much do you typically charge for goodwill planning (i.e. tax planning from capitalizing the value of goodwill and creating a director's loan account when incorporating a sole trader or partnership business)?

Some firms in the survey have a minimum price which they will never go below (which is what the first part of the graph shows) and the second part of the graph shows the typical prices that firms charge:

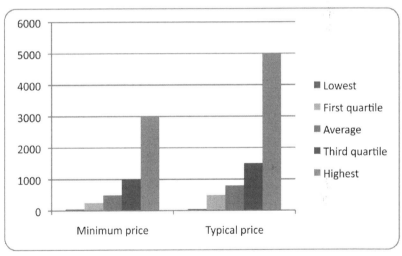

Figure 6 – Prices firms charge for capitalising goodwill on incorporation

The numbers behind figure 6 are:

Goodwill	Minimum fee	Average fee
The bottom practice charged	£50	£50
The worst 25% of firms charged	£50 - £250	£50 - £500
The below average 25% of firms charged	£250 - £500	£500 - £800
The average firm charged	£500	£800
The above average 25% of firms charged	£500 - £1,000	£800 - £1,500
The best 25% of firms charged	£1,000 - £3,000	£1,500 - £5,000
The top firm charged	£3,000	£5,000

We also asked those firms the highest prices they had been able to charge. 27 firms in the survey had charged £3,000 or more; this is further broken down as follows:

13 of these had successfully charged between £3,000 and £5,000

8 of these had successfully charged between £5,001 and £15,000

4 of these had successfully charged between £15,001 and £25,000

And 1 firm had successfully charged £30,000

So once again, there is no such thing as "the market price" for this type of tax work.

How much do firms charge for their company car planning service?

This is the question that was asked in the survey:

Survey question

How much do you typically charge for company car tax planning (i.e. how much would you charge for looking at the most tax-efficient way of treating cars, assuming you are looking at a business that has two cars)?

Some firms in the survey have a minimum price which they will never go below (which is what the first part of the graph shows) and the second part of the graph shows the typical prices that firms charge:

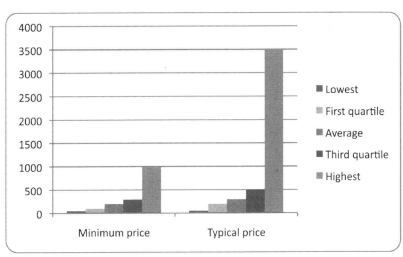

Figure 7 – Prices for company car tax planning where there are two cars

The numbers behind figure 7 are:

Company car tax planning:	Minimum fee	Average fee
The bottom practice charged	£50	£50
The worst 25% of firms charged	£50 - £100	£50 - £200
The below average 25% of firms charged	£100 - £200	£200 - £300
The average firm charged	£200	£300
The above average 25% of firms charged	£200 – £295	£300 - £500
The best 25% of firms charged	£295 - £1,000	£500 - £3,500
The top firm charged	£1,000	£3,500

We also asked those firms the highest prices they had been able to charge. 12 firms in the survey had charged more than £500, with one successfully charging £7,000.

Once again, nothing in the research suggests that there is a market price for this type of tax work.

The implications for the way firms should price

The evidence is clear:

- The market does not set price; firms do.
- In other words, prices are a choice made by practitioners.
- Some firms are much better at making pricing choices than others.
- The way firms make those pricing choices has a fundamental impact on their profitability and success.
- By studying how the most successful firms price other practices can transform their results.

Time and time again we see that firms that fully understand value pricing (and that doesn't mean simply giving a fixed price in advance of doing the work) get superior results.

15

Chapter 15
The role of guarantees and risk reversal in pricing

Offering a guarantee is an incredibly powerful and proven process for helping a client to say, "Yes."

It is also an extremely effective way to charge higher fees. And it gives you a way to charge value based fees, and make those fees compellingly attractive to clients.

This is the question that was asked in the survey:

Survey question

Do you usually offer – and explain to clients – a guarantee when providing a quote for tax planning work? (Note: a contingent fee where you only charge the client the fee if the planning is successful is a form of guarantee)

115 responded with "No" and 56 responded with "Yes", i.e. 32.7% of firms in the survey offer guarantees and/or contingent fees.

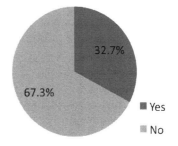

Figure 8 – Firms that offer a guarantee

An example of a tax planning guarantee that achieves all of this is:

"We promise that we will restrict our invoice to [25%] of the amount of tax we actually save you which means that in the event that we are unable to secure any tax savings for you we will not charge you a single penny."

Guarantees are sometimes referred to as "risk-reversal." What this means is that you are removing the risk from the client, i.e. the tax benefit will always be greater than the fee, and if you cannot obtain any tax saving then you will not charge for the work. Since the client cannot possibly be worse off it is very likely that they will ask you to carry out the work.

Of course, unlike traditional time-based billing the risk now sits with you because if you are unable to secure a tax saving for the client you will not be able to raise a bill. So your risk is that you may not be able to recover all or some of any time costs. And this is how it should be... you should only charge clients to the extent that you can add value.

The reality is that the risk of not being able to help the client save tax is very low. And whilst this may happen from time-to-time, it is very likely that the value-based fee you generate from other tax planning (perhaps with other clients) will more than compensate.

In other words, research and experience shows that firms charging value-based fees and removing the risk from the client by building in a guarantee are able to charge very significantly more on average than firms that charge time-based fees with no guarantees.

Case study – Meades & Co

On 2 July last year practitioner Paul Meades sent us the following story in an email (which he has kindly agreed we can share with you):

> "...I just wanted to say thanks for earning me £5,000 this week. Let me explain. A few weeks ago I noticed an opportunity to potentially save a client around £53,000 in VAT for about half a day's work. When I offered him the chance for us to utilise the opportunity, rather than charge for the hours at about £500 all in, I charged

him 10% of whatever we could achieve in a refund (remembering what you keep telling me and the lessons from the Masterclass). Last week he received a cheque for £53k plus £2k interest so we billed him accordingly and he happily paid us the full fee as previously agreed, we even earned a cut of the interest!"

The morals of the story are clear... when we systematically and proactively invest our own time looking for ways to save clients money then:

a) We provide all of our clients with excellent service, and
b) The clients who act on our advice will happily share the benefits by paying us value-based fees that recoup the speculative time cost we invest in providing this kind of proactivity to all our other clients.

So everybody wins.

16

Chapter 16
The 12 key lessons you must learn from this book

Key lesson 1

Whether you are new to value pricing or one of those firms that are already getting much improved results (like the firms that have kindly shared their stories within this book) it is always worth taking a step back and looking at the big picture. And so my suggested first action after you finish reading this book is to look at the numbers for your practice.

Take the numbers from your firm's latest accounts and carry out some 'what-if' analysis. See what will happen to your bottom line profits if you can increase your prices by 10%, 20% or even 40% on average. Perhaps factor in losing some clients. The results will almost certainly make you think and will hopefully make you realise that focusing your efforts on pricing is likely to yield a much quicker and better payback than any other marketing activity.

I have come across dozens of stories of accountancy practices that have increased their prices across the board by these sorts of amounts and lost very, very few clients as a result.

Key lesson 2

Having done some 'what-if' analysis I would suggest you then think about strategy and positioning. Are you going to be a cheap accountant? Are you going to be an average accountant? Or are you going to build a profitable and rewarding practice working with great clients by pursuing a strategy of differentiating yourself, adding value to your clients and in the process charging a premium price.

Make a decision now and stick to it. Build your whole pricing around your chosen strategy.

Without a clear strategy you are likely to fall into the trap of sometimes charging value based fees with some clients (often your better ones), but using more conventional billing methods and offering cheap prices to your smaller and more price-sensitive clients in the hope of keeping everyone happy. The trouble with this is that you are unlikely to have the systems and cost-structure in place to make a worthwhile profit from the price-shoppers and the extra resources these clients will consume will prevent you from focusing on adding value to the better clients who would be willing to pay for that. It also prevents you from spending time building a marketing strategy for acquiring more premium clients.

If you currently have a practice with a very mixed client base, i.e. some A clients that you can add massive value to and who will pay a premium price and some D clients that constantly complain about price and service then you will need to think carefully about your strategy. I know of a number of firms that have made the very brave decision to sack the D clients and have never looked back.

A really useful exercise is to look at the numbers. Analyse your client base between different categories of client and look at the gross fee income you earn from each segment. Very often you will find the 80:20 rule holds true, i.e. the top 20 clients account for 80% of your total practice fees. Conversely it is likely that your D clients will account for a very, very small proportion of your total practice fees. And so the impact of losing them as clients is likely to be very small in terms of the effect on your turnover and profits, but very large in terms of improving the morale of your team, your margins and your scarce time resources.

Key lesson 3

You should continually test your prices. Test your prices and measure. I work with one of the UK's leading experts in R&D Tax Credits. Her name is Alison. Alison has been specialising in this niche area for 11 years and has built up a stunning reputation and close relationships with HMRC (which help her get amazing results for her clients).

Six months ago we talked about how she prices her services and I suggested that she increase her fees by 25%. Despite a huge reluctance I encouraged Alison to test.

Several months later Alison reported back to me that she had received no price resistance to her new pricing structure and yet the impact on her bottom line profit has been massive. At the time of writing Alison is now testing a further increase of 20% to her prices.

What is the worst that can happen?

Clients start to complain and she stops winning work. In which case Alison will revert back to the price structure before the latest 20% increase at a one-off cost of losing out on a few jobs.

What is the best that can happen?

There is no adverse feedback, Alison wins every job and her bottom line profits go through the roof… not just now but every year from now on.

What is the likely outcome?

The likely outcome is somewhere in between. Yes, at the new pricing structure Alison might lose some work. But she will also win lots of work at these new prices (simply because she is the best at what she does and she has a very powerful guarantee). So margins and profits will go up (and for those clients that say "No", she could always revert back to the previous price structure just for them… remember, different customers are willing to pay different prices).

Key lesson 4

Make a decision on how you are going to price going forward. Will you retain the old-fashioned time-based billing? Will you move to fixed prices up front as a now very significant proportion of accountants do? Or will you move completely to value based pricing?

The latter isn't always easy, but the rewards are massive.

I really hope this book provides you with many practical ideas for helping you on that journey. And if you want further help or want to meet up with other accountants who are on that journey (so you can learn from them) go to the "Further help" chapter that follows this one.

Key lesson 5

The first of the 3 keys to value pricing is increasing the value of what you do. A good understanding of the value equation is essential here. You should then apply everything you have learned from the value equation to every product and service that you offer.

A simple and practical way to do this is to focus on one service offering at a time (so for example, you might start with your payroll service) and then, over lunch time or perhaps over dinner in the evening, take your team out and run a brainstorming session. You will find that when you involve other people, the list of benefits you arrive at will be much, much greater than if you do this exercise on your own.

Key lesson 6

This, and the next lesson, is based around the second of the keys to value pricing, i.e. explaining the value.

Remember the 3 pricing emotions. You will get price resistance so accept that. If you don't you're too cheap. You will have clients experience buyers' remorse, and a great way of dealing with this is the use of guarantees. And you will experience payment resistance so review your payment terms and build them into your pricing systems.

Key lesson 7

You have probably heard of WIIFM on many marketing courses (just in case you haven't, it stands for '*what's in it for me*'). This applies just as much to communicating the value of what you do. Don't just tell your clients the "features" of what you do. Tell them the "benefits."

Every time you list a benefit in any quotes or price sheets ask yourself "So what?" For example, if your consulting service will help the client increase their sales. So what? Well, that will increase their profits (assuming of course they maintain their margins). But so what? Well, that will put more money into the client's bank account. So what? That will help them pay off their mortgage within 3 years. And it's that last bit that the client is probably much more emotionally connected to.

It is likely to be much more compelling to say, "When you go through our structured business improvement process we will help you to pay off your mortgage in less than 3 years" than to say, "When you go through our structured business improvement process we will help you increase your sales."

I talked about a process for setting out your fee proposals. You should get the price out of the way early in the proposal and then spend much of the rest of the proposal setting out the benefits to the client. The more relevant benefits you list and the more compelling those benefits are to the client the more they will want to buy from you and the less they will be thinking about price.

Key lesson 8

The third key to value pricing – having increased the value and effectively communicated that value to the client – is to link the price to the value.

Where the value is quantifiable (such as tax planning and corporate finance work) it is relatively easy to come up with a 'formula'. However, value is sometimes subjective, and so it becomes harder to do this. Nevertheless, with some thought, it is always possible to find ways to link the price to the value. In the chapter on 'iterative digital pricing' I went through a practical way of doing this for compliance work.

Other things you could do include charging a premium price for faster turnarounds. For some clients, getting their accounts completed within 2 weeks is really important. So if they value this they will pay a higher price. Some clients perceive greater value if the assignment is carried out by a more senior member of your team, so this could be another option. Bearing in mind that different customers are willing to pay different prices, by offering options, the clients will select those options that represent value to them.

Key lesson 9

There are many different ways for charging different customers different prices and perhaps the simplest and certainly one of the most effective for accountants is menu pricing.

So for each service you offer, e.g. payroll, think about how you can break it down into 3 different service offerings. Think carefully about how you price each bundle and how you communicate the value. This simple idea has transformed the results for many, many firms that I have worked with. For example, many firms that used to charge £200 - £400 for an incorporation service now use the ideas in this book (together with appropriate systems) to charge £1,000 - £20,000.

And remember the power of top down pricing. Present your top level bundle first.

Key lesson 10

You will always get price shoppers. However, the reality is that most people don't really buy on price. They are looking for value. So if you think you have a practice full of price shoppers, the reality is, you haven't given them any other reason to buy other than price.

Further, you will always find competitors in your market place (very often the unqualified firms) who are willing to compete on price.

If you have chosen a strategy of differentiation and adding value, rather than low-cost leadership or simply being average, then you need to create strategies for dealing with the competition so I suggest you revisit the "When your competitors are cheaper" chapter. And if your clients appear to be price shoppers...

Key lesson 11

... you must develop some objection handling scripts. These will become a powerful tool for helping your clients understand the value and deflect them from focusing just on price.

You will of course still have some genuine price buyers, so you need to have a strategy for dealing with them.

Key lesson 12

I have attempted to make this book as practical as possible because I want you to get results. And I'd love you to share your successes with me... it gives me a huge sense of pride and satisfaction when I hear stories of accountancy firms that have taken my ideas and made them work (so please email info@4p-marketing.co.uk whenever you get any successes, it will be much appreciated).

However, you are not going to get those results unless you TAKE ACTION.

Hopefully, the action you have taken as a result of "key lesson 1" above has made you realise how important pricing is to your future success. So block out some time in your diary right now to start implementing the stuff you have learned from this book.

You might recall that in the preface to this book I said, "... you can never know everything. Learning is a continual process and if we want to get better results, we need to keep learning to find a better way." Well, I guess the fact that you have got this far through the book suggests that you fully believe in the message. So in the next chapter on "Further help" I set out some ways that you can continue your learning process...

... I sincerely hope to have the pleasure of working with you at some point in the future and helping make a difference, not just to your profits, but also your life.

So let me leave you with this case study which I things sums up much of what I have talked about in this book and really demonstrates what is possible.

Case study – Harvey Smith & Co

In 2010 Harvey Smith & Co, an 8 person practice in Essex led by sole practitioner Alan Cowperthwaite, increased its turnover by 29%. According to Alan, most of that improvement is a consequence of "being even more professional in the way we help clients, and being even more commercial in the way we price for that help".

Getting it right with incorporations

As an example of being more professional, he has introduced a new system whereby every time his team produce a set of accounts for an unincorporated business they run the numbers through their Incorporation Tax Planner software to see whether there are any potential tax savings from incorporation. And if there are, the team use the software to produce a plain English report that Alan can discuss with the client.

This may not seem like rocket science, but the straw polls my colleague Steve Pipe has conducted with over 500 accountants at our recent seminars suggest that less than 5% of practices even claim to do this. Of course, most of the firms surveyed say they do it some of the time with some of their clients. But less than 5% claim to do it every year with every client. And yet one or more of the client's profits, drawings aspirations, attitude and tax regime may well have changed. So surely we have a professional responsibility to consider it every year for every unincorporated client?

Winning when other firms don't get it right

Alan's systematic approach to giving professional incorporation advice is not only paying dividends with existing clients. It is also helping him to win good quality new clients, as he explains:

"A sole trader with a highly respected professional qualification, and seven of employees, was referred to me. He had been with his accountant for a long time, but had never been advised to consider incorporating. So when I met him I opened up our Incorporation Tax Planner software and showed him that he could save about £28,000 a year in tax by incorporating, with a further c £70,000 over the next five years or so if he also capitalised goodwill.

I think he was shell-shocked, and astounded that he had never been given that advice before. After all, by not giving him this advice years ago, his accountant had literally cost him tens of thousands of pounds.

I then went on to use our pricing software to show him how much our 3, 4 and 5 star services would cost him. There was an audible gulp when he saw the 4 star price of £5,500, since he had previously been paying only £2,000 for what was notionally a very similar service. But, even so, he appointed us there and then because he knew that we were going to leave no stone unturned in serving him properly, and that the fee was tiny compared to the value we would bring.

I should also stress that the £5,500 agreed fee is only for the ongoing annual work. I will be having a separate conversation with him in due course about the fee for helping him to incorporate."

All of that was very professional. But what impressed me even more was that immediately afterwards Alan called a meeting to debrief his team on why the other accountant had lost this client by letting them down, and to re-focus their energies so that Harvey Smith & Co never lost a client in a similar way. In my opinion it is that sort of attention to detail that is the mark of a true professional. And it is therefore no surprise that the practice is enjoying such success.

Pricing more commercially

According to Alan, the second key to their 29% growth rate is that they now set their prices more commercially. And there are two main elements to this: their pricing methodology and the actual prices they charge.

Their new pricing methodology involves using software to give clients a choice of three different service bundles:

- 3 Star - which covers the basic compliance work
- 4 Star - which adds in tax planning, and
- 5 Star - which is more all singing and all dancing.

Rather than just take last year's fee and add a bit for inflation, they also took a long hard look at the current fee every client was paying, and used their new methodology to arrive at a proper commercial fee. Where this was significantly more than the historical fee, they then had a one to one meeting with the client to explain that the fees were too low and that out of fairness they needed to be adjusted. And, as Alan explains, the results of this process were very positive:

"Even though we're in the jaws of a recession, pretty much the only clients we lost were the smaller ones where we had never priced properly. All our good clients stayed. And some of the fee increases were pretty big. For example, I had one client where the fee went up from £2,000 to £4,000 and he said to me afterwards that it was still 'very reasonable', and another where due to their growth the fee went up from £1,500 to £7,000 and he settled it the very next day. So our experience is that when you serve clients properly, and explain the situation carefully, fee resistance melts away."

Further help

This section lists some of the key resources available to help you implement many of the ideas within this book and emulate the results of the firms that feature in the case studies.

"Your blueprint for a better tax practice" – To get a free copy of this ground-breaking survey worth £295 and find out how some accountants are setting the standards for best practice, serving their clients better and making better pricing choices, please visit **www.FreeTaxResearch. co.uk/acc**.

Free proactivity training – You are strongly recommended to attend a "Proactivity" seminar. This is presented by Steve Pipe and Mark Wickersham, and will reveal the precise "how to's" for getting the very best from many of the actions recommended in this book. Places are usually £200 each, but as a reader of this book you can attend as our VIP guest. To claim your free VIP guest place go to **www.AccountantsSeminars. co.uk/Pricing** and enter your details so that we can contact you to arrange your free place.

Support, training, software and advice – For a very modest investment membership of both the Tax Club and Accountants Club provide you with the opportunity to learn and share best practice and help you to build on the ideas contained within this book. Please visit **www. MyTaxClub.co.uk** and **www.MyAccountantsClub.co.uk** for details.

Sales leads and new clients - The 4P Marketing seminar - *"Proven, practical, professional and painless marketing for accountants"* - is a two-day residential course for accountants covering everything you need to know to grow your accountancy practice fast (including how to price accountancy services for maximum profit). It is regarded as the most important and powerful seminar ever created for practices that want to grow. To find out more please go to **www.4p-marketing.co.uk**.

About AVN

Mark Wickersham and Steve Pipe of AVN are passionate about helping the UK's accountancy firms become the most successful and enjoyable to run in the world. All over the UK, hundreds of accountants have joined this association and are using AVN resources, tools and support to help them become more successful, more profitable and enjoy what they do much, much more... and to do the same for their clients.

About 4P Marketing

The 4P Marketing programme has been developed to address a need amongst UK accountants to market their practices using tried and tested marketing systems with measurable results.

The two-day 4P Marketing seminar is packed with tips based on more than 10 years' experience of what works for accountants, combined with the latest thinking in the area of digital marketing. You'll leave with a full list of actions for you to implement in your practice straight away.

I really hope you've enjoyed reading this guide. Even more, I hope you take some action.

If you need more help with implementing any of the ideas in the book, or would like to find out more about our marketing programme just for accountants, then please contact us at **info@4p-marketing.co.uk**.

4P Marketing – Proven, Practical, Professional and Painless marketing solutions for accountants

Bibliography

Michael V. Marn, Eric V. Roegner, Craig C.
   Zawada, *The Price Advantage*

Reed K Holden and Mark R Burton, *Pricing with Confidence*

Robert B. Cialdini, *Influence: Science and Practice*

Robert J. Dolan and Hermann Simon, *Power Pricing*

Ronald J. Baker, *The Professional's Guide to Value Pricing*

Ronald J. Baker, *Pricing on Purpose*

Steve Pipe and Elisabeth Wilson,
   Stress Proof Your Business and Your Life

Steve Pipe and Mark Wickersham,
   Your Blueprint for a Better Tax Practice. The Tax Club

Steve Pipe, *The Good, The Bad and The Ugly.*
   Accountancy Magazine July 2008

Thomas T. Nagle and John E. Hogan,
   The Strategy and Tactics of Pricing

Thomas J. Winninger, *Full Price*

Tony Cram, *Smarter Pricing*

TITANS

How Superheroes Can Help Us
Make Sense of a Polarized World

by
ARMOND BOUDREAUX
with COREY LATTA

CASCADE *Books* · Eugene, Oregon

TITANS
How Superheroes Can Help Us Make Sense of a Polarized World

Pickwick Publications
An Imprint of Wipf and Stock Publishers
199 W. 8th Ave., Suite 3
Eugene, OR 97401

www.wipfandstock.com

PAPERBACK ISBN: 978-1-5326-0400-3
HARDCOVER ISBN: 978-1-5326-0402-7
EBOOK ISBN: 978-1-5326-0401-0

Cataloguing-in-Publication data:

Names: Boudreaux, Armond Joseph | Latta, Corey

Title: Titans : how superheroes can help us make sense of a polarized world / Armond Boudreaux and Corey Latta.

Description: Eugene, OR: Pickwick Publications, 2017 | Includes bibliographical references.

Identifiers: ISBN 978-1-5326-0400-3 (paperback) | ISBN 978-1-5326-0402-7 (hardcover) | ISBN 978-1-5326-0401-0 (ebook)

Subjects: LCSH: Superheroes in literature—Philosophy | Comic books, strips, etc.—Political aspects | Comic books, strips, etc.—Moral and ethical aspects | Superheroes—Religious aspects—Christianity | Superhero films—History and criticism | Motion pictures—Moral and ethical aspects

Classification: PN6728 B682 2017 (paperback) | PN6728 (ebook)

Manufactured in the U.S.A.   06/23/17

www.armondboudreaux.com
https://www.facebook.com/armondboudreauxthathemayraise/
https://aclashofheroes.wordpress.com

This book is for my parents: for my Mom, who has always been my biggest fan; and for my Dad, who will always be my hero.

—Armond Boudreaux

To my boys, Justice and Gus.

—Corey Latta

An empire toppled by its enemies can rise again. But one which crumbles from within? That's dead … forever.

—Helmut Zemo in *Captain America: Civil War*

Wondrous conflagration spread through Chaos,
and to eyes and ears
it seemed as though what they saw and heard
was the collision of the Earth and the wide Sky above.
For so vast a crash could only arise
if earth collapsed under collapsing sky;
such was the uproar of the battling gods.

—Hesiod
Theogony

Contents

ACKNOWLEDGMENTS

A lot of people contributed to this book. First and foremost, I'd like to thank my wife, Leah, who is my constant reader, supporter, and critic. I'd also like to thank several others whose help has been invaluable: Stephen Slimp, a good friend who read many of these pages and offered helpful criticism; my friend and colleague Alan Brasher, whose excellent conversation has helped to hone many of the ideas presented here; and all the students who have taken my Critical Thinking course at East Georgia State College—especially Victoria Powell, Jordan Whorley, Rance Powell, Brianna Powell, and Skyler Wilkes, as well as others too numerous to name—who during class discussions have helped me work through my ideas about superhero mythology. I am grateful to all of you.

Last (but certainly not least), thanks to my friend Corey for contributing chapters on *Daredevil* and *Batman v. Superman*.

—Armond Boudreaux

Thanks to Armond, friend and primary author of this book, for inviting me to write about characters and stories as meaningful to me as they are fun to talk about.

—Corey Latta

ix

A Word about Comic Book Citations

The publication of comic books can be a complicated business. Each individual issue of a comic has an issue number, and most comics also have a volume number. In footnotes, we cite comics by noting their issue numbers, and when a series has multiple volumes, we also note the year in which that volume began. For example, *Captain America* #333 (1968) refers to issue 333 of the volume of *Captain America* that *began* in 1968. (That issue was published in 1987, but its volume began in 1968.)

If a series only has one volume, we do not note the year of the volume (for example: *Kingdom Come* #4 or *The Dark Knight Returns* #1).

Introduction, Part 1
Superheroes as Myth

Armond Boudreaux

Why We Need Superheroes

Why are superhero stories important? Some people will say that they aren't. Recently, one of my college freshmen said to me that a movie like *The Avengers* "doesn't have anything to do with the real world. It's just dumb entertainment." I had to forgive this student for such an outrageous statement. She's new to college, and I have no control over whatever subpar education that she received before now. What in the world do they teach in schools these days?!

So why *are* superhero stories important? Some people would tell my student that superheroes give us something to aspire to. Zack Snyder's film *Man of Steel* deals with this idea. Jor-El, Superman's biological father, tells him, "You will give the people of Earth an ideal to strive toward. They will race behind you. They will stumble. They will fall. But in time, they will join you in the sun, Kal. In time, you will help them accomplish wonders." And we could all certainly do worse than to emulate Superman, Captain America, or Spider-Man. Each embodies ideals of human behavior that we could all learn from.

But while this view of superheroes isn't *wrong*, it's only one answer to the question—and it might not even be the most important one. More important than being moral exemplars, superheroes can also do for us what mythology did for ancient cultures like the Norse, the Greeks, and the Egyptians. Other writers have made this argument before, but here I'd like to describe two particular features of mythology (both ancient and modern), because they are important to the argument of this book.

The Moral Playground

The word "mythology" gets used in different ways by different people, but to most people today it means something like "false belief." For example, Christians might refer to the beliefs of the ancient Egyptians as "myth" in comparison to biblical theology, or a scientist might describe geocentrism as a "myth."

But that's not how we're going to use the word "myth" in this book. It comes from the ancient Greek word *mûthos* (μῦθος), which means "story." In spite of its common usage today, "myth" doesn't originally refer to some belief that turns out to be false. Instead, it refers to *stories*—especially stories that dramatize the beliefs, values, and fears of a culture.

We can find a good example of this in Greek stories about sons betraying their fathers or taking away their fathers' power. These myths reflect certain beliefs and fears about mortality, about the passage of time, and fatherhood. For example, in Hesiod's *Theogony*, an ancient Greek poem about the beginning of the world, Ouranos, the sky-god, rejects his children and prevents their birth by pushing them back into the womb of their mother, Gaia. But Kronos, the eldest son, uses a sickle made of a mythical metal called *adamant* (yes, think of *adamantium*, Wolverine fans!) to castrate his father and allow him and his siblings to be born.

The cycle of conflict between fathers and their children continues when Kronos, now the king of the Greek pantheon, consumes his own children as they're born because he believes that they are destined to overthrow him. But his wife Rhea hides their youngest son, Zeus, from him, and when the child grows up he forces Kronos to vomit up the children that he consumed. After he saves his brothers and sisters from the belly of Kronos, Zeus and the other gods of his generation wage a war against the Titans (a conflict called the *Titanomachy*).

Interestingly, the name *Kronos* seems to be related to one of the ancient Greek words for "time." This is one clue to tell us that myths are more than just fanciful stories. *Kronos* is related to the idea of "time" because ultimately, that's what his story is about. All children are reminders to their parents that one day, they will die and be replaced. (Think of Ultron's sermon to the Maximoff twins in *Age of Ultron*: "Everyone creates the thing they dread. . . . People create . . . children—designed to supplant them, to help them end.")

The Greeks seem to have been particularly concerned with the generational struggle between parents and their children, and they dealt with this problem through their myths: in *Theogony* and in later works like the play *Oedipus the King*. Stories like these helped them to work out the possible consequences of their fears, to dramatize those fears in a way that helped them to better understand what they were afraid of.

Superhero mythology can do the same thing for us that myths did for the Greeks, Romans, Norse, Babylonians, and others. Myths about Superman and Ms. Marvel and Black Panther dramatize the things that we think are most important. In other words, they turn the things we care about the most into *story*. They give us interesting and engaging ways to think about what it means to be good—*really* good. They often confront us with difficult questions like: *Who has a right to exercise power? When should we obey, and when should we stand up to authority? What is the nature of identity?* They give us a playground where we can freely answer those questions and see the consequences of our choices.

Though comic books have had a certain philosophical sophistication for a while now, recently the films have taken on a similar sophistication. For example, *The Avengers* presents audiences with a difficult moral problem: is the obligation not to kill innocent people so important that we should obey it even when doing so might result in the death or enslavement of many people (maybe billions)? When an alien race called the Chitauri invades New York, the Avengers try to protect the city while the World Security Council orders Nick Fury to launch a nuclear missile at the alien army—knowing that it will kill everyone in New York. "If we don't hold them here," says one Councilman, "we lose everything." Nick Fury responds that if he launches a nuclear weapon at the island of Manhattan, then "we already have [lost everything]." Though the film clearly favors Fury's position, the scene still presents viewers with a difficult question: is it better to risk the whole world to save a few, or is it better to sacrifice the few in order to ensure the safety of the many?

While some might call such a moral dilemma outlandish and sophomoric, a not dissimilar dilemma arguably confronted American leaders at the end of World War II—and more importantly, this kind of intellectual or ethical puzzle is characteristic of ancient myths: *Is Oedipus free or fated? Is he culpable for his crimes? Should Agamemnon have refused to sacrifice Iphigenia? How do we explain the way Zeus and Poseidon treat the Phaiakians after they help Odysseus?*

We ask ourselves these kinds of questions in order to help us better understand our lives and our world. We need these kinds of puzzles to work out how to best handle the real-world problems that confront us. And the stories we tell about the X-Men, Captain Marvel, Green Lantern, and the rest all seem especially good at giving us vehicles for exploring those questions. As Mark D. White puts it,

> Luckily, literature—and by "literature" I mean comic books—provides us a way to discuss [moral problems] without having to experience them. We don't have to . . . have a real-life Batman and Joker. That's what the thought experiments are for—they let us play through an imaginary scenario and imagine what we should and shouldn't do.[1]

Serving as a kind of "moral schoolyard" seems to be one of the oldest functions of stories. They help us figure things out without hurting ourselves (though our heroes often suffer a *lot* while we make sense of ethical or spiritual problems).

The Modern Myths

Walk into your local comic shop and browse the new comics, the trade paperbacks, or the used bins, and you'll find plenty of examples of the kinds of stories that I've just described:

- *Superman*: The Man of Tomorrow's origin is a mythologized version of the story of immigrants to America (as well as the stories of Moses and Jesus). Kal-El's parents send him away from their doomed home planet of Krypton just before it is destroyed, and he arrives on Earth as a refugee. Though Kal looks human, though his adopted parents raise him as their own son, he can never quite shake the sense that he is somehow an outsider in this world. But by his devotion to virtues like humility, fairness, and justice, he grows up to use his powers to help the world in the best way he can. His story speaks to the experience of many immigrants, who also often feel like outsiders and who use

1. White, "Why Doesn't Batman Kill the Joker?" 15.

their talents in the best way that they can in order to prove their worth to society.

- *Batman*: In the story of the Dark Knight we find the ancient pagan story of the indomitable will: the human drive to fight on, even though we know we will ultimately lose the war. We see this ethos in classical stories like *Antigone* and the poetry of Homer, as well as in northern European literature like *Beowulf*. And even though it is a very old value, it still has a lot of purchase for people today. We live in a world full of threats that seem unconquerable, and Batman represents our drive to be unyielding in the face of overwhelming obstacles. He can't ultimately defeat crime in Gotham—he is only a man, after all; he will die some day—but he achieves a kind of victory simply by his refusal to give up.

- *Spider-Man*: It might be tempting to think of Peter Parker's story as a teenage boy's power fantasy, but scratch the surface and we find something more: the story of many young people in the modern world who, despite their feelings of social awkwardness, find themselves empowered through unexpected means.

- *The X-Men*: The Children of the Atom give mythological weight to modern rejection of racism and prejudice. Though mutants often suffer persecution and bigotry because of their differences, the X-Men prove their value by protecting a world that often hates them, embodying the principles of men like Martin Luther King, Jr. Meanwhile, the Brotherhood of Mutants, led by Magneto, take a more radical stance, rejecting the idea of integration with normal humans.

I could cite any number of examples, but thankfully, superheroes, both in comics and on the screen, have gained some of the legitimacy that they deserve over the last several years, taking their rightful place as the modern world's Olympians and Asgardians.

Evolving Stories

Ancient myths changed over time. This happened in part because they were passed down orally, and stories told that way are bound to see some alterations. This will happen simply because people don't always pass along information reliably, but also because different people might interpret a story differently. They might adapt it to suit the needs of their time or their audience. For example, the story of Oedipus, the king of Thebes doomed to kill his own father and marry his own mother, was most famously told by Sophocles, but variations of that story show up in Homer and in other writers. When Oedipus appears in *The Odyssey*, Homer doesn't mention a prophecy that destines Oedipus to kill his father and marry his mother. But when Sophocles takes up the story of the doomed king, the prophecy becomes very important—not just to the plot, but to the major themes of the play. *Oedipus the King* is very much about what determines human destiny: are we fated to whatever end we come to? In other words, Sophocles takes a traditional Greek story and uses it to explore questions that concern him most.

Superhero mythology also has the same kind of applicability or adaptability. Different writers and artists can reinterpret familiar superhero stories so that they can use them to speak to the relevant questions of their time.

Maybe the best example of a superhero who has changed with his times is Batman. The Caped Crusader first appeared at the beginning of World War II, and in his first appearances, he was dark, remorseless, and sometimes brutal. During the optimistic fifties, however (partly because of the restrictions placed on superhero publishers by the Comics Code Authority), he took on a lighter, more child-friendly persona—a persona made famous by the 1960s television series. Batman kept this light-hearted tone through the Silver Age of Comics, but when Frank Miller wrote *The Dark Knight Returns* in 1986, the character took on a much darker, more adult tone. Miller used the Batman myth to write a withering critique of the politics, pop-psychology, mass media, and popular culture of the 1980s. With *The Dark Knight Returns,* the character became mature, darker, and more cynical.

In Christopher Nolan's 2008 film *The Dark Knight*, Batman's story takes on a new dimension in light of post-9/11 geopolitics. In Nolan's Gotham, the Joker becomes a terrorist, while Batman, Jim Gordon, and Harvey Dent find themselves in dangerous and uncertain territory in their response to his crimes. In this way, the film reflects the problems that global terrorism poses against the nations of the West. How do you fight against an enemy who is completely unpredictable, immoral, and lawless? How far can we go in the fight against terrorism? Can we justify spying on average citizens in order to keep them safe? And if so, who can we trust with that kind of power? What kinds of interrogation tactics can we legitimately use in order to get the information that we need? And how does a figure like Batman—someone who operates outside the established order—fit into society's response to radical terror?

This adaptability in our myths allows them to change to suit the needs of the time. It allows them to speak to the values that are important or in question for new generations. And superheroes have proven remarkably able to adapt to the problems and societal changes of each generation without fundamentally changing as characters.

Think of Captain America, for instance. When he first appeared in 1941, he represented simple patriotism. The first image of him that the public saw—Cap delivering a right cross to Adolf Hitler—spoke to the spirit of the time. But as Steve Rogers learns when he wakes from the ice, America and the rest of the world have changed a lot since the 1940s. Though Cap remains a symbol of national pride, he is no longer an instrument of the United States government. Instead, he stands as a guardian of American ideals. That position leads him to oppose American institutions on a number of occasions when they fail to live up to the ideal. In *Civil War*, for example, he opposes the Superhuman Registration Act because he believes that it violates the rights of the individual. People who have only a passing familiarity with Steve Rogers might assume that he would support a bill like the SHRA. After all, it passes with overwhelming support. It is designed to defend the American public. And let's face it: the guy wears the flag as a costume. But as he has grown, it has become clear that Captain America is not a stooge of the United States government or of whoever happens to be in power at any given time. He is the Sentinel of Liberty, and he will oppose anyone who threatens freedom or equality.

In some periods, such as in the 1940s when he fought the Nazis and in the 1950s when he fought communism,[2] Cap's enemies were foreigners trying to destroy American values. But recently Cap has had to fight against insiders who seek to destroy America from within. In the Russo Brothers' 2014 film *Captain America: The Winter Solider*, for example, Hydra tries establish a new political order from inside America using the military and

---

2. Since then Marvel has retconned the Captain America of the 1950s to be a well-meaning but mentally-unbalanced impostor, but this does not change the point: like any other myth, the Captain America story adapts to its time to help people make sense of their values, fears, beliefs, etc. ("Retcon"—an abbreviation of "retroactive continuity"—refers to what happens when writers change, alter, or ignore some established element of a story, character, or fictional universe.)

intelligence power of S.H.I.E.L.D. These Hydra operatives are not outsiders coming in; they're American officials, politicians, and intelligence operatives. Sometimes the enemy is already inside the gates.

Some Objections

Some people might raise objections to my view that superheroes constitute a new mythology. For example, someone might argue that since we already have the classical myths, we don't *need* a new mythology. If we want to explore the question of freedom and fate, we've got *Oedipus the King* and *The Odyssey*. If we want to think about warfare, we've got *The Iliad*. If we want to think about masculinity and femininity, we might turn to *Agamemnon*. If we want to think about power and the individual's relationship to the state, we've got *Antigone*. Why do we need these new myths? Why spend time reading comic books when the ancient myths will do?

My first answer is that while the classical writers did pretty well cover just about every major human concern, that does not mean that it isn't worthwhile to apply those questions to modern contexts. For example, Marvel's 2006 series *Civil War* takes the idea of *civil disobedience* that we find in *Antigone* and places it into a very contemporary situation. In doing so, it raises questions about gun control, the regulatory power of government, the ability of science to predict human behavior, and other important topics that weren't necessarily an issue for the ancient Greeks. That doesn't make *Civil War* "better" or "more relevant" than *Antigone*. Instead, it makes it clear that the questions raised by *Antigone* haven't been put to rest or answered satisfactorily, and it gives us an opportunity to apply those questions to contemporary political life.

My second answer is that this new mythology doesn't have to *replace* the old one. We can read and appreciate both. Now someone might object, "But nobody has the time to read all of the classics, let alone both the classics and this 'new mythology,' so why devote time to the newer, inferior works?" But even if we grant that new literature is inferior to ancient literature, this kind of thinking leaves us having to say that nobody should write anything new. One of the great beauties of humanity is that we must constantly be creative, even if that creativity means taking ancient ideas and presenting them in new ways.

Another serious objection to the idea that superheroes are a modern mythology is this: unlike Prometheus and Re, Batman and Captain

America and the rest of the superhero pantheon are products to be bought and sold. They are created by multi-million-dollar companies for the primary purpose of making money. They are featured not only in works of art like comic books and films, but also on T-shirts, lunch boxes, children's toys, and on popcorn bags at movie theaters. It seems absurd to argue that such blatantly commercial characters can rise to the level of mythology.

Even worse, the behavior of the companies who produce comics and superhero movies undercuts the idea of a superhero mythology. In a recent blog post, philosophy professor Mark D. White complained about the crass way in which the editors and writers at Marvel decided to kill off a character in one of their major story events:

> Representatives of both the Big Two [Marvel and DC] comics companies like to say how superheroes comprise our modern mythology. However, that also makes the Big Two the stewards of that mythology and the characters that ground it, and stewardship implies responsibility. Create characters, change characters, kill characters, . . . they're all fine if done well, but please do so with a little more respect for those who want to revel in the mythology.[3]

If superheroes are mythology for our culture, then they deserve a kind of respect not afforded to some other kinds of fictional characters. It is hard to imagine characters who are subject to every whim of the creators (or worse, editors and company administrators) existing on the same level as Beowulf or Odysseus.

But this objection leaves out an important characteristic of comic book characters: because of the nature of the creative and publication processes, over time these characters have taken on lives of their own. Even though he would not exist without Jerry Siegel and Joe Schuster, Superman no longer belongs to any one creator. He has taken on a life outside the minds of his original creators, outside the mind of any creator since then, and has become a myth, a *story*, in the public consciousness. Though creators have some control over individual changes to Superman and his story, his evolution is under the control of no single person. A toy company can make a Superman action figure, a cereal company can put images of him on cereal boxes, and Gene Luen Yang can de-power him[4]—but the Big Blue Boy Scout, the refugee from Krypton, the Man of Tomorrow remains

---

3. White, "*Civil War II*: How the Comics Sausage is Made . . . ."

4. See *Superman* #41 (2011) and *Action Comics* #41 (2011).

a fixed part of American mythology apart from (and sometimes in spite of) the creators and company who own the rights to publish him.

The New Titanomachy

This book exists primarily because we believe that superhero mythology can help people better understand a major problem in contemporary life. Unless you've been on a long vacation in the Negative Zone (or the Phantom Zone, if you prefer the Distinguished Competition) for the last twenty years or so, you've noticed how deeply divided the political and social life of Americans has become. I'm not just talking about the differences between Republicans and Democrats. Like the Divide in Marvel's 2015 version of *Civil War,* there seems to be a real schism running right down the middle of our country that nobody can cross.

People of every political persuasion seem ready and even eager to think the absolute worst that they can of anyone who disagrees with them: "Hillary Clinton wants to destroy America!" "Donald Trump wants to kill all immigrants!" "You disagree with me about X, so you must be a bigot! Or a socialist!" We can't seem to be able to grasp the possibility that people might be convinced that they have good reasons to believe what they believe. Worse, we can't fathom the idea that we ourselves might be wrong about something. If someone disagrees with us, the only *possible* explanation has to be an irrational fear, a sinister prejudice, an unforgivable bigotry, a willful stupidity.

Besides our seemingly unbridgeable divides, there is the problem of reconciling two principles that are equally important to the American ideal: compromise, and standing by your convictions. I think that most people can see the value in both approaches, but the two are in constant tension with one another. So how do we reconcile them?

It might be tempting to say that people should be more willing to meet each other half-way, that politicians should be more willing to compromise in order to get things done, but there are plenty of important issues on which compromise isn't really possible. There are times when we *have* to stick to our principles, when there is no possibility of compromise. To use an example that nobody should find controversial, there was no way for the northern and southern states to compromise with one another about slavery. Either slavery was acceptable, or it is unspeakably evil. There is no middle ground.

Even though many politicians are inept and selfish, many (is it too much to say "most"?) of them believe that they are acting for the "greater good." I hear people say all the time that politicians should stop bickering over their particular interests and do what is best for the people. But the problem isn't really that public officials aren't working for the good of the people. The problem is deciding what the "greater good" *is*. Republicans, Democrats, Libertarians, and Socialists all believe that they know how to achieve the greatest good for the greatest number of people, but they hold some incompatible ideas about what that "greater good" *is*—not to mention how to reach it. Politics means rational people deliberating about how to best order their lives together—but how do people who have fundamentally different beliefs about humanity and about right and wrong deliberate about *anything*?

In this book, Corey and I will try to show how superhero mythology, especially stories in which good people find themselves in conflict with other good people, can help us better understand the modern political and social situation. To do this, we will look at superheroes both on the page and on the screen, and we will discuss heroes from DC and Marvel. In the end, we hope that we can find something in superhero myths that might help us be better neighbors and better citizens. Very often, however, what we'll see are dire warnings about the frightening consequences of our political and social choices.

Introduction, Part 2

Sometimes Superheroes Best Say What Needs to be Said

Corey Latta

That superhero films and comic books often address weighty and politically relevant ideas will come as no surprise to those familiar with stories about Superman, Batman, Spider-Man, Captain America, and others. To comic book readers it need not be said that comics have taken up serious themes since the Golden Age of Comics. Death, the existence and nature of God, the possibility of the afterlife, the problem of evil, one's identity and its meaning in society, the abusive nature of power—comics have explored all of the major questions and issues that matter to human beings.

But to the casual comics fan or the average moviegoer just looking for a popcorn flick, it might not be obvious why comics visit crucial political and philosophical topics so frequently and so effectively. In 2016 alone we saw superhero films take up such important issues as civil disobedience, the problem of evil and theodicy, the relationship of the individual to the state, and the role of myth in the creation of society. How can movies about people who can't possibly exist help us to think about such issues?

Famed fantasy writer and renowned literary critic C. S. Lewis might be able to help answer that question. He once said that in some cases, with some messages, fantastic stories—or what he called "fairy stories"—can do a better job of saying what the author means to say than more realistic stories. Speaking of his fantasy series *The Chronicles of Narnia*, Lewis said that for the kind of story he wanted to write—one that required "no love interest and no close psychology"[5]—the fairy tale proved ideal. Each genre comes with its unique virtues. For Lewis, virtues such as the fairy tale's brevity, restraints on description, and its traditionalism, made it the ideal form for what needed to be said: "I wrote fairy tales because the Fairy Tale seemed the ideal Form for the stuff I had to say."[6] But then he came to a more profound realization: "I thought I saw how stories of this kind could steal past a certain inhibition which had paralyzed much of my own religion in childhood."[7]

Knowing that some people might accuse the religiously allusive *Chronicles of Narnia* of being preachy, Lewis thought that the fairy form might allow him and his readers to avoid any obligations to feel overtly religious sentiment. Lewis concluded,

> But supposing that by casting all these things into an imaginary world, stripping them of their stained-glass and Sunday school associations, one could make them for the first time appear in their real potency? Could one not thus steal past those watchful dragons? I thought one could.[8]

In other words, to project important and weighty ideas onto an imaginary world is to remove stereotypical and stigmatic associations from the subject, allowing one to see the thing anew.

The fondness that comic and superhero scriptwriters have for heavy philosophical ideas is due to the freedom their form allows. Hence, a miniseries like *Kingdom Come* can explicitly explore Christian eschatology without reading like a work of systematic theology. A reader can forget that behind the aged Justice League's war with the metahumans is an exploration of traditional morality versus the amorality of postmodernism. The very presence of figures like Superman and Captain Marvel encourages readers to disassociate themselves from entrenched ideas of universal morality and the ethics of violence by depicting those ideas in an unfamiliar and fantastic setting.

Likewise, a film like *Captain America: Civil War* asks that viewers consider afresh what it means for one's personal convictions when public consensus demands that those convictions be compromised. Within the

5. Lewis, "Sometimes Fairy Stories May Say Best What's to Be Said," 47.
6. Ibid., 47.
7. Ibid.
8. Ibid.

complexities of Captain America's disagreement with Iron Man stands an age-old tension—the conflict between the state and individual—yet because the idea is projected onto an imaginative form, the idea of civil disobedience steals past the watchful dragons of preconception and prejudice. By wearing a mask, the struggle between the personal and the public can be approached as a stranger and seen as if for the first time. Where a realist exploration of a political idea brings in real entanglements of partisan bias that discourage critical thought, an imaginative approach unfetters the subject from familiarity.

To understand how exactly a superhero film causes ideas like civil disobedience to appear for the first time in their real potency, I turn to J. R. R. Tolkien—author of *The Lord of the Rings*, friend of C. S. Lewis, and fellow member of the Oxford intellectual community known as the "Inklings." In a masterful essay, "On Fairy-Stories," Tolkien writes that fantasy—of which I include *Civil War* as an example—"is founded upon the hard recognition that things are so in the world as it appears under the sun; on a recognition of fact, but not a slavery to it."[9] The premise behind *Civil War* is that the fact that things are wrong ought not enslave one to the idea that they should remain wrong. *Civil War*'s chief aim is to show that the world as it appears under an encroaching governmental sun needs saving by free men and women not beholden to it. Tolkien ascribes three functions to fairy stories—recovery, escape, and consolation—which shed light on how the superhero film achieves that purpose. We can use these concepts in order to understand how a movie like *Captain America: Civil War* explores a theme like civil disobedience so effectively.

Tolkien says that fantasy's first operation can help us to see something about reality more clearly: "Recovery (which includes return and renewal of health) is a re-gaining—regaining of a clear view."[10] In *Civil War*, the fundamental object of recovery is the moral fortitude required to resist power. As tensions heighten between Captain America and Tony Stark over the Sokovia Accords, which place the Avengers under the authority of a government bureaucracy that Cap fears can be corrupted, there arises an imperative for moral courage. Ironclad policy must be met by unbreakable personal conviction.

9. Tolkien, "On Fairy-Stories," 144.
10. Ibid., 146.

When Sharon Carter speaks at the funeral of her Aunt Peggy, she becomes an agent of recovery by describing the moral courage that Cap will have to show:

> I asked [Aunt Peggy] once how she managed to master diplomacy and espionage at a time when no one wanted to see a woman succeed at either. And she said, "Compromise where you can. Where you can't, don't. Even if everyone is telling you that something wrong is something right. Even if the whole world is telling you to move, it is your duty to plant yourself like a tree, look them in the eye, and say, 'No, *you* move.'"

That final imperative—"No, *you* move"—becomes the new lens through which Cap regains sight of moral conviction. Agent Carter cleans the window, as Tolkien describes the act of recovery, of perspective for Captain America, and gives him a new vision of a familiar conviction.

The second way *Civil War* goes about exploring political ideas is through what Tolkien labels "escape." According to Tolkien, this second function of fantasy draws the audience out of time-bound provincialism and particulars so that the timeless truths of the story might appear. Fairy stories, Tolkien says, have "more permanent and fundamental things to talk about."[11] It's on this point that *Civil War* as a story operates most effectively. In its imaginative presentation—even in ancillary things like Ant-Man's ability to change his size or Iron Man's newest gadget—the story is loosed from the constraints of realism and allowed to stand on the legs of its ideas. By presenting its ideas in a fantastic way, *Civil War* allows us to see politics in a fresh and unfamiliar light.

The final way *Civil War* fulfills its role as a work of fantasy is in what Tolkien calls "consolation." Tolkien says that the truest form of consolation comes in what he coins the "eucatastrophe," the story's upward turn.[12] In the arc of a story, the eucatastrophe comes with dire consequence. Often veiled by catastrophic circumstance and loss, the eucatastrophe is that unexpected promise of fulfillment, comfort, even joy. This, according to Tolkien, is a story's highest function—to promise the reader that in spite of the conflict and loss that we suffer, better things lie ahead than behind. Tolkien writes, "In such stories when the sudden 'turn' comes we get a piercing glimpse of joy, and heart's desire, that for a moment passes outside the frame, rends

11. Ibid., 149.
12. Ibid., 153.

indeed the very web of story, and lets a gleam come through."[13] In *Civil War*, this upward "turn" is hard won, the joy earned by pain. The eucatastrophe comes in a poignant letter that Steve writes to Tony at the end of the film:

> I know I hurt you, Tony. . . . I wish we agreed on the Accords. I really do. I know you're doing what you believe in, and that's all any of us can do. That's all any of us should. So no matter what, I promise you, if you need us—if you need me—I'll be there.

Conflict need not lead to despair. In *Civil War*, "the joy of the happy ending"[14]—what Tolkien calls the consolation of the fantastic—lies in the very moral conviction the film aims to recover. The moral conviction that leads Captain America to stand against Tony is the same conviction that compels him to promise future loyalty. For Cap, and for the film, civil disobedience is an inflexible commitment to what the conscience confirms as right. On the issue of the Sokovia Accords, Cap's convictions lead him to opposition. On the issue of friendship, his convictions insist upon fidelity. As consolation, *Civil War* seeks to bring peace to rival factions by reclaiming harmony between friends.

What makes *Civil War* an effective political statement about civil disobedience is the genre in which the statement is made. I've here tried to argue that the thing said is only as good as the way in which it is said. In a superhero story that deals with important ideas, we see those ideas in light of their ideal forms. When we look at the reflection of political or social themes in comics, we're meant to see not only what a thing *is*, but also what it *should be*. Lewis writes that fantasy stories seek "to generalize while remaining concrete, to present in palpable form not concepts or even experiences but whole classes of experience, and to throw off irrelevancies."[15] That is what *Civil War* and other superhero stories can do for us. They can say best what needs to be said.

---

13. Ibid., 154.
14. Ibid.
15. Ibid., 48.

Part I

Heroes on the Page

by Armond Boudreaux

Creon: I say to you at the very outset that I have nothing but contempt for the kind of Governor who is afraid, for whatever reason, to follow the course that he knows is best for the state; and as for the man who sets private friendship above the public welfare,—I have no use for him, either.

Antigone: Your edict, King, was strong,
But all your strength is weakness itself against
The immortal unrecorded laws of God.
They are not merely now: they were, and shall be,
Operative for ever, beyond man utterly.

—Sophocles
Antigone

1

Two Americas

The Fight for Captain America

Who Is Captain America?

In some ways, no hero's legacy has been more contentious over the years than Captain America's. To whom does he belong? Does he belong on the left or the right side of the political spectrum? In what way does he represent America and her values? Is he an instrument of the American government? Does he stand for the American Dream? Is he truly the Sentinel of Liberty, or does he simply fight to maintain an unjust status quo? Many different people—creators, fans, and critics—have come up with different answers to these questions. Those of us who care about him have fought for possession of Captain America in much the same way as the Greeks and the Trojans fought over the body of Patroklos in the *Iliad*. And given Cap's status as a symbol of American values and ideals, this ought to surprise no one. Whatever we decide Captain America means, that will be what America herself means, as well.

Through the Years

If the 2016 election season taught us anything, it's that the nation is as divided as it has ever been—socially, ideologically, economically, theologically, morally, politically, intellectually. Everyone seems to know what it means to be an American and what America stands for, but the divisions that separate us from one another prevent any kind of consensus about what American ideals truly are. Presidential candidates promise to restore America to some past greatness that has been lost—but people will disagree about what it is that ever made America a good nation to begin with. Others promise to "stand up to the billionaires" and tell them, *You can't have it all!"* But often these promises seem dubious at best because those who make them are very well-off and divided by wealth and privilege from the people they claim to represent. Still others promise to represent "all Americans"—even as their actions and policies show that they're just as biased as the politicians that they criticize. Segments of the public, interest groups, religious groups, social organizations, and others struggle for a voice in how we order our lives together. Though the forces behind them are complex, most of these conflicts can be reduced to disagreements over the basic values that define America.

In many ways, the history of Captain America has been a history of that struggle. Since 1941, we've seen dozens of Captain Americas: Steve Rogers, the original, who is the "true" Cap for many fans; William Burnside, the 1950's Captain America; Bucky Barnes, who acted as Captain America while Steve Rogers was "dead" in the late 2000s; Sam Wilson, one of the two current Captain Americas; Isaiah Bradley, who was part of a government program that attempted to re-create the Super-Soldier Serum;[1] William Naslund and John Walker, who were appointed by the U.S. government to replace Rogers (Naslund when Rogers was presumed dead after WW II,[2] and Walker when Rogers stepped down from the position after becoming disillusioned with the government[3]); and several others. Even Clint Barton wielded the shield at one point (for just a single outing).[4]

Most of the stories involving alternate versions of Cap result from crises and conflicts about what Captain America means—who he belongs to and what he stands for. Naslund's and Walker's tenures as Captain America, for example, speak to the question of whether or not Cap's title and position should be a function of the U.S. government. These stories ask whether Cap is merely appointed to carry out the will of the state, or if he represents

---

1. *Truth: Red, White, and Black* (2003).

2. *What If?* (1977).

3. *Captain America* #333 (1968).

4. *Fallen Son: The Death of Captain America* #3 (2007).

values and ideals that transcend political structures. Rogers's opposition to government regulation in *Civil War*, his "death" at the end of that conflict, and Bucky's struggle to understand his role as the new Captain America in the Brubaker run also raise interesting and often difficult questions about who or what Captain America stands for. And most recently in the Nick Spencer run on the title, Cap has been transformed by the Red Skull into a Hydra sleeper agent, raising deep questions about whether or not America is still a force for good in the world. Almost always, these stories end up pitting Cap against other heroes. Even more significantly, they often pit him against *other* Captain Americas.

The Man without a Country

In *Captain America and the Falcon* #175 by Steve Englehart and Sal Buscema, Cap and the Falcon (Sam Wilson) have been fighting the Secret Empire, an off-shoot of Hydra that has been kidnapping mutants in order to use their powers as energy for running their "flying saucer," a weapon that the Empire hopes will bring the U.S. to its knees. At the end of that issue, Cap, Falcon, and Marvel Girl defeat the Empire and their weapon on the White House lawn. Number One, the leader of the Empire, flees into the White House, and when Cap catches him and unmasks him, the villain shoots himself in the head. Though we never see Number One's face, Cap's shocked reaction to the man's true identity and Number One's dialogue show that he is a highly-placed government official, strongly implying that he is actually the president—an implication that has been confirmed by Englehart.[5]

When this issue was published in 1973, the American public was reeling from the Watergate scandal and the revelation of corruption in the government reaching all the way to the highest levels. Cap's shock and disillusionment at the realization that the president himself is guilty of treason, hypocrisy, and corruption reflects the feelings of the nation at a time when faith in America and its ideals had suffered a painful wound. More importantly, it leads Cap to give up the name of Captain America and his shield and brings him into conflict not only with villains like Viper and Cobra, but also with his closest friend, the Falcon.

At the beginning of #176, still reeling from the revelation at the end of #175, Cap stands with his fists clenched and his face turned dramatically

5. Englehart, "Captain America II."

toward the sky to exclaim, "Captain America must die!" Over the next few pages, Steve recalls Project: Rebirth and his origin as Captain America. He remembers the awe and tremendous sense of responsibility that he felt when he fully understood what he had become, but then a two-page spread interrupts the regular six-panel layout of the issue to reveal Cap with his head down and his hand over his face, the whole history of his life since the Super-Soldier Serum laid out across the page: the loss of his original partner, Bucky; the Red Skull; his entombment in ice; the Avengers; and the Secret Empire's leader with a gun pointed at his temple. "But so much has happened since then," Cap says. He might have been able to believe in patriotism and heroism during the 1940s when the divisions between the "good guy" and the "bad guy" were much clearer, but now Cap is the Man Out of Time.

Aware of his disillusionment, some of Cap's fellow Avengers try to dissuade him from giving up heroism. Thor argues that a man is "most fully alive" and full of "true nobility" when he fights "for the right," and that without his masked identity, Steve will give up the most important part of himself. Iron Man argues that Steve's powers obligate him to use them for the good of others. As Uncle Ben might say, with great power must come great responsibility.

But while Thor and Iron Man are calm and patient with Cap as he works through his despair at the corruption of the institution to which he has devoted his life, Falcon barges into the room and angrily accuses him of going off the "deep end." He says that Cap is letting everyone down—including all the people in the country who look up to him—by giving up his identity and his role as a hero. To Sam, Captain America is more than just a superhero name, and Steve is more than just a super-soldier. He is the Sentinel of Liberty, an icon who represents the best of America and unites its citizens.

But the usually idealistic Steve remains unpersuaded by the arguments of his friends. For him, the very idea of America has died. The government that the people elected to represent them has become corrupt, and the people themselves are divided:

> There was a time, yes, when the country faced a clearly hideous aggressor, and her people stood united against it. But now, nothing's that simple. Americans have many goals—some of them quite contrary to others! In the land of the free, each of us is able to do what he wants to do—think what he wants to think. That's

as it should be—but it makes for a great many different versions of what America is. So when people the world over look at me—which America am I supposed to symbolize?

This speech ends with a panel that shows the ethnic and racial diversity of 1973 America: black, white, Hispanic, Middle Eastern, Asian—and in the middle, a Captain America who has been broken under the weight of his role. One man, he concludes, can't embody of the spirit of such a diversity of people, and they have nothing but a corrupt government to unite them. So at the end of #176, Steve renounces the name of Captain America and retires from heroism altogether.

While his fellow Avengers accept this decision, the Falcon sees Steve's abandoning of his role as a betrayal not only of the principles that Steve claimed to stand for, but also a betrayal of Sam himself. Steve trained him and inspired him to be a hero, to be the kind of person who sets an example for others to follow, and besides being partners in their work, they are also friends. So when Steve quits, Falcon feels it as a slap in the face. Steve has betrayed his principles and their friendship. When Steve happens upon a battle between the Falcon and a group of killer robots, Steve intervenes and rescues Sam just as he is about to be defeated. Sam, however, isn't happy about Steve's help:

> Couldn't help yourself, huh? You couldn't be bothered to be my partner, no matter how much I pleaded—but you were right there to be my nurse maid! Well, listen, big man. I thank you for my life this time—but from now on, I'll thank you to leave the Falcon strictly alone! Got it?[6]

Sam's animosity toward Steve continues through issue #184. Believing that there has to be a Captain America, even if Steve won't do the job anymore, Sam takes on a sidekick named Roscoe Simons, who dons the Captain America costume and shield. Meanwhile, believing himself to be a man without a country but unable to set aside superheroics, Steve returns to heroism under the name Nomad.

Just a Kid from Brooklyn

What finally drives Steve to take up the shield again is a realization: despite corruption in the government he has pledged to serve and despite the

6. *Captain America* #178 (1968).

deep divisions in American culture, the one quality that can define Captain America is service. In fact, his desire to serve has always been Steve Rogers's defining characteristic. The great power that he wields is indeed extraordinary, but what is truly remarkable about Captain America is the fact that both before and after he becomes a super-soldier, Steve Rogers seeks only to serve others.

The 2011 film *Captain America: The First Avenger* perfectly captures this. When we first meet Steve in that film, he is a scrawny, patriotic young man so eager to fight that, though he is medically ineligible, he tries several times to enlist only to receive a 4F stamp. He finally catches a break when Abraham Erskine overhears a conversation between Steve and his best friend, Bucky Barnes. "Why are you so keen to fight?" asks Bucky. "There are so many important jobs." Steve's response impresses Erskine: "There are men laying down their lives. I got no right to do any less than them." When Steve tries to enlist that night, Erskine personally evaluates him and makes him part of the super-soldier program.

At first, Steve has no idea why Erskine chooses him. He struggles through boot camp, barely able to do the required training and frequently victim to the bullying of the other cadets. The turning point comes when Colonel Phillips, annoyed that Erskine has chosen Rogers for the first super-soldier experiment, throws a dummy grenade into the middle of a crowd to prove that other cadets are better candidates, that "you don't win wars with 'niceness.' . . . You win wars with guts." When all the other cadets scatter, the weakling Steve leaps onto the grenade to shield others from the blast. Though Colonel Phillips continues to feign skepticism, the grenade incident proves to everyone present what has been clear to Erskine since he first laid eyes on Rogers at the recruitment office: Steve Rogers's character and desire only to serve others makes him the ideal candidate for the super-soldier program.

On the night before the experiment, Steve asks Erskine "the only question that really matters": "Why me?" Indeed, why Steve? He is undoubtedly brave, but courage is not enough to win a war. The other cadets in the program are already strong, fast, and obedient to their superiors. By the measure of most people who understand military matters, almost any cadet would be a better candidate for the super-soldier program than Steve Rogers, who is obedient but lacks almost all other soldierly attributes. And yet Erskine looks for something in the test subject besides his physical strength:

> The serum amplifies everything that is inside, so good becomes great; bad becomes worse. This is why you were chosen: because the strong man who has known power all his life may lose respect for that power, but a weak man knows the value of strength and knows compassion.

Though Steve seems unsure whether he should understand Erskine's words as a compliment, we know that the scientist has in fact greatly praised the skinny weakling in front of him. He has said that of all the men in the U.S. military, Steve Rogers is the one man to whom he will entrust this tremendous power. Rogers is a rarity among men precisely because he is weak and does not pursue power—only the opportunity to give what he has in the service of others.

This is the realization that makes Steve abandon his Nomad identity and take up the mantle of Captain America once more in *Captain America* #184. When he discovers that the Red Skull has killed the new Captain America in order to draw him out, Steve cries, "I don't want to be Captain America!" But as he goes over in his own mind his reasons for abandoning the shield in the first place, he realizes that "there has to be somebody who will fight for the dream, against any foe." That, he concludes, is what defines Captain America.

Throughout issues 175–84, others try to take up the role of Captain America—a baseball player named Bob Russo; a member of a biker gang named Scar; and Roscoe Simons—but none of them succeed. Russo and Scar don't take the job seriously enough, and they want it for the wrong reasons. Roscoe takes the role and the responsibility seriously, but he isn't physically up to the challenge. Even though Steve says that he doesn't *want* to be Captain America anymore, he realizes—perhaps in part because of Roscoe's death—that there *must be* a Captain America, and the one best suited to the job has the responsibility to do it.

The Commission and the Captain

In 1987, Cap goes through another crisis of identity that in some ways is the reverse of the dilemma that he experienced in 1973. This time he has no doubts about the ideals that he represents as Captain America. Even though the nation is run by a government that has often been corrupt, Cap understands that America as an ideal transcends the state that represents her. Instead, he finds himself being forced to choose between the ideals and the symbol itself.

In *Captain America* #332, Steve Rogers gets hauled in front of the Commission, which one of its members describes as "a specially appointed task force operating under the direct command of the president," whose "specific purview is the nation's 'special operatives,' namely those who the media have dubbed 'super-people.'" Even though Captain America has been operating independently of the government ever since he emerged from the ice in *Avengers* #4 (1963), the goal of the Commission is to bring him under their direct control:

> You will *resume* your official position as America's super-soldier, and have all of your activities coordinated by this office. . . . Your uniform, your shield, and the very name of Captain America, as we said, are rightfully ours.

The Commission gives Rogers one day to decide whether or not he will continue to wear the mantle of Captain America, warning him that if he chooses not to submit to their directives, they will find a replacement for him.

The events of issue #332 mark another moment of crisis for Cap, but unlike before, when he became Nomad, Rogers is not uncertain about what it means to be Captain America:

> Those men [i.e., the Commission] are not my country. They are only paid bureaucrats of the country's current administration. They represent the country's political system—while I represent those intangibles upon which our nation was founded: . . . liberty, justice, dignity, the pursuit of happiness. . . . That, really, is my major stumbling block with their plan for me. By going back to my wartime role as a glorified agent of America's official policies, I'd be compromising my effectiveness as a symbol that transcends mere politics.

So instead of submitting to bureaucratic authority, Steve hands over the shield and uniform to the Commission. Unlike before when he gave up the role of Captain America to become Nomad, Steve gives up being Captain America out of respect for the symbol—not as a rejection of it. He doesn't want to participate in the politicization of America's ideals.

In issue #333, the Commission recruits John Walker to be Steve's replacement as Captain America. Walker, who as the masked hero Super Patriot had been a harsh critic of Captain America, eagerly takes on the new role. Unfortunately, he proves to be unsuited to the role that the Commission wants him to play, and after a group of right-wing domestic terrorists called the Watchdogs kill his parents, he goes off the deep end, murdering several of the Watchdogs as well as nearly killing two of his former friends, Jerry Johnson and Hector Lennox.

Meanwhile, Steve Rogers takes up a new superhero persona, dubbed simply "the Captain." He wears a costume reminiscent of the Captain America uniform with a red, white, and black color scheme and a matching vibranium shield, and he continues to act exactly as he did before the Commission forced him to give up the name of Captain America. As he tells the members of the Commission, "I have learned these past months that I can serve my ideals—the ideals of this great country—even without that uniform! I've learned that it's the man that counts, not the clothing!"[7] Whereas his discovery of government corruption in the 1970s made him question the very idea of America, Steve now believes that America is more than any one person or institution that claims to speak for her.

What makes Steve take up the mantle yet again is the revelation that the Commission has been manipulated by the Red Skull in order to discredit the Captain America persona and to disgrace Steve himself. When Steve exposes the head commissioner as having been working with the Red Skull, the Commission forces John Walker to step down from the position and offers it to Steve, who initially refuses. But John begs him to become Captain America again, arguing that Steve is the only man for the job: "Take the [uniform and shield] back—to prevent [the Commission] from getting yet another poor slob to try to do the job you do so easily."[8] Yet again, responsibility drives Steve to take up the Stars and Stripes and the shield—not because he desires the role, but because the name of Captain America belongs to the one who best understands its meaning and who is most capable of living up to it.

Captain America vs William Burnside

Ed Brubaker's run on *Captain America* from 2004–12 brought about some of the most interesting developments to the character in his history. First, he brought to the character a spy-thriller, espionage tone that was in keeping with post-9/11 paranoia. Second, he brought Cap's old partner Bucky

7. *Captain America* #350 (1968).
8. Ibid.

back from the "dead," revealing him to have been captured and brainwashed by the Soviets and employed as the super-assassin Winter Soldier for the entirety of the Cold War. And third, Brubaker killed Steve Rogers at the end of the superhuman Civil War, ushering in a period in which Bucky Barnes took up the mantle of Captain America before Rogers's return from the dead.[9] It's no exaggeration to say that Brubaker's time as the scribe for the *Captain America* titles resulted in some of the best stories about the Sentinel of Liberty ever written.

But in addition to developing the character and reviving reader enthusiasm for him, Brubaker's run also had stories with interesting political implications. And not surprisingly, one of the most important of these involves a conflict with another Captain America: William Burnside, the Captain America of the 1950s.

Though the original Captain America title (by creators Joe Simon and Jack Kirby) ended in 1949, Cap was revived in the 1950s in three different books: *Young Men, Men's Adventures,* and *Captain America Comics* #76–78. True to the spirit of the time, these stories depicted Cap and Bucky fighting Communists (including a Soviet Red Skull) instead of Nazis. But these stories were never very successful, and when Stan Lee revived Captain America again in 1964, he chose to ignore the 1950's books and gave us the story that most people know today: Captain America was frozen in ice and fell into a state of suspended animation in 1945 before he was revived by the Avengers in 1964.

The 1950's Captain America stories remained non-canonical for the entire Silver Age of Comics,[10] but in 1972 Steve Engelhart revisited the 1950's stories. He revealed that the man who operated as Captain America in the 1950s was an impostor who—along with his sidekick, James "Bucky" Monroe—underwent an imperfect reproduction of the super-soldier program. The procedure made him physically stronger than the original Captain America, but it also slowly made him paranoid and mentally unbalanced, turning him into a white supremacist who saw a Communist in anyone who didn't appear to be his idea of the perfect American. When his paranoia and bigotry go too far, the government captures him and Bucky and put them into suspended animation. "They used to be heroes, but now they're insane," one official says of them. "Officially we disapproved of

---

9. It has nearly become a cliché to note that death rarely lasts in comic books.

10. The period of comics history that lasted from the late 1950s to roughly 1970.

them, but they meant a lot to America before they went bad."[11] During the Brubaker run, the 1950's Cap falls under the influence of the Red Skull and Doctor Faustus, and his true name is revealed to be William Burnside.[12]

Steve Rogers comes into conflict with this impostor Captain America in *Captain America* #155–65, when the 1950's Cap and James Monroe are released from their suspended animation and go after Steve, believing that he is a traitorous successor to the original Captain America. Though Steve ultimately beats Burnside (while Falcon and Sharon Carter take down the deranged Monroe), the fight rattles him. Standing over the unconscious Burnside, Steve tells Sharon, "He'll be fine. . . . The authorities will put him and Bucky back in their suspended-animation tanks, until a cure can be found—*if* one can be found. And I'll go back to fighting for a better America while they sleep. But all the time, I'll be thinking . . . that he could have been *me*."[13]

Burnside resurfaces later during the Brubaker run when the Red Skull and Doctor Faustus try to position him as the new Captain America after Steve Rogers is presumed dead. Burnside escapes their influence, though, and returns to his hometown of Boise, Idaho, where he becomes disillusioned with what America has become since the 1950s and joins an antigovernment group called the Watchdogs. He tries to blow up Hoover Dam as the start to a revolution, but Captain America (Bucky Barnes) and the Falcon foil the plot. Bucky tries to reason with him, promising to get help for him, but in the end he has to shoot Burnside with a machine gun in order to keep him from setting off the bomb, and Burnside's body falls over the dam into the Colorado River.

The story of the 1950's Captain America is really the story of America's reflection upon the politics of the Cold War. After World War II, our fight with Communism united us, but as the long years of the Korean and Vietnam wars dragged on, as McCarthyism took its toll, and as socialism and communism took root in the academy, many Americans began to reevaluate America's position in the world, as well as rethinking the existential conflict between capitalism and communism or democracy and totalitarianism. When Marvel brought the 1950's Captain America into continuity with the rest of Cap's stories and turned him into a deranged impostor, they did so in keeping with the attitude that a large segment of the citizenry

11. *Captain America* #155 (1968).
12. *Captain America* #602 (1968).
13. *Captain America* #156 (1968).

had come to adopt. They had come to reject many of the values that had driven the Cold War up to that point. As always, the evolution of Captain America's story reflected the evolution of the nation's self-image.

Friends Divided

In 2014, during the Rick Remender run on the title, Cap battles a villain called the Iron Nail, who hates America and the West and sets out to discredit Cap and S.H.I.E.L.D. by hijacking a helicarrier and using it to attack the Eastern European nation of Nrosvekistan. Cap defeats the Iron Nail, but not before the villain siphons away all of Steve's strength and his youth, leaving him a frail old man. Steve passes on his shield and the title of Captain America to his longtime friend Sam Wilson, while Steve himself takes up a new role as an advisor and commander for S.H.I.E.L.D.

With Nick Spencer now writing the *Captain America* titles, things don't always go well for Sam as the new Captain America, and his relationship with Steve suffers some setbacks. All this comes from Sam's decision in *Captain America: Sam Wilson* #1 to wade into politics, which his predecessor always tried to avoid doing.[14] Instead of taking sides in policy disputes, Steve tried to remain above the fray, but Sam believes that he can't—and maybe even *shouldn't*—do that, so he decides to wade into partisan politics as Captain America:

> Red and blue, black and white, Republican and Democrat, North and South—feels like we're constantly at each other's throats. . . . And it used to be—even if we didn't *agree* on what to do in our communities, we could at least unite in fighting common enemies. Everybody's okay with beating up Hydra. Even *that's* not so simple anymore. . . . But the even bigger, scarier problem for me? In all these debates, all these things tearing us apart—I *have* a side. That's right. I have opinions, strongly held beliefs, even.[15]

Rejecting the approach to politics that Steve has usually taken, Sam decides to become a super-powered warrior for social justice. He sets up a hotline that will allow the general public to contact him about "injustice" or about "a wrong that needs to be righted."[16] And though he gets inundated with

---

14. With some very notable exceptions, of course. For example, see chapter 2.

15. *Captain America: Sam Wilson* #1.

16. Ibid.

bogus requests—one guy wants to meet Taylor Swift because he "knows" that they will have a "connection"—he acts on the first legitimate call that he gets. A woman named Mariana Torres calls him about her son, Joaquin, who has been helping illegal immigrants by providing food and water for them as they cross the desert into the United States. Mariana believes that Joaquin has been taken by the latest iteration of the Sons of the Serpent, a racist nationalist group that has plagued the Marvel universe for years. Sam tracks Joaquin and intervenes when the Sons of the Serpent attack him and a group of immigrants, but doing so makes him run afoul of Steve Rogers and S.H.I.E.L.D., who have also been investigating the Sons of the Serpent.

Sam and Steve also find themselves at odds with one another over the Whisperer, a hacker who has been leaking S.H.I.E.L.D. data to the public in order to expose corruption and unethical activities.[17] One of the most important things that the Whisperer leaks is information about Kobik, a S.H.I.E.L.D. program that involves using a Cosmic Cube to rewrite the histories of supervillains in order to "reform" them. Since a Cosmic Cube has the power to alter all of reality at a whim, any use of it is extremely dangerous. What makes Kobik even worse is that S.H.I.E.L.D. has turned the fragments of a broken Cosmic Cube into a sentient version of the reality-altering object. In other words, Kobik is a little girl with the power to make any of her thoughts into reality.

Maria Hill, the director of S.H.I.E.L.D., wants the Whisperer apprehended and prosecuted for breaking the law. Though Steve and Sam both agree in their opposition to the Kobik program, Steve supports his prosecution for breaking the law, while Sam believes that he is a hero and thinks that he should go free. Steve offers to testify on behalf of the Whisperer when he's caught, but this isn't good enough for Sam, and the division between the two friends grows deeper.

RIP Steve Rogers (1918–2016)?

As of May 2016 and for the foreseeable future, Captain America is dead. That is, Steve Rogers, the original Captain America, is dead in the post-*Secret Wars* Marvel Comics universe.

---

17. The Whisperer turns out to be Bruce Banner's old friend, Rick Jones, who *Captain America* scribe Nick Spencer uses as an analogue to Edward Snowden, who similarly exposed NSA secrets in 2013.

But he's still alive, someone might object. *He's even got his own book right now.*

No, he wasn't killed by a supervillain. No, he didn't finally croak of old age. But he's dead, all the same. Death in comics doesn't usually last more than a few years, so I won't say that he can't come back in some future story. But the death that Cap suffered in 2016 is different from other comic book deaths.

On May 25, 2016 Marvel released *Captain America: Steve Rogers* #1, the first issue in a new series whose tagline promised "a hero reborn." This was the issue that featured a Steve Rogers newly restored to the youth and strength that he had before he was turned into a weak old man by the Iron Nail. The beginning of the issue promises that now the Marvel universe will have *two* Captain Americas. Sam Wilson will continue to wield the classic round shield, while Steve Rogers has a new uniform and a new, triangular shield. But throughout *CA:SR* #1, we see hints here and there that something is wrong with the new status quo: Steve constantly wants to fight alone, to get away from his friends, and in a series of flashbacks, we learn that when Steve was a kid, he and his mother were introduced to Hydra (which is presented as a community organization). At one point, Steve tells Sharon Carter, "I feel like a stranger in my own body."[18] Then, at the end of the issue, Steve tosses one of his fellow heroes, Jack Flag, from a flying plane (regretting that he has to kill him in the service of a larger cause), and in the last panel, we see a sinister-looking Cap say, "Hail Hydra."

When the issue hit the stands, the entire internet made a collective, "*WHAT?!*"[19] Cap *had* to be brainwashed, or mind-controlled, or he *had* to be working as a triple agent. There was no way that Captain America—a hero created by two Jewish men[20] specifically for the purpose of fighting Hitler—could *really* buy into the repugnant doctrines of Hydra, a fascist terror organization that was based in part on the Nazi Party!

As is often the case in comics, things are not as the seem. *CA:SR* #2 reveals that Steve has become a victim of Red Skull, who gained influence over Kobik[21] and used her to rewrite Steve's past. In this new history, Steve and his mother were inducted into Hydra when Steve was just a child, and Captain America was secretly a Hydra spy during World War II.

18. *Captain America: Steve Rogers* #1.

19. Actually, what we all said was a little more vulgar.

20. Joe Simon and Jack Kirby.

21. During 2016's *Standoff* storyline, also written by Nick Spencer.

The resulting story has been one of the most gut-wrenching ever written about the Sentinel of Liberty. As I write these pages, *Captain America: Steve Rogers* is up to issue #8, and so far we've seen Steve plot to take over S.H.I.E.L.D.; try to kill fellow hero Jack Flag;[22] brutally murder a supervillain named the Red Ghost; manipulate his friends during the second superhuman Civil War;[23] join forces with Helmut Zemo; and work behind the scenes to undermine his best friend, Sam Wilson.

But what makes all of this so much worse is that in spite of the fact that he's acting like a supervillain, it's very much Steve Rogers doing these things. Unlike the Red Skull, who seeks only world domination for his own sake, the Hydra Captain America believes that what he is doing *really is* for the greater good of everyone. Moreover, he often acts with genuine compassion—the same compassion that he has had for his entire history. Yet after Kobik restores him to his youth and strength, everything that Steve does is in the service of Hydra—or, at least, what Steve believes Hydra should be. But the Hydra that he wants to restore to its former glory isn't the organization run by the Red Skull, Zemo, or Baron Strucker. As Steve tells Erik Selvig (who has also been made an agent of Hydra by Kobik),

> The *true* Hydra isn't a collection of marauding thugs, preaching *blind hatred* and *intolerance*. It isn't conquest for conquest's sake. And it certainly wasn't built to glorify *one man*.[24]

After this speech, Steve tells Selvig his true plan. In addition to using S.H.I.E.L.D. to take control of American foreign policy, he plans to kill the Red Skull, who he believes is a disease that has undermined Hydra's true mission: "peace through strength."[25]

No, Really: Who is Captain America?

At the time of this writing, we can only guess at Spencer's ultimate goal for his two Captain America titles. Two things seem to be looming on the horizon, both of which will be absolutely heart-wrenching for anyone who loves the characters of Steve Rogers and Sam Wilson, and both of which will have enormous political significance for the Marvel universe.

22. As of issue #8, Jack is still alive and in a coma after his fall from the plane.
23. See Chapter IV.
24. *Captain America: Steve Rogers* #4.
25. Ibid.

First, a major conflict between Steve and Sam is almost certainly coming soon. One of the story arcs in *Captain America: Sam Wilson* is ominously called *#TakeBackTheShield*. That title comes from a hashtag that becomes popular early in Sam's tenure as Captain America. A large portion of the population disapproves of Sam's very public political positions and wants the "real" Cap, Steve Rogers, to take back the round shield, which he asked Sam to keep when Kobik restored Steve to his strength. In addition, a number of congressmen have been working behind the scenes to try to force Sam to give up the classic shield, even asking U.S. Agent[26] to go after Sam and take the shield from him. And at the end of *Captain America: Sam Wilson* #13, we learn that Steve himself is behind the plot to *#TakeBackTheShield*. Though his goal is to force Sam to give it up, he tells U.S. Agent that he can't take the shield back himself: "We both know how this will look—me telling him to stop being Captain America. . . . I just don't know that the country can take that kind of *division*." Even though Steve isn't in his right mind, this is one of the most painful betrayals ever witnessed in comics, and it points toward a looming fight between Steve and Sam.

Second, at the time of this writing, Marvel has just begun a major event story called *Secret Empire*. In that story, Steve sets into motion his plan to take over America in the name of Hydra. In *Secret Empire* #0, he orchestrates a worldwide catastrophe that achieves several goals: it places the U.S. under a state of martial law with emergency powers handed over to Steve and S.H.I.E.L.D.; it traps most of Earth's strongest superheroes in space; and it isolates most of the rest of the world's heroes in a magical dimension. Now that he has removed from play anyone who can oppose him, he will begin a new era of Hydra ascendancy. As he tells his gathered Hydra army:

> Through Hydra, we will be made strong, together. We will fight to forge a better world. . . . A world where no one is put above any other—where all work together for a common cause—ever expanding, ever increasing. We will expose those who claim to lead us—we will lay bare their weakness, and their corruption! We will bring order and strength to chaos! This is the hour, this is the place—now, everything changes.[27]

---

26. John Walker, the one who takes up the role of Captain America when the Commission forces Steve to give up the mantle in *Captain America* #332 (1968).

27. *Captain America: Steve Rogers* #16.

Now that the world at large knows of Steve's true allegiance, and now that he has succeeded in taking power of the U.S., perhaps the most important question is whether or not people will know that Steve has been manipulated and transformed by Kobik, or if they will believe that Steve has always been a Hydra agent. If the latter proves to be the case, then the damage to America herself will almost certainly be deep and long-lasting.

Captain America has long been the moral center of the Marvel Universe in the same way that many have seen America as a moral compass for the real world. But that moral center has been undermined by the very enemy of everything that Captain America has stood for, and in that way, both of Nick Spencer's *Captain America* books reflect the way many Americans have felt for the last several years.

It doesn't matter what your political persuasion is—it should be hard for anyone to look at the state of American politics without the sneaking suspicion that something or someone has been trying to hijack the values at the core of the nation. Like the Red Skull altering Steve Rogers' past in order to make him into a Hydra sleeper agent, something seems to have changed the very makeup of what it means to be an American. And it doesn't matter whether you're a progressive, a conservative, or a libertarian; we all ought to agree that something fundamental has gone wrong.

If art reflects life, then let's hope that someone or something restores Steve Rogers's true identity soon. Goodness knows we need him.

2

DC's Kingdom Come

Superheroes as Despots

Warring Factions

Kingdom Come, the 1996 miniseries by Mark Waid and Alex Ross, offers some important insights into the conflicts that can arise between good people who hold very different opinions about how to achieve and preserve order. The book serves as a warning about what it takes to fight against chaos, showing the deep dysfunctions that can appear in a society when people who disagree about basic ideas like freedom have to confront crises. Though the major players in *Kingdom Come* all want to restore peace and freedom, they find themselves resorting to tactics that seem antithetical to their goal in order to achieve it.

Kingdom Come tells the story of a dystopian near-future when the old-guard superheroes—Superman, Wonder Woman, the Green Lantern, and others—have withdrawn from public service, leaving a void that quickly fills with new metahumans who are not dedicated to public safety as their predecessors were. They are exceedingly violent and fight just for the sake of fighting. As the book's narrator, a minister named Norman McRay, says,

> The world . . . is filled not with [the heroes of yesterday], but with their children and grandchildren. They number in the nameless thousands, . . . progeny of the past, inspired by the legends of those

who came before, . . . if not the morals. They no longer fight for the right. They fight simply to fight, their only foes each other. The superhuman boast that they've all but eliminated the super-villains of yesteryear. They are challenged, but unopposed. After all, they are our protectors.[1]

The public lives in fear of these new "heroes," who cause untold damage throughout the world. It appears that what they lack is a good example, a moral guide to emulate, someone to show them a better way.

When the metahuman crisis has nearly reached a catastrophic intensity, Wonder Woman convinces Superman to leave his retirement in the Fortress of Solitude and to join the rest of the older generation of heroes. They return to public heroics, policing the new generation and trying to lead by example. Some problems arise.

The first is that most of the new metahumans are not eager to follow in the footsteps of Superman and the rest of the Justice League. They see this older generation as out of touch with the realities of contemporary life (sound familiar?).

The second is that two major parties emerge in competition or conflict with the Justice League over the best way to respond to the metahuman crisis. Batman, Oliver Queen, and some other heroes resist Superman's program of providing a moral example and enforcing the peace when necessary. (Oliver Queen calls their philosophy the "democratic response."[2]) Meanwhile, Lex Luthor, Captain Marvel, and several former villains join forces in order to orchestrate the "human" response to not only the new generation of metahumans, but *all* superheroes. They call themselves the "Mankind Liberation Front." Each of these parties sees the Justice League as tyrannical, and each has its own agenda and interests.

Power and Order

The conflict in *Kingdom Come* arises primarily from a lack of order and a shared desire on all sides for the power to create order out of chaos. Superman believes (or rather, hopes) he can create order by providing a good example for metahumans to follow, and if that doesn't work, by enforcing peace. When he and the newly re-formed Justice League address the United Nations after ending a battle at Ellis Island, Superman tells reporters:

1. *Kingdom Come* #1.
2. *Kingdom Come* #3.

> In our absence, a new breed of metahumans has arisen, . . . a vast
> phalanx of self-styled "heroes" unwilling to preserve life or defend
> the defenseless, . . . a legion of vigilantes who have perverted their
> great powers, . . . who have forsworn the responsibilities due them.
> We have returned to teach them the meaning of truth and justice.
> Together, we will guide this new breed with wisdom . . . and if
> necessary, with force. Above all, we will restore order.[3]

Though Superman means precisely what he says—that he wants the metahumans to freely choose to follow the example of the Justice League—we
could easily put his words into the mouth of a supervillain who intends
to subject others to his will. It shows just how bad things have gotten that
Big Blue, the one who stands for Truth, Justice, and the American Way, is
talking like a tyrant.

But he's not talking about average citizens, someone might object. *He's
talking about rogue metahumans, people who have been causing tremendous
fear, destruction, and loss of life.* Yes, that's true, but consider the actions that
Superman has to take as the story progresses. For wisdom and advice, he
consults Orion, the son of Darkseid and the unwilling tyrant of the desolate
planet Apokolips. Orion suggests that Superman deport all of the metahumans to Apokolips—"They cannot be more challenging to me than my own
subjects"—but Superman turns him down, saying, "Given the nature of my
own struggle, I had hoped that Orion . . . could lend some wisdom. . . . But
I was mistaken. I can learn nothing from you."[4]

Instead, Superman turns to Mister Miracle and Big Barda, who have
become something like teachers to the people of Apokolips, encouraging
them to become free citizens rather than subjects. Finding their methods
more palatable than Orion's, Superman asks for their help in the creation
of the Gulag, a facility for the imprisonment and reeducation of rogue
metahumans.

Superman isn't Darkseid, the evil tyrant of Apokolips. He isn't even
Orion, its reluctant despot. But in *Kingdom Come,* he finds himself doing things he might never have believed himself capable of. He seems to
recognize this early on, although he is reluctant to admit to himself that
somewhere in the process of reforming the earth's metahuman population
he has crossed some kind of line. Wonder Woman tells him, "You said it
yourself once: . . . We are warriors. We have an obligation to wage combat."

3. *Kingdom Come* #2.

4. *Kingdom Come* #3.

Superman responds, "Given who we are, Diana, . . . given the power we possess, . . . we have a greater obligation to keep the peace. Only the weak succumb to brutality."[5] Here Kal sounds more like he's trying to convince himself than convince Wonder Woman. No matter how hard he tries, he will find himself becoming more and more like Orion than he would have believed possible:

> Superman: We shouldn't have to fight this hard.
>
> Wonder Woman: You said it yourself, Kal. We do what we have to do.
>
> Superman: And yet, we're ending up with more captives than converts.[6]

Just as Orion finds the people of Apokolips so unable to cope with their own freedom that he has to become the tyrant that he despised in his father, Superman finds more and more that he has to resort to the tactics of a despot in order to bring about order.

The other players in this conflict don't fare much better. Batman, for example, has long ago become the clandestine ruler of his city. When the Spectre first shows Norman McRay a vision of Gotham, they witness several robotic Bat Knights, an army of patrol and enforcement machines that an elderly Bruce Wayne controls remotely from the Batcave, take down a gang of teenagers. Bruce's self-appointed role as Gotham's protector has led him to create a police state. As the Spectre tells Norman McRay, "Batman has his city under control."[7]

When Superman goes to see Bruce in the Batcave in order to ask him to join the Justice League, his old friend notes the new black background for the symbol on his chest, suggesting that Superman has a dark side. Bruce tells him that Genosyde not only destroyed Arkham Asylum and everyone in it, but also Blackgate and Bellereve Prison:

> Bruce: Not an action I'd condone, but tell me the thought of it doesn't give your invulnerable skin a little tingle.
>
> Clark: I don't have *that* dark a side.[8]

5. Ibid.
6. *Kingdom Come* #2.
7. *Kingdom Come* #1.
8. *Kingdom Come* #2.

Bruce goes on to criticize the League's methods—which he says amount to "punching *now*, asking questions *later*"[9]—comparing them unfavorably to his own method, which he says involves more "finesse." But one can hardly call Bruce's police state in Gotham a model of freedom compared to the Justice League's tyranny. As Superman points out, scaring the citizens of Gotham into obeying the law makes them into a "cowardly, superstitious lot."[10] Batman might get results, he might have created what he calls a 'Utopia," but the kind of fear that he has created in the Gotham of *Kingdom Come* seems entirely incompatible with freedom.

Interestingly, the Mankind Liberation Front, led by Lex Luthor and made up primarily of villains and former villains, might be the least despotic of the three major parties in the conflict of *Kingdom Come*. Their primary goal is to escalate the war between the new metahumans and the Justice League so that the MLF can exploit the conflict and wrest control of the world from them. As Luthor puts it, "Once Superman and his toadies are out of the way, the Mankind Liberation Front can seize power and [once Batman has restored peace] return the reins of civilization to the humans."[11]

Now, it might be doubtful whether or not Luthor really means to "return the reins" to humankind (especially given his history), but the MLF as an organization seems truly devoted to what they see as the cause of freeing humanity from the despotic rule of metahumans of all generations.

But then both Batman and Superman also believe that they are acting for the greater good. More problematically, like Luthor, Supes and Bats believe that they are fighting for "freedom."

If this strikes you as odd, consider the major political positions in the United States. Republicans, Democrats, and Libertarians all claim to be the party of freedom, but they each have different (sometimes *very* different) ideas about what "freedom" means and what it takes for people to be free. They also regularly accuse one another of despotic tendencies (well, Republicans and Democrats do, anyway; it would be very difficult to accuse a libertarian of having aspirations to tyranny). The same is true for the major players in *Kingdom Come*.

---

9. Ibid.
10. Ibid.
11. *Kingdom Come* #3.

The Freedom to Be a Hero

Superman seems to believe primarily in the form of freedom that we could call *freedom for* or *freedom to*. We might use the term coined by the Latvian-British philosopher Isaiah Berlin: *positive liberty*. When Supes tries to recruit new members for the League at a dance club or bar for metahumans, he tells them,

> I'm here because the world's in bad shape. We have a lot to do and not a lot of time to do it in. I want you to join the League . . . willingly. Before you do, you should know that we have rules. Heroes act in a certain way. This isn't it. Those of you who take up with us . . . *willingly* . . . will be expected to be as *responsible* as you are *powerful*. You'll be expected to behave *better*. Those who *don't* . . . will be *dealt* with.[12]

Though these words certainly veil a threat, Supes really does mean that he wants them to *choose* join the League. He's asking these metahumans to make a choice *for* something. Until now, they've been free in the sense that they operate according to no one's rules. No one tells them what to do. But now Superman offers them another kind of freedom: the freedom to be a hero.

This might strike some people as strange. After all, modern Westerners seem to primarily think of freedom in terms of a lack of restraint. Instead of *freedom to*, most people seem to believe in *freedom from*—freedom from rules, regulations, limits. *Nobody tells me what to do.* And while this isn't wrong, it's probably an incomplete understanding of freedom.

For example, let's say that I believe that "freedom" means *freedom from rules.* And let's say that tomorrow I decide to give up my teaching gig and go into something more lucrative. So I decide that I am going to be a hip-hop artist. That seems to be a better-paying job than teaching, so what the heck? But since I'm *free*—meaning that nobody tells me what to do—I'm not going to be a rap artist like every other rap artist. So I notice that most rap songs have electronic percussion in them, and I think, "I'm not going to do what everybody else does. I'm *free*. I do my *own* thing." So instead of electronic percussion in my music, I just have a guy playing a set of bongos (maybe Sheldon from *The Big Bang Theory*?). I also notice that most rap lyrics are about urban life, and since nobody tells me what to do, my lyrics are going to be about literature and philosophy. After all, why not? I'm free,

12. *Kingdom Come* #2.

right? Finally, I question the very idea of rapping the lyrics at all. I mean, why should I conform to conventions? If I simply do what's expected, then I'm not truly free, right? So instead of rapping, I sing—in the style of an Italian *aria*.

You see where this is going. I might be free from the rules and conventions that "govern" rap music, but if I refuse to conform in this case, I am not free to be a hip-hop star. The problem isn't that nobody would buy my music; the problem is that the music itself will not *be* hip-hop. Therefore I'm not free to make rap music if I'm not willing to obey the "rules" of rap music.

The same is true for being a hero. As Superman points out, the metahumans are free in the sense that they can choose to act in whatever way they please, but they are not free to be heroes as long as they do not do understand and follow the "rules" of being a hero. Those rules are not written down anywhere, but anyone can easily know them through reason and experience: heroes saves lives; heroes act selflessly; heroes try to minimize the damage that their actions can cause; heroes use their power for the good of others and not for personal gain.

The difficulty that arises for Superman—and the reason that he ends up taking stances that some would call *tyrannical*—is that most of the people in the world of *Kingdom Come* don't want to be free in the way that Supes proposes. They don't need to aspire to his version of freedom—a freedom that makes demands on them—because they are perfectly content with freedom from rules, restraints, and interference.

Freedom through Fear

In the Gotham City, "freedom" takes a very different form. Bruce Wayne, long ago motivated by the grief and fear that the murder of his parents caused him as a child to become a vigilante, now rules his city through fear. From the dark confines of the Batcave, he uses his Bat Knights to terrorize Gotham's criminals into obeying the law.

This might strike us as the total opposite of freedom. After all, fear kills liberty.[13] If I am afraid of my government, then I don't speak my mind about laws that I think are unjust. If I have a colleague who is also married to my boss, then I might be afraid to disagree with a proposal that he makes

---

13. Think of Steve Rogers in *Captain America: The Winter Soldier*: "This isn't freedom. This is fear."

for our department because I'm afraid of offending my boss. If I'm a student, and I'm afraid of receiving a bad grade if I hold the wrong opinions, I'll be afraid to speak up when I disagree with the professor about some political issue.

But even though we reject the idea that fear somehow leads to liberty, most people will recognize the need for law-enforcement, which ensures obedience to the law through the fear of arrest and punishment. Many would argue that such fear is necessary for liberty. If I live in fear of all my neighbors, they would say, then I can't live a truly free life. A strong authority, like government and law enforcement, ensures that both my neighbors and I can live freely.

Thomas Hobbes, the seventeenth-century political philosopher, might agree with such reasoning. He said that in our natural state, people are all equal, not in the sense of rights or dignity, but in our vulnerability. We're all vulnerable, and we are all in competition with one another, so we live in constant fear of others. The only way to erase that fear is for the group as a whole to submit themselves to what Hobbes called the *Leviathan* state. By surrendering some of our freedoms to the state, we can have stability and order in our lives. The fact that each of us lives in fear of the Leviathan means that we don't have to fear each other.

Ultimately, Waid and Ross don't tell us enough about the Gotham of *Kingdom Come* for us to decide how justified Bruce is in holding such a tight grip on his city. But let's assume that in this dystopian future, the people of Gotham have abused their freedom so much that the only thing left to maintain order is for Batman to become something more than just a vigilante. Maybe what they need for peace and stability is the army of Bat Knights watching over them. Maybe Batman's "police state" is the only thing that saves the city from destroying itself (and in the chaotic world of *Kingdom Come,* that isn't hard to imagine). In that case, Batman has become Hobbes' Leviathan, creating civilized order out of the chaos of humanity in its natural state.

Even so, it's difficult to believe that a society controlled by fear is truly free—or *good*. People too afraid to exercise their freedom can't develop the virtues of a good citizen. And people who don't develop the virtues necessary for good citizenship will need a progressively stronger authority to rule them. Bruce might believe that he is the "democratic response" to the tyranny of the Justice League, but when we look closely at his methods, they're not very different from what Supes and the rest of the League have to do in order to restore peace. In fact, given the kind of order that he and his network of allies have created (from Gotham "all the way to Star City,"[14] he says), Bruce's criticisms of Superman and the League sound almost laughably hypocritical:

> I have allies. *Human* allies more in *tune* than *your* friends to humanity's needs. *We* don't *want* to rule the world. We just want to straighten it *out . . . our* way, by *ourselves*.[15]

Bruce clearly implies here that Superman and the Justice League *do* want to rule the world, while he and his friends merely want to "straighten it out" in "our way." But what does it mean to "straighten it out"? What *can* that mean except to say that since people don't behave the way he wants them to, he's going to force them to?

Freedom as Power

Another understanding of freedom is that it means the power to have one's will enacted. Let's say I want to possess a piece of property that has woods for hunting, a clean and reliable water source, and a field for farming. If I have the power to make it happen, then I have freedom. Or if I want to buy a vehicle that will comfortably carry my family of six, and I save up the money to buy that vehicle, then I have freedom. If I want to raise public support for some political cause—say, an end to the death penalty, an expansion of Medicaid benefits, or tighter restrictions on abortion—and I have the ability to enlist others to my cause, then I have freedom.

In this view, freedom means the power to do what I choose to do, to have what I choose to have, to control what I choose to control. It means having a say in how society is ordered. It doesn't just mean a lack of outside limits or interference; it means having the ability to assert myself, to make real changes to the world—to have control over not only my own affairs, but the functioning of society as well.

But in *Kingdom Come*, we see a world where the average person feels completely disempowered. This is a world where normal people look into the sky to and see gods, angels, monsters, and demons determining the outcome of world events. Yes, sometimes the metahumans save the humans from danger. But more often they are the source of the danger. More

---

14. *Kingdom Come* #2.

15. Ibid.

importantly, their existence is a permanent reminder of just how little power normal humans have. Even compared to a man like Bruce Wayne, the average person must feel helpless—what about compared to people of immense power like Wonder Woman, Green Lantern, or Superman?

In *Kingdom Come,* this understanding of freedom is best reflected by the delegates of the U.N. and by the Mankind Liberation Front.

When Superman and the newly-reformed Justice League make their first speech at the United Nations, the Secretary General asks a delegation of representatives, "Is anyone here delighted with what we've just heard?"[16] The Spectre points out to McRay that the appearance of the League has confirmed the fears of mankind:

> Long have these mortals suspected that they are no longer the captains of humanity's destiny. Their suspicions have just been confirmed.[17]

It might be a stretch to think of a massive bureaucratic body that has authority over many nations as representative of the human race. But the response of the Secretary General and the rest of the U.N. delegates to the return of the Justice League speaks to the resentment people often feel toward those who have more power than they do. For the last decade or more, for example, Americans have seen tremendous unrest among voters who believe that a small number of people in power have a disproportionate amount of control over the state of things. And the feeling of powerlessness—whether it is justified or not—can often lead to a great deal of resentment and irrational decisions.

We see this point emphasized when Wonder Woman and Superman meet with the U.N. in the middle of issue #3 of *Kingdom Come.* When they arrive, the Secretary General snarks that he and the delegates are

> flattered that the mighty Justice League has finally deemed the human race worthy of conversation. . . . We're simply no longer accustomed to being advised or consulted. Imagine our surprise, for instance, to learn that the center of the U.S. now harbors a metahuman prison. . . . We must begin to decide some things for ourselves. Good day.[18]

16. Ibid.
17. Ibid.
18. *Kingdom Come* #3.

His dismissal of the Man of Steel and Wonder Woman perfectly sums up the resentment that humans must feel about living in a world full of people with tremendous power. As a solution to the metahuman problem, Superman has taken on an almost parental authority over society, and though he thinks that he is helping, he finds that people reject his help. If they need it, then that means that they don't have control over their own lives.

This resentment goes so deep that when the Justice League gather at the Gulag to stifle a prison riot, the U.N. tries to wipe out the whole superhuman population by launching a nuclear missile at them. When the secretary general proposes nuking the Gulag, many of the delegates protest that using a weapon of mass destruction in the heart of the Midwest is "irrational," and the secretary responds,

> These are not rational times! We are at the flashpoint of human existence! My God . . . you can hear the battle from here! At any moment, it threatens to spread forth and engulf the world! What then? . . . What then? The only way to ensure that future generations remember this as humanity's final option is to ensure that there will be future generations. . . . Let us strike while we still can.[19]

If the U.N. speaks for the human race, their extreme response to the crisis at the Gulag shows just how desperate that crisis has made people in general. They want control over their own lives again, so much so that they are willing to rain down fire on their fellow human beings. Sure, we're talking about *meta*humans, *super*humans, vigilantes, saviors, gods—but they're human nonetheless.

Though nobody in the real world is proposing that we nuke our fellow citizens, we see a similar kind of desperation in contemporary geopolitics. Out of a desire for power—over other people or even over their own lives—terrorists do horrifying things, inhuman acts of violence, to their fellow people.

Closer to home, Americans have found themselves driven to one extreme or the other in order to regain some sense of control over their society and their lives. In the 2016 presidential election, for example, two of the most popular candidates were men who would have been unthinkable in previous elections.[20] We have reached this point because, whether they're right or wrong, many people feel disempowered.

19. *Kingdom Come* #4.
20. Donald Trump and Bernie Sanders.

Like the U.N. delegates, the Mankind Liberation Front is guided by a belief that "freedom" means "power." Luthor and his partners want to rid the world of metahumans in order to return the "reins" of society to humanity again. But where we might understand why the U.N. would use a nuclear weapon in response to the Gulag crisis (even if we disagree with it on moral grounds), the MLF's aims and methods are much more sinister.

The problem is that by "humanity," Luthor doesn't seem to mean *all* people or humanity as a *whole*. He merely means *some* human beings—ultimately himself and his few companions. He proves this in *Kingdom Come* #2 when Vandal Savage crushes the throat of Luthor's secretary because she doesn't put two sugars in his drink. Luthor's response is to complain, "I just had her trained." Never mind the secretary's life; what matters is Luthor's investment of time and money in her.

Luthor's idea of a free society is one in which the few possess power over the many. When he objects to superhumans having power over "humanity," he merely means that only humans (meaning non-superpowered *homo sapiens*) have a right to control human affairs.

A Dire Warning, But No Solution

One disturbing fact in *Kingdom Come* is that the book doesn't really offer a solution to the problem that it shows us; it only issues a warning about its effects and causes. The theories of French philosopher René Girard can help us better understand the problem that the book warns us against.

According to Girard, human beings are locked into an endless cycle of memetic desire that leads to conflict, violence, and finally to scapegoating. What happens, he argued, is that because humans are primarily imitative creatures, we imitate each others' desires (say, for a particular kind of house, shoe, piece of land, etc.). But since resources, goods, and commodities are scarce, people end up in competition with one another. And when that competition continues long enough, it results in violence. The competition will often last long enough that the people forget the object of their competition and just fight with one another for the sake of fighting. What finally ends the cycle and restarts it is the sacrifice of a scapegoat, a single individual who becomes the target of violence for all sides of the conflict. This act of sacrificing the scapegoat satisfies everyone's bloodlust for a time . . . until the cycle begins again. Hatfield applies Girard's theory to *Kingdom Come* and argues that Captain Marvel (Shazam/Billy Batson) is the scapegoat who finally ends the conflict at the Gulag.[21]

When the U.N. launches the nuclear weapon at the Gulag, Superman asks Marvel to decide whether or not he should stop the bomb. If he doesn't, it will kill them all. If he does, then the metahumans will "run rampant across the globe."[22] He asks Marvel to make the decision because, he says, Marvel belongs to "both worlds": human and superhuman. Before Batson can answer, Superman flies into the air to stop the warhead. But Captain Marvel flies after him, catches him, throws him back to the earth, and stops the bomb himself. He pushes it into the upper atmosphere, where it explodes and kills him. His sacrifice saves a small remnant of the metahumans, but the shockwave kills the rest.

Believing that he is the only one who survived, Superman flies to the U.N. in a rage, ready to destroy the building and kill everyone inside—and he might have done it had Norman McRay, Wonder Woman, and Batman not arrived to stop him. But because they do, Superman has a sudden change of heart:

> I no longer care about the mistakes of yesterday. I care about coping with tomorrow . . . together. The problems we face still exist. We're not going to solve them for you. . . . We're going to solve them with you, . . . not by ruling above you, . . . but by living among you. We will no longer impose our power on humanity. We will earn your trust . . . using the wisdom one man left as his legacy. I asked him to choose between humans and superhumans. But he alone knew that was a false division . . . and made the only choice that ever truly matters. He chose life . . . in the hope that your world and our world could be one world once again.[23]

After he gives this speech, Supes hangs Captain Marvel's gold cape from a flagpole at the U.N. Then we see the fruits of the peace that Marvel has won for the world: new alliances forming between metahumans and world powers; Wonder Woman restored to her royal place among the Amazons; Wayne Manor turned into a hospital; Superman tilling the soil of the ruined Midwest and restoring it to fertility.

---

21. Other writers have already seen Girard's ideas at work in *Kingdom Come.* In "The Problem of Violence in *Kingdom Come,*" for example, David Hatfield applies Girard's thought in order to explain the conflict between the Justice League, the Outsiders, the U.N., and the MLF. Collected in *Superman and Philosophy,* edited by Mark D. White.

22. *Kingdom Come* #4

23. Ibid.

It all sounds too good, too tidy. In fact, the whole ending of *Kingdom Come* rings falsely. But that isn't a flaw in the story—it's part of the point. If Girard's theory of mimetic violence and scapegoating is true, Marvel's sacrifice doesn't truly solve any problems; it only resets the process, restarts the cycle. Because he did not—and *cannot*—change human nature, the cycle will begin again: a period of relative peace, mimetic desire, competition, opposing sides, mimetic violence, and finally . . . another scapegoat.

We might like to think that Marvel's selfless act could permanently bring people together, but it only shocks the humans and metahumans into cooperation. That cooperation can't be perpetual because people's notions about what it means to be free, to have power, and to lead are not likely to change. Superman says that he wants them all to "cope" with "tomorrow . . . together," but notably, he never says precisely what that means. As good as it sounds, his speech at the United Nations after Marvel's death is little more than a few platitudes. It isn't that he doesn't *mean* what he says. No one can doubt that Superman *means* to stay true to his word. But whether he will be able to actually put what he suggests into practice is another question altogether. Crime won't go away. People won't stop being envious. The ambitious will not stop desiring power. And those problems will always complicate out attempts to cooperate with one another.

But more importantly, good people will continue to disagree about the best way to respond to those problems. They all desire order and peace, but because they disagree fundamentally about the best way for us to order society, their attempts to achieve it will be frustrated by stalemates and competition. Girard would argue that this is just the cycle at work.

Gazing into the Abyss

It would be mistaken to try to see a one-to-one correlation between people or groups in *Kingdom Come* and people or groups in the real world. We can't say that the Justice League stands for Republicans while Batman and his allies represent Democrats, or vice versa. But I think that the book does dramatize the very real human instincts and desires that animate our political debates and conflicts.

We all desire freedom, but we disagree not only about how best to ensure freedom, but more importantly, what freedom *is*. We see this kind of question come up in disagreements between people who advocate for a broad understanding of freedom of speech and people who believe in the right of minorities or persecuted groups not to be subjected to speech that they find offensive or hurtful. On the one hand, some people believe that freedom guarantees our right to say what we think without restriction, while others think that freedom guarantees us a right not to be hurt by what others say. There is little room for compromise between the two extremes in that debate. If you think like Batman and you believe that freedom means an absence of something (in his case, the threat of crime; in our case, it might be offense or hurt), then we might have to side with those who want to restrict speech in order to ensure that nobody ever has to feel judged or rejected.

If we accept the view of freedom espoused by Superman—the idea that true freedom means *freedom to* or *freedom for*—and we believe that the purpose of freedom is to allow us to be good citizens (whatever we decide that means), then is it right to compel people who don't conform to our ideas about being a "good citizen" in the same way that Superman tries to force metahumans to be "heroes"? Can we compel people to behave in a certain way in order to make them more "free"?

Or what if we believe that "freedom" really means "power"? In that case, we might have to accept a tyranny of the majority. In a democracy, power rests in the hands of the voters who cast the winning votes. But if "freedom" means simply "power," then those who have it can do whatever they want—even if their freedom does violence to the rights of the minority. *Kingdom Come* offers no easy answers to the problems I've just raised (and political philosophy isn't necessarily more helpful). Each of the ideas about freedom that we find in the book has its merits and its flaws, and each can be held up as the standard that should guide society. The most valuable thing that *Kingdom Come* can tell us about them is that the pursuit of any one of these views can result in despotism. To paraphrase the German philosopher Friedrich Nietzsche, when we fight monsters, we should make sure that we don't become monsters ourselves. Or—as in the case of Superman and Batman—when we fight against anarchy we should be careful not to become despots or something worse.

3

MARVEL'S CIVIL WAR

Tocqueville, Burke, and Civic Virtue

The Fundamental Questions

In Marvel's 2006 crossover event *Civil War*, the entire Marvel universe becomes embroiled in a conflict about questions that ought to be very familiar to modern Westerners. Though the outward issue is the registration of superhumans with the United States government, the story raises questions essential to any modern, free society: *what is the just arrangement of power structures? to what extent can the individual act independently of the government? what is the danger of too much government oversight, and how do we guard against that danger without becoming reactionaries?*

Readers have often seen the Superhuman Registration Act as an allegory for gun control, and that can certainly be a helpful way to read the book. Guns give people a kind of superhuman power, and most people believe in some form of government regulation of that power. Yet reasonable people (as well as some unreasonable ones) have very serious disagreements about how far the government's regulation of guns should reach.

Others have pointed out the way in which the book speaks to the political atmosphere in the years immediately following 9/11 and the way in which the terrorist attacks revived the old debate over freedom and security. I write these words on the day after the fifteenth anniversary of the attacks at the World Trade Center and the Pentagon, and in many ways the traumatic events of *Civil War* and its immediate aftermath do reflect the state of the world in the years after 9/11. A television spot produced by the Ad Council that aired in the months following the attacks claims that "on September 11th, terrorists tried to change America forever." The ad then shows a neighborhood in which every house has an American flag. "Well," the narrator says, "they succeeded." But while a renewed patriotism might be a good thing, not all of the changes that occurred in America (and the West generally) following 9/11 were for the best. The War on Terror and all of the changes to American society that it entailed might well have been necessary, but American society isn't necessarily *better* or *freer* because of them. One could argue that the Patriot Act, PRISM, and similar programs make Americans safer from terrorism than they might have been; but one cannot argue that we are otherwise better off or more free because of an increase in intelligence and in government spying.

It is true that *Civil War* and the stories that followed it—*The Initiative* and *Dark Reign*—in many ways reflected the debate Americans have had about freedom and security following 9/11; and it is also true that one can easily see the question of gun control reflected in the idea of superhuman registration. But instead of reading *Civil War* as an allegory for any particular political problem—be it guns, terrorism, government regulation, freedom and security, etc.—I want to suggest another reading, one that explores the basic philosophical principles that underlie the specific issues that others have already seen represented in the book. *Civil War* raises questions about all sorts of very specific political problems, but at the heart of these questions are deeper, even more fundamental questions about the relationship of citizens to each other and to their government.

The Conflict

When the New Warriors go after a group of supervillains in Stamford, Connecticut, a superhuman called Nitro causes an explosion that destroys half the town and kills more than six hundred people—including sixty children at a nearby elementary school. This event turns public opinion against superheroes and causes congress to renew its push for superhuman regulation—an idea that had been floated and debated previously in the Marvel universe.[1] The Superhuman Registration Act passes with overwhelming

---

1. For example, see *Uncanny X-Men* #181 (1981) and *Fantastic Four* #335 (1961).

public and congressional support, and the Marvel heroes find themselves divided right down the middle.

Though in the past he opposed similar legislation, Tony Stark (Iron Man) now supports registration. Though some fans will complain that Tony is acting out of character in supporting the SRA, in fact his support of registration is a natural progression of his personality and a direct result of his experiences as Iron Man. First, he's a progressive—in other words, he believes that through the intelligent application of human ingenuity, we can perfect society. Second, he's a pragmatist. He believes that he is making the best of bad circumstances, doing what he has to do in order to prevent something worse from happening. Third, he's just gone through the events of the *Execute Program* story arc. In that series, Tony becomes bodily integrated with his armor (because of the Extremis serum), and the son of Ho Yinsen manages to hack into Tony's armor *and mind* and use him to assassinate several world leaders. At the end of the story, Tony experiences what he thinks of as a revelation: both his armor and his body are weapons that can be used like a gun. Guns can be used responsibly or irresponsibly:

> Sal: Your armor is like a gun. It was Yinsen's son that aimed it and pulled the trigger.
>
> Tony: You're right, Sal. But I'm not the only gun lying around. Whether they go bad or they're co-opted like I was, the result is the same . . . an unacceptable loss of innocent lives. *Every* super hero is a potential gun . . . and the last time I checked, guns required registration.[2]

Though some of us might doubt the logic that leads Tony to this conclusion, he decides that oversight might have been able to prevent the *Execute Program* incident—or at least it might not have gotten so bad if he had been registered and employed by a government body or S.H.I.E.L.D.

Captain America, on the other hand, opposes registration from the outset, viewing it as a dangerous violation of the civil rights of the heroes. When Maria Hill orders him to lead a team of S.H.I.E.L.D. agents tasked with taking down heroes who refuse to register, she tells him that his job is to "obey the will of the American people." Cap's response tells us a lot about what motivates him:

2. *Iron Man* #12 (2005).

Don't play politics with *me*, Hill. Superheroes need to stay above
that stuff or Washington starts telling us who the *super-villains*
are.[3]

Throughout his history, Cap has seen over and over again the danger of
government corruption, of good institutions being infiltrated by people
who—whether they are well-intentioned or not—turn those institutions
into instruments of corruption, tyranny, and evil.[4] Sharon Carter, Sally
Floyd, and others accuse him of acting irrationally, of being merely a re-
actionary who is stuck in the past. But even if we think that Cap's values
are old-fashioned or outdated, we have to admit that of all the heroes in
the Marvel universe, Steve Rogers is the one who has the most reasons to
distrust government oversight.

But while Stark and Rogers have their ideological battle over the merits
and dangers of the SRA, one important issue that few people acknowledge
or discuss is the way in which free citizens develop discipline, restraint,
and civic virtue. What kind of society best encourages its citizens toward
excellence? Is it one in which the government tries to foster good behavior
and habits through regulation? Or is it better for people to be free to develop those habits and virtues on their own, either in private or through
voluntary associations? On this point, we can look to the political thought
of Alexis de Tocqueville, Edmund Burke, and other writers for help.

Tocqueville and Civic Virtue

Alexis de Tocqueville was a nineteenth-century French thinker and dip-
lomat who wrote one of the earliest modern works of political science,
Democracy in America. In that two-volume work, Tocqueville describes
and analyzes American government and society: the behavior, beliefs, and
associations of its people; the structure of its civic and government institutions; the relationship between those institutions; the paradox of slavery
existing in a nation whose founding principles are freedom, justice, and
equality; and the peculiar dangers that threaten the freedom of citizens in
a democratic republic.

In a chapter entitled "What Type of Despotism Democratic Nations Have to Fear," Tocqueville describes a particularly dangerous form

---

3. *Civil War* #1 (2006).

4. For more on this topic, see Chapter 1.

of despotism that, paradoxically, democratic republics have a tendency to become. It is a soft despotism, more dangerous even than the tyranny of a Roman emperor, because where Caesar's greatest power was limited to a small number of people, the power of the soft despotism extends to all, hidden and unnoticed because it is disguised by the illusion that the people maintain control over their own lives:

> I see an innumerable crowd of similar and equal men who spin around restlessly, in order to gain small and vulgar pleasures with which they fill their souls. . . . Above those men arises an immense and tutelary power that alone takes charge of assuring their enjoyment and of looking after their fate. It is absolute, detailed, regular, far-sighted and mild. It would resemble paternal power if, like it, it had as a goal to prepare men for manhood; but on the contrary it seeks only to fix them irrevocably in childhood; it likes the citizens to enjoy themselves, provided that they think only about enjoying themselves. It works willingly for their happiness; but it wants to be the unique agent for it and the sole arbiter; it attends to their security, provides for their needs, facilitates their pleasures, conducts their principal affairs, directs their industry, settles their estates, divides their inheritances; how can it not remove entirely from them the trouble of living?[5]

Tocqueville thought that the citizens of a democracy didn't have to fear tyrants as much as they did "tutors," by which he meant a state that treated its subjects as an overprotective parent treats her children. Children raised by parents who never allow them the freedom to make mistakes often don't grow into competent adults who make sound decisions, but rather remain children all their lives. The same could be said for citizens: the more dependent we become upon the state, the less able we will be to make sound decisions, and therefore the less free we are. And more importantly, the greater the role the state has in our lives, the greater a role it wants—until it has all the power of a tyrant without the warning signs that accompany tyranny. Instead of working for the misery of its subjects, as we would expect from a despotic government, it makes their happiness its business. Such a government doesn't have to be sinister in nature in order to be despotic. In fact, the more benign and benevolent its officials are, the more likely it is to turn into a soft despotism.

The greatest danger of Tocqueville's soft despotism is that without actively seeking to dominate people, it gradually reduces their freedom until

---

5. de Tocqueville, *Democracy in America*, vol. 2, 1249–50.

they no longer see the need to exercise their right to choose in the first place. They become more docile, less likely to recognize and oppose injustice or stand up to the overreach of institutions, and more and more unwilling to bite the hand that feeds them. Such a people are not true participants in a democracy. Their government works diligently to remove from them all the risks associated with freedom, and without those risks, they are not truly free—free to choose how to order their lives, or more importantly, free to become *good*. Indeed, the more dependent people become upon this soft despotism, the less able they are to develop the virtues necessary for democracy.

One of the things that impressed Tocqueville the most about American democracy was the prevalence of voluntary associations among its people. In European society, Tocqueville saw little to separate the sphere of the state from the private sphere of the family and local community, but in America he saw an intermediary power between those two areas of life: voluntary associations that encouraged people to participate as free citizens in public society. To Tocqueville, these associations performed two functions for democracy: they discouraged the social isolation that resulted from excessive individualism; and they encouraged the citizens to cooperate in order to do for themselves what would otherwise be left to the government.

But the soft despotism that worried Tocqueville tends to eliminate competition. As the power and purview of the state increases, the power and number of these voluntary associations will tend to decrease. For example, in a nation where the state provides few welfare benefits, the need for a social safety net is increased. The burden falls on churches, families, and other small units of society to provide help to the poor (and those organizations usually rise to the challenge). But as the state begins to provide welfare benefits, it not only decreases the need for voluntary associations, but it also sees the need to increase its regulatory power over those voluntary associations that remain, sometimes hindering their ability to provide services to the needy.[6] This can cause individuals to give up on voluntarily participating in public life and increasing dependency on the government for all kinds of public services.

An example of the way in which voluntary associations can come into tension with the state is the so-called Cajun Navy that rescued thousands of flood victims during the 2016 Louisiana floods. Though it took federal

---

6. For example, see the fight between the Little Sisters of the Poor and the Obama administration over the Affordable Care Act.

relief days to respond to the flooding, the Cajun Navy, a well-organized, volunteer-based group of people with boats, took to the floodwaters immediately after the rain and rescued many people before FEMA could even organize. These regular citizens proved to be at least as effective as government relief services, and they acted much more quickly than their official counterparts.

After the floods, however, the Louisiana government proposed requiring civilian rescuers to have training, permits, and licenses. Even though the senator who made the proposal argued that the potential legislation would "empower" rather than restrict volunteers, the incident exemplifies the tendency of the state to oppose the people acting independently of itself. This opposition is usually couched in language about safety and proper training, but it generally amounts to the same thing: as the state grows, it becomes less and less tolerant of citizens organizing and acting outside of what it takes to be its purview—especially when the citizens prove more effective than the government can be.

It's true that disasters can bring out the worst in people. I lived in southern Mississippi when Hurricane Katrina hit the Gulf Coast states in 2005, and I saw a lot of ugliness: people hurting each other over gasoline, food, and even over bags of ice. But times of crisis can also bring out the best in people. The Cajun Navy is a good example of this. People who act freely for the good of others have the opportunity to develop virtues that others who act under coercion or as employees of government institutions are less likely to have. This doesn't make government employees bad people, of course; nor does it mean that a FEMA worker can't be courageous or generous. But risking your life to save others because they're part of your community and risking it because that's the job you're paid to do—these actions tend to produce different kinds of virtues, and Tocqueville was convinced that a society that relies on the actions of local citizens freely cooperating with one another rather than on government employees will be more virtuous and therefore more free.

Civic Restraint

But there is another side of this coin. Where Tocqueville thought that a free civil society and voluntary associations balanced government power and guaranteed individual liberty, many people have argued that citizens can only maintain their freedom from tyrannous rule by ruling over themselves, by freely restricting their own freedom. In other words, if we don't want the government to over-regulate us and to become the soft despotism that Tocqueville warned against, then we have to regulate ourselves.

Perhaps the most famous expression of this idea comes from Edmund Burke. Writing about half a century before Tocqueville, Burke was an Irish statesman and a member of the English Parliament in the late eighteenth century. He is most well-known for his support of the American Revolution and for his pamphlet written in opposition to the French Revolution: *Reflections on the Revolution in France*.

In his "Letter to a member of the National Assembly, 1791," Burke described the importance of people's willingness to rule themselves:

> Men are qualified for civil liberty in exact proportion to their disposition to put moral chains on their own appetites—in proportion as their love to justice is above their rapacity;—in proportion as their soundness and sobriety of understanding is above their vanity and presumption;—in proportion as they are more disposed to listen to the counsels of the wise and good, in preference to the flattery of knaves. Society cannot exist unless a controlling power upon will and appetite be placed somewhere, and the less of it there is within, the more there is without. It is ordained in the eternal constitution of things that men of intemperate minds cannot be free. Their passions forge their fetters.

Burke's point is that no matter what, human behavior *will* be subjected to some limiting power or principle. We can limit ourselves, or we will be limited by the state. The less we're willing to place what Burke calls "moral chains" on our own appetites and desires, the more we will be subjected to the regulations and restrictions of the ruling power.

The American founders were particularly concerned with the idea that a system of self-rule can only work if the citizenry do in fact *rule themselves*. For example, in a message to the Massachusetts Militia in 1798, John Adams argues that

> Our Constitution was made only for a moral and religious people. It is wholly inadequate to the government of any other. . . . [W]e have no government, armed with power, capable of contending with human passions, unbridled by morality and religion. Avarice, ambition, revenge and licentiousness would break the strongest cords of our Constitution, as a whale goes through a net.

Many people have used this passage to support the idea that the U.S. was founded as a Christian nation, but my interest here is not in that question. Rather, what I am interested in is Adam's belief that for the American system to work as he and the other Founders intended, the American people must be a fundamentally "moral and religious people." He thought that the American system—with its checks and balances, its limits on government, its subsidiarity, and the large degree of liberty that it affords to the individual—could work and its people remain free only if they ruled themselves by their free adherence to a system of religious and moral codes of behavior.

We've seen this borne out in a number of areas of American life: guns, drugs, speech, cars, business dealings—each of these things has seen greatly increased regulation over the course of American history primarily because individuals increasingly refused to regulate themselves. *Laissez-faire* capitalism gives way to government regulation of business because of monopolies, for example. One might say that there is a paradoxical direct relationship between the power of individuals and the power of the state. When the citizens do not freely limit their own power by their adherence to morality, they contribute to the increase of the state's power and the contraction of their own freedom. Indeed, citizens who refuse to freely regulate themselves make it necessary for the government to regulate them—thus increasing the size and power of the state and reducing the power of the citizens.

Freedom, Virtue, and Moral Chains

Self-regulation, then, is key to remaining free from Tocqueville's soft despotism, and one would be hard-pressed to find a better example of a self-regulating group of citizens than the Avengers. They have made their fair share of mistakes, but Earth's Mightiest Heroes have always been models of Tocqueville's free association. And if all heroes acted like the Avengers, there would be no need for legislation like the SRA. But not every hero has the morals of Captain America. The New Warriors are a good example of this.

In the fourth volume of *New Warriors*, the team becomes the subject of a reality TV show that documents their exploits as they fight super-crime in small-town America. (After all, taking something good and worthwhile and commercializing on it—that's what popular culture is best at, right?) At the beginning of *Civil War*, the Warriors have tracked a group of b-list and c-list villains—Cobalt Man, Coldheart, Speedfreek, and Nitro—to a hideout in a residential area of Stamford, Connecticut. The show's producer points out that one of those villains "almost took down the Hulk," and Microbe wants to back out: "Those guys are totally out of our *league*, man. No *way* we should be going in there." Ignoring the danger to themselves and to the people who live in the area, Speedball says, "But think about the *ratings*. . . . This could be the best episode of the entire second season."[7]

The Warriors attack and disable most of the villains fairly easily. Speedball knocks out Speedfreek; Namorita and Night Thrasher take down Coldheart; and Microbe defeats Cobalt Man. But Nitro escapes the fighting and runs toward a local elementary school before Namorita knocks him down. The Atlantean thinks that she has subdued him, but Nitro points out that she's "playing with the big boys now" and explodes, destroying the elementary school and killing hundreds of people.

Collateral damage is never completely avoidable. That's simply the nature of crimefighting of any kind. But the New Warrior's reckless endangerment of the people of Stamford is inexcusable: they know the risks before they engage with the villains; they know that Speedfreek nearly defeated the Hulk; they know that Coldheart had gone toe-to-toe with Spider-Man; and they know that Nitro—a man whose powers came from a Kree[8] experiment—killed Captain Mar-Vell. And the film crew captures footage of Speedball saying that his concern is ratings for the reality show. Because of the negligence of the New Warriors, the Stamford incident becomes the catalyst not only for the SRA, but also of a massive change in public opinion about superheroes.

Though his teammates are killed in Stamford, Speedball himself survives and becomes the face that everyone associates with the abuse of superhuman powers. Nitro's explosion has a reaction with Speedball's kinetic powers and sends him flying hundreds of miles before he comes to rest in a farmer's field. When a representative of S.H.I.E.L.D.'s Anti-registration Terrorist Violation Squad offers him a deal that will allow him to escape jail, Speedball refuses because signing the agreement amounts to an admission of guilt. "We did everything by the book," he reasons.[9] "I'm not the one who exploded. I was the one trying to *stop* him."[10] His actions in Samford

---

7. *Civil War* #1 (2006).

8. An alien race who have a habit of experimentally enhancing human beings.

9. *Civil War: Frontline* #1.

10. *Civil War: Frontline* #2

were perfectly acceptable under the status quo that had existed in America since the emergence of superheroes in the 1930s, and the explosion was caused by Nitro, a supervillain that he and the New Warriors were trying to subdue. But the S.H.I.E.L.D. representative doesn't see it that way: "You're bring offered a one-time chance to escape punishment for the crimes committed by yourself and your former teammates," he says. When Speedball protests and insists on his right to a lawyer, the rep responds, "You're an unregistered combatant, Mister Baldwin. *I* define your rights."[11]

And during a transfer from one holding facility to another, a soldier assaults Speedball because he blames him for the death of a family member:

> Soldier: I got a cousin in Stamford, Connecticut. I *used* to have. And she died 'cause some attention-seeking moron in a costume decided to record a crime-fighting spree on national TV.
>
> Speedball: It wasn't our fault. It was Nitro. I'm sorry for what happened to those people—
>
> Soldier: Not like you *will* be, boy![12]

It isn't enough that the New Warriors were the "good guys" in Stamford. What matters is that they acted irresponsibly. They refused to regulate themselves, so now Speedball and the rest of America's superheroes have to pay the price.

The price proves to be very high, not only for Speedball, but also for other heroes as well. For example, when Johnny Storm, the Human Torch, goes to a nightclub soon after the Stamford incident, he gets attacked by a group of civilians who think that he's guilty by association. Meanwhile, not only do the heroes who refuse to register lose their freedom to operate independently of the government, but they also lose other things, too. Captain America, for example, tells his partners about an appointment he had made with a kid from the Make A Wish Foundation to play baseball in his back yard. Now he can't do it because, he says, "the place is probably crawling with cape-killers."[13]

11. Ibid.
12. Ibid.
13. *Civil War* #2 (2006).

Philosopher Kings in the Technocracy

Registration is ultimately about whether or not people in general are trust-worthy and whether or not it is likely that people will use their freedom to develop the virtues that make for a good society. If the world can trust the majority of the heroes to do what is right, then there is no need for the SRA. On the other hand, if the heroes selfishly and irresponsibly exercise their freedom and do not exercise self-discipline and restraint, then some controlling power becomes necessary.

But even if we accept the reasoning at the heart of the SRA, what about the regulators themselves? As Juvenal (and Alan Moore) has asked, *Quis custodiet ipsos custodes?* (Who will guard the guards?) One of the basic assumptions behind the SRA or any other form of regulation is the belief that the regulators themselves know what is best for society and what people will do under certain circumstances. For example, a free economy promotes competition and growth. But a *laissez faire* economy leaves selfish people free to create monopolies and discourage competition. Moreover, experience and history tell us that people in fact *will* form monopolies, so it becomes necessary for the government to create regulations to discourage or prevent monopolies. But our knowledge of what people will do in an economy only goes so far. That is why Communist Russia's economy ulti-mately failed. The Soviet central planners knew in theory how to manage their economy and yield optimal production, but they overestimated their ability to understand the immense complexity of human interaction that is involved in any economic system.

Similarly, the SRA depends upon its creators and managers assuming a certain understanding of human behavior. It is no accident that three of the Marvel Universe's greatest scientific minds fall on the pro-registration side the conflict. Tony Stark, Reed Richards, and Hank Pym all believe that the scientific method can solve the world's problems. And in theory, they are right about the SRA. With S.H.I.E.L.D. managing the world's security and directing the country's superheroes, accidents and collateral damage will be kept to a minimum.

When Sue Richards objects to putting "half [her] Christmas card list" in prison, Reed agrees that the SRA will lead to some unpleasant conse-quences. But he points to several whiteboards of mathematical equations that he has done in order to show the consequences of not regulating superheroes:

> Reed: Just take a look at my projections if you need to see the social dangers [the anti-registration heroes are] creating.

> Sue: What are you *talking* about? This is gobbledygook.

> Reed: No, it's the exponential curve the number of super beings is following and the *apocalypse* we're facing if unlicensed activity isn't brought under control. Tony's secret plan is an amazing opportunity for us, darling. You should hear the ideas he and Hank Pym have been tossing around. They're like *concept-machines*. I don't think I've ever seen people this super-charged.[14]

Even worse, Reed hides the centerpiece of his and Tony's plans from Sue. She sees a disk labeled "42" on his desk, and when she asks about it, Reed says that it's "classified." As we later learn, 42 refers to a superhuman prison built in the Negative Zone—an alternate universe made of negatively charged matter.

This kind of thinking—the belief that a special few can predict human behavior; that those few have the right to make decisions for society without people's consent—has shown up in one form or another since ancient times, and it always leads down a dark path. From Plato's *Republic* to Stalinist Russia, the philosopher kings have thought that they know better than everyone else. But societies run by those kinds of people are never good, even if the philosophers themselves are well-intentioned. Reed, Tony, and Hank all believe that they know what's best, but it takes real arrogance to believe that one can mathematically determine how to best order a society, and such arrogance ultimately leads to hubris.[15]

Just as importantly, a society run by people like Tony Stark and Reed Richards will not be free enough to allow the average person to develop the essential virtues necessary for a good society. If we accept the premise that a few technocrats can scientifically predict and manipulate human behavior, then we must dispense with the notions of liberty and equality bequeathed to us by the American Founders and acknowledge that we live in a technocracy, not a democracy. Freedom requires not only options, but knowledge as well. The power of government can only rest in the citizenry if those citizens understand how their society runs and can make important decisions based upon that understanding. But whether or not they would be comfortable putting it this way, Reed, Tony, and Hank believe that their

14. *Civil War* #2 (2006).

15. For more on the subject of using data analytics to predict the future, see Chapter 4.

status as scientific and technological geniuses means that they are better qualified than the average person for making the decisions most important to society. (In fact, Tony and Hank are responsible for the creation of the Illuminati, a secret group of super-intelligent heroes formed precisely for the purpose of making decisions for humankind that we can't make for ourselves.) They aren't dictators or despots in the traditional sense, but their decisions are part of the general move toward Tocqueville's soft despotism—a society in which the average person neither can nor wants to do the work of maintaining society and is not free enough to develop the virtues of a citizen.

4

CIVIL WAR II

Freedom and the Surveillance State

In 2016, Marvel published an eight-issue crossover event entitled *Civil War II*. Many critics derided the story as a money-grab meant to capitalize on the ten-year anniversary of the original *Civil War* and the release of *Captain America: Civil War*. There's no doubt that Marvel meant the book to make money (they are a business, after all), but it doesn't deserve the critical bashing that it got. It features beautiful artwork by David Marquez, tells an emotionally gripping story that has real consequences for the future of the Marvel universe, and—most importantly for the purposes of this book—explores ideas that reflect the hopes and worries of our society.

Like its predecessor, *Civil War II* asks what seems like a fairly straightforward question: is it actually possible to predict what people are going to do before they do it, and if so, *should we*? But where the original *Civil War* approached its questions about freedom and security from a purely political point of view, *Civil War II* uses the problem that it confronts as a jumping-off point for deeper, more purely philosophical questions. As is often the case, though, the philosophy isn't content to remain abstract or devoid of practical consequences. In fact, the political implications of *Civil War II* are just as relevant to its own time as *Civil War* was a decade ago.

The Problem of Foreknowledge

The premise of *Civil War II* bears some resemblance to the Philip K. Dick story "The Minority Report" (and its film adaptation, *Minority Report*). A new Inhuman[1] named Ulysses emerges who seems to be able to predict the future. When Ulysses predicts the destruction of New York in an attack by a cosmic being, the Avengers, the Ultimates, and the Inhumans are able to stop the attack and save the city. Impressed with his ability, Captain Marvel (Carol Danvers) decides to use Ulysses to not only predict disasters, but also to prevent crimes before they happen. But when he realizes what Carol has planned, Tony Stark raises some concerns. First, he thinks that it is irresponsible to use Ulysses to predict the future without first knowing more about him and how his power actually works. Second, he points out that whatever Ulysses' visions reveal to him, it isn't *the* future; it can only be a *possible* future:

> Tony: You have an Inhuman with a power to predict "*possible*" future events.
>
> James Rhodes (War Machine): It wasn't a possible future, Tone, it was *going* to happen. . . .
>
> Tony: But it didn't happen because we stopped it. So it wasn't the future he saw, it was a possible future. Think about it.[2]

In other words, if Ulysses' vision of the cosmic being destroying New York had been *true*, then the Avengers, Ultimates, and Inhumans would not have been able to stop it. But Carol argues that it doesn't matter whether or not the prediction was technically *true* because it saved lives and stopped a disaster:

> It *doesn't matter* how it works. The point is it *does*. And everybody wants to be high-minded and take a stand on principle here, but that's not where we live. We *punch* people for a living. And we do it for a good reason. Hell, I'm not even sure what the *choice* is here. If this kid tells us *Los Angeles* is about to be wiped off the map—we're supposed to, what? *Ignore* him?[3]

1. Inhumans are the descendants of people who were the subjects of genetic experiments by an alien race called the Kree thousands of years ago. When people who are carriers of the Inhuman gene are exposed to a substance called "Terrigen," they develop abilities beyond those of normal humans.

2. *Civil War II* #1.

3. *Captain America: Sam Wilson* #11.

She has a point. When the attack on New York happens in *CWII* #1, the Avengers and the Ultimates know about it ahead of time, but they don't know until afterward that the information came from a prediction of the future. And even if he had known beforehand that the tip came from an Inhuman who predicts possible futures, Tony certainly wouldn't have refused to act on the information.

But the problem for Tony isn't alien invasions; the problem is the moment when Ulysses has a vision of some individual committing a crime. It's easy for the Avengers, Ultimates, and Inhumans to congratulate themselves on stopping a "big cosmic monster"[4]—but what if Ulysses predicts that Tony or Carol will commit a crime? Or what if he predicts that some straight-laced, well-mannered, law-abiding civilian will some day be involved in a criminal conspiracy (which in fact happens in *Civil War II* #4)? If Ulysses' visions are merely predictions of *possible* futures, does Carol have a moral right to act on them?

In some ways Tony and Carol take surprising stances on the issue of whether or not to use Ulysses' power to stop crime and alien attacks. Tony has always prided himself on being a "futurist"—in fact, one of his motivations in the first *Civil War* is that he believes in the ability of science to predict how people are going to behave.[5] And though she suffered many emotional and personal traumas early in her career, Carol has lately become an intensely moral character. So the fact that Tony is worried about the morality of relying on Ulysses' ability while Carol seems entirely unconcerned about it might strike some people as out-of-character behavior.

In another sense, though, the stances that Tony and Carol take are exactly right (one might even say "predictable"). Tony is a futurist who puts a lot of faith in the power of information to improve the world, but he also understands that we have to think critically and ethically about our use of technology—and he recognizes early on that Ulysses' power is more comparable to technology than to the supernatural power of prophets. Carol, on the other hand, lives every day with the responsibility of protecting the world and with the possibility of failure: "What if one day we're just not enough?" she asks Doc Samson before Ulysses emerges.[6] If we have the chance to know about disasters before they happen and use that knowledge to save lives and prevent crimes, shouldn't we do it?

4. *Civil War II* #1.

5. For more on this issue, see Chapter 3.

6. *Civil War II* #0.

The Conflict

Whereas Captain America's refusal to go along with the Superhuman Registration Act immediately leads to violent conflict in the original *Civil War*, at first the disagreement between Captain Marvel and Iron Man about Carol's use of Ulysses seems to be simply academic. Tony explains his objections, Carol tells him that he's being foolish—"I am stunned by that man. Again," she tells the gathered Avengers and Ultimates[7]—and then they both seem to move on.

The conflict doesn't become violent until it becomes personal. Three weeks after the New York incident, Ulysses sees a vision of Thanos coming to earth in order to find a powerful object known as a Cosmic Cube. He warns Carol about the threat (Thanos is one of the most vile beings in the Marvel Universe, and Cosmic Cubes are among the most powerful and dangerous objects), so Carol and the Ultimates thwart Thanos' plan. But Tony's best friend, Col. James Rhodes (War Machine) also joins the fight, and though the team stops Thanos, Rhodey dies in the process. Tony blames Carol for the death of his friend, and in response, he kidnaps Ulysses in order to test him and find out how and why his power works.

Predicting the Future?

What Tony learns from his scan of Ulysses' brain confirms his earlier suspicions. Ulysses' power doesn't enable him to accurately predict the future. Instead, his brain unconsciously calculates probabilities based on all the available information. Ulysses' mind has the ability to "absorb . . . data and energies cascading over the entire world. . . . He's *not* seeing *the* future because it is not there. He's creating an algorithm of a *possible* future."[8] In other words, Ulysses' brain operates like an extremely advanced version of the kind of algorithm that Google, Facebook, Amazon, and other sites use in order to predict users' buying habits and sell relevant advertisements.

As others have noted, social media and websites like Facebook and Google do not really provide their services for free. Instead, we pay for the services that they provide—not with money, but with information about ourselves. Those companies use that information in order to predict what

7. *Civil War II* #1.
8. *Civil War II* #4.

we like and want and then use that information to sell ads and create more software and services that they predict that we will want.

Though some of us might find it a little creepy to search for a book at an online retailer and then start seeing advertisements for it in our social media news feeds, the use of our data for advertising isn't at all surprising. But if technology analysts are to be believed, advertisements are only the beginning. Already streaming music services try to predict (with varying degrees of success) songs that we will want to listen to. Online retailers use our past purchases in order to make new recommendations to us. And our electronic devices recommend applications based on the time and our location. For example, I use an app to take attendance in my college classes, so when I arrive at work for my first class, my tablet recommends my attendance app, and it does so based on my location and the time. In other words, it keeps track of my movements and my app usage in order to provide useful information to me. But as useful as such tracking and recommendations might be, there is a real danger to uncritically accepting the fact that our devices monitor us constantly.

Meanwhile, police and government officials seem to be working hard to make use of the treasure trove of data that people have been putting onto the web for the last three decades. Revelations about the National Security Agency's PRISM program have shown that the U.S. government uses data-gathering from private emails, social media, video chats, and other communications in order to combat terrorism,[9] and police departments around the country have been engaging in "predictive policing" that purports to "identify people and locations at increased risk of crime."[10]

Everything Sticks

The use of data in order to sell ads; to predict what products and services we'll want to buy; to guess what books we'll want to read and what movies we'll want to see; to make music recommendations to us; to know what apps we'll want to use in what place (and when); to predict whether or not we'll become criminals or victims—we could say that these things are merely the application of the scientific method to human behavior. It's a logical extension of the foundational theories of psychology and sociology: we can use

9. Gorman and Valentino-Devries, "New Details Show Broader NSU Surveillance Reach."

10. Perry et al. "Predictive Policing."

scientific methods in order to understand why people behave in the ways that they do, and as long as we know enough about them, we might also be able to *predict* their behavior, as well. And if our ability to use the data that is available about us makes our lives safer and more convenient, why not?

But there are a number of problems with the use of data in this way. Probably the greatest and most discussed problem with it is the fact that it violates our privacy. When Edward Snowden first leaked classified information about PRISM to the public, many people were outraged by the notion that the government could access the private communications and activities of its citizens without a warrant. The ability to monitor people's private emails, video chats, and other communications is a tremendous and frightening power, and in giving the government the ability to do these things, we are giving up more than just a little privacy. One can imagine all sorts of ways in which unsupervised technicians might abuse their access to people's private communications and devices; but there are more insidious risks, as well. If our data can be used to predict our behavior, it might also be used to manipulate and coerce us. Moreover, in a society like ours where freedom of thought and expression have come under increasing threat, our private online data could also be used to punish us for believing or saying the wrong things. After all, nothing that we do or say electronically is completely safe. As Selina Kyle tells Bruce Wayne in *The Dark Knight Rises*, "Everything we do is collated and quantified. Everything sticks."

The Problem of Induction

As important as privacy is, however, *Civil War II* raises another problem with the kind of prediction that both the NSA and Ulysses engage in. This problem has to do with *epistemology*, which is the branch of philosophy that deals with theories of how we know things.

In *Civil War II*, Ulysses' brain unconsciously collects information from a vast quantity of sources. As Tony explains to Carol and Steve Rogers,

> Everything in the world puts out energy, everything and everyone. [Ulysses] take[s] it in and the kid—he spouts it back at us . . . in the form of these visions. . . . He's creating an algorithm of a possible future. Yes! Maybe a *very* possible future. But, and you have to hear me on this, it is *only* an algorithm. It's math. It's *guesswork*.[11]

11. *Civil War II* #4.

In other words, like the work done by the NSA and data-gathering websites, Ulysses simply collects information and uses a kind of algorithm to predict future events and behavior based upon past behavior. And it isn't unreasonable to use knowledge of the past and present in order to predict what someone will do in the future. Most human knowledge depends upon our ability to make judgments about the future based on the facts and information that are available to us. In fact, the validity of scientific knowledge depends upon predictability and repetition. If I think that A produces result B, then science says that I should be able to reproduce result B by repeating A.

But we ought to take note that there is a difficulty with our assumption that what happened in the past can tell us what will happen in the future. As the Scottish philosopher David Hume argued,[12] the fact that A was followed by B in all past observations does not logically prove that A will *always* be followed by B. Or the fact that I have observed something happening frequently in the past does not mean that it will continue to happen frequently in the future.

For example, imagine a long hallway with doors on either side for as far as you can see. Each door is numbered so that at the beginning of the hall, door number 1 is on your right, and door number 2 is on your left. You open door number 1 and find a pink elephant inside. After you get over your surprise at seeing a pink elephant, you close the door and open door number two and find . . . another pink elephant. You try several more doors, and behind each one you find a pink elephant. After about fifty doors, you come to the conclusion that each of the doors hides one of the animals. But do you *know* what you will find behind each door? Most people would say no, but most of us would say that it is reasonable to think that we do.

But let's say that you keep going. You open a hundred doors and find a hundred pink elephants; two hundred; three hundred. This goes on for door after door until you reach the last door, number 1,000, at the end of the hall. Behind the first 999 doors, you found pink elephants. When you open door number 1,000, you feel certain that you will see another pink elephant. But do you *know* that you will?

The most logical answer is still no. You *don't* know that you will find a pink elephant behind the 1,000th door.

Though that example is simplistic, it illustrates the problem. Much of what we call "knowledge" comes from *inductive reasoning*. Induction

12. For example, in his 1748 book, *An Enquiry Concerning Human Understanding*.

means making generalized judgments based on specific observations. For example, if I walk into a college classroom and notice that all of the students are female, I might conclude that this is a women's college. And though that seems like a reasonable conclusion, there could be other explanations for the lack of males in this particular class. In other words, induction can't necessarily give us the kind of certainty that we would like for it to provide.

Now none of this is to say that induction is useless or even very unreliable. *Much* of what we call "knowledge" is the result of inductive reasoning. But as Hume and other philosophers have pointed out, it is a leap of logic to say with absolute certainty that because B has always followed A in my past observations, B will always follow A in the future, too.

So here is Tony's problem with Ulysses' power: even though it is complex and superhuman, Ulysses' ability to predict the future is nothing more than a ultra-sophisticated form of induction. His brain processes the "observations" that it absorbs through the energy produced by every object in the world and draws conclusions from those observations. Those predictions might be highly likely, but they're still only possibilities—which means that they could be wrong.

And even though it is an indispensable source of our knowledge, induction certainly isn't a foolproof means of thinking about human behavior. In fact, it can be downright dangerous when used unethically. For example, some people who are concerned about the threat of terrorism will point out that the majority of terrorist attacks committed in the last few decades have been done by Middle Easterners. They might use this observation to conclude that people of Middle Eastern descent tend to be dangerous and then use such reasoning to come up with all sorts of bad or dangerous policies.

Logicians might say that this is an example of a hasty generalization. The number of Middle Easterners who have committed acts of terrorism is too small for us to use it to make a judgment about Middle Easterners in general. But "hasty generalization" is merely a way of describing inductive reasoning that we happen to find unconvincing. And there is no objective test that we can apply in order to show whether our reasoning is sound or if we've committed a hasty generalization. What we find convincing or persuasive can be entirely subjective.

More importantly, while induction depends upon consistency and predictability, people are not always predictable or consistent. In fact, people change quite often in any number of ways: their friends, their political or social views, their religious convictions, their taste in food or movies.

When I was younger, for example, I listened mostly to heavy metal music. Now I can't stand that kind of thing. Instead, I listen mostly to classical, bluegrass, and jazz—in other words, music that I couldn't stomach fifteen years ago. Likewise, when I was younger, I enjoyed large gatherings and loud talking, but now I prefer intimacy and quiet conversation. My political views have also changed in many ways over the years. And I'm not just describing myself here. Most people would have to agree that they are in some ways different people than they were years ago.

Fine, you say, *but a guy who was a jerk all of last week is likely to be a jerk this week.* In other words, at any given point in their lives, people's behavior is basically consistent; they act according to their character and personality. Though we often repeat ourselves and usually act in ways that are consistent with our overall character, we are also capable of surprising each other. For instance, as a teacher I often look at the way students behave at the beginning of the semester and think that I can predict how those students will perform in the class. And often my predictions prove correct, but sometimes students surprise me. I've had a number of students who started out the semester very well but still ended up failing the class because they simply quit trying. Similarly, I might think that a student has performed so badly in the beginning of the semester that he's a lost cause, but then suddenly he gets his act together, starts to turn in good work, improves his attendance and behavior, and manages to pull his grade up by the end of the semester. That certainly doesn't happen always, but it happens often enough that it isn't really fair to write off poor students as lost causes. We might think that it is possible to use what we know in order to predict other people's behavior, but the fact that people often surprise us casts serious doubt on our foreknowledge.

Captain Marvel's line about Tony in issue #1 is a good illustration of what I'm talking about: "I am *stunned* by that man. Again." If someone *stuns* us, it is because he or she has defied our expectations. If you had asked her ahead of time what Tony would think of using an Inhuman to predict the future and stop disasters before they happen, she probably would have said that she expected him to like the idea. The fact that Tony defies that expectation is what *stuns* her. But then she adds that word "again." In other words, this isn't the first time that Tony has "stunned" her. In fact, it probably happens on a regular basis. One might wonder, then, why she continues to be surprised by his behavior. The answer is that even though

Carol has known Tony for years, her expectations (or predictions) of his behavior are not reliable.

You Need Proof

The problem of induction also comes to the forefront in issue #4 when one of Ulysses' visions shows that a woman named Alison Green—who works in finance, has a father on the Chicago police force, and "really loves karaoke"—is a "high-ranking deep-cover operative" of Hydra "working on a multi-pronged violent plot" to destroy America's financial institutions. Though S.H.I.E.L.D. combs Alison's life and finds no evidence that she has ties to Hydra or any other criminal organization, Carol remains convinced of her guilt because she believes in the accuracy of Ulysses' prediction. After questioning her, Carol tells the terrified Alison, "I have the legal right to hold you here indefinitely" and leaves her in the interrogation room. But Black Panther and the usually aggressive Maria Hill remained unconvinced:

> Hill: You need proof.
>
> Carol: We'll find it.
>
> Hill: Carol.
>
> Carol: *We'll find it!*

Because of her faith in Ulysses' predictions and her own ability to *know*, it doesn't even seem to cross her mind that she might be wrong about Alison. In her determination to keep people safe, Carol seems to be verging on mania. In her state of mind, she might very well believe that *any* evidence supports her belief that Alison is guilty.

The Clash Paradox

In addition to highlighting the difficulties with our ability to know anything about the future (like that Alison will be part of a Hydra plot to disrupt U.S. financial institutions), *Civil War II* also points to the paradoxical nature of foreknowledge and asks to what extent our predictions affect what will happen. Do our efforts to predict the future in some way *cause* the future?

That is the major theme of the *Civil War II* tie-in miniseries *Civil War II: Amazing Spider-Man*. Now the head of his own technology corporation, Spider-Man (Peter Parker) employs some of his former enemies in order to allow them a second chance at life. One of those men is Clayton Cole, the former supervillain Clash. At Parker Industries, Cole is working to develop a "sonic-based system" that will allow flying cars to detect dangerous obstructions in their paths. Though he previously worked as a henchman for the Owl, Cole has reformed (with the help of Peter Parker) and now devotes his genius-level intellect to working for the good of other people.

But when Spider-Man brings Ulysses to Parker Industries, the Inhuman has a vision of Clayton wearing the Clash suit and fighting Spidey. "You have to remember, not everything I see comes true," he tells Spider-Man. "I mean, almost all of it does, but . . . ."[13] At first, Peter is reluctant to act on the vision in any way because he is convinced that Cole has truly reformed. He worries that confronting his friend with the information might be what causes him to return to crime.

Meanwhile, things take a downward turn in Cole's personal life. Though he has given up crime and has a good job at a major technology company, Cole's parents treat him like a child. And worst of all, the woman that he hopes to marry breaks off her relationship with him because she's afraid that her son, who idolizes Cole, will one day find out about Cole's criminal past. None of this is enough to drive Cole back to crime, though. Through all of it, what sustains him is the confidence that others put in him:

> Rohan (one of Cole's co-workers): Your life can't be over as long as you've got *Spider-Man* going to bat for you, can it?
>
> Cole: Yeah. And Mr. Parker. He believes in me, so I have to believe in myself, right?[14]

Though we can't *know* that Cole would be alright as long as Peter continues to have faith in him (remember the problem with induction?), we can reasonably assume that he will.

What ultimately pushes him over the edge is that Cole notices Spidey and Ulysses acting suspicious toward him and begins to feel paranoid. In issue #2, Cole uses a device called a "retroactive recorder" to eavesdrop on Spidey's conversation with Ulysses. The device "pick[s] up sound waves still bouncing around the room," so he is able to hear Ulysses tell Spider-Man that "he's gonna go bad. He's gonna put on a costume and fight you."[15] When Spider-Man catches Cole using the recorder (which was designed for po-

13. *Civil War II: Amazing Spider-Man #1.*
14. *Civil War II: Amazing Spider-Man #2*
15. Ibid.

lice and isn't supposed to be used without a warrant), Cole becomes angry and quits Parker Industries. Cole's response to Spider-Man highlights the problem of induction:

> Cole: I know what [the retroactive recorder] is! I *made* it! Along with a dozen other things that have brought in a *fortune* for this company! But after all that, you're gonna take the word of some punk who can't even grow facial hair—who doesn't even *know* me!—that I'm gonna go bad?

> Spider-Man: Clayton, it's not that simple. He—keep this quiet, but he's got *powers*. He—

> Cole: I don't care if he's *Captain America*! I helped you against the Zodiac![16]

Cole believes that his time and service to Peter Parker and Spider-Man[17] are enough evidence to show that he has truly reformed, and he accuses Spider-Man of believing that he will return to crime because of insufficient evidence. And since Ulysses has already admitted to Spider-Man that his predictions aren't always correct,[18] Cole might well have a point. In any case, Ulysses' prediction about Cole ends up being a self-fulfilling prophecy—not unlike the prophecies about Oedipus and Macbeth.[19] When Cole learns about the prediction, it makes him believe that Peter Parker has lost faith in him, and that drives him to become Clash again.

What makes all of this even more complicated, however, is that Cole doesn't *actually* "go bad," as Ulysses predicts. When a supervillain called Robot Master asks Cole to join him in a plot to steal ideas from Parker Industries, Cole pretends to be open to the proposition; but when he creates a new Clash suit and meets Robot Master at his lair, he attacks the villain in order to prevent him from carrying out his plan. When the fight spills out into the streets of New York, Spider-Man joins Clash, and together the two of them stop Robot Master and his drones.

---

16. Ibid.

17. Cole doesn't know that they are the same person.

18. In *Civil War II: Amazing Spider-Man* #1.

19. These are two of the most famous self-fulfilling prophecies in literature. In Sophocles' play *Oedipus Rex,* the Oracle at Delphi prophesies that Oedipus will kill his own father and marry his own mother—but it is Oedipus' attempts to escape this fate that ultimately brings it about. In *Macbeth*, the title character kills the king so that he might ascend to the throne, but only after three witches prophesy that he will become king.

Afterward, Spidey tells Cole that he can come back to Parker Industries and that both he and Peter still believe in him. But he also tells him that he has to turn over all of his Clash technology over to Parker Industries and promise never to work in sonics again. This drives Cole into a rage, and he attacks Spidey: "I don't [have a choice]," he reasons. "The vision that *Ulysses* kid had . . . it came true. Which means *none* of us have a choice. The future's set."[20] Spider-Man points out that he has prevented several of Ulysses' visions from coming true and that Cole always has a choice. But just when it looks like he's getting through to Cole, Robot Master attacks them again, and Cole abandons Spider-Man to the fight:

> Sorry, you're right. My future's in my hands. And I don't want the life that got me tossed in jail. But y'know what else I don't want? The life I've had the past few days. I'm on my own. So are you.[21]

Even though Cole is violating his parole by taking up the Clash identity again, he doesn't seem to be going back to a life of crime. In fact, he tells Spidey, "I wanted to prove that I was on the right side. That I could make the right choice!"[22] While Spider-Man argues that Cole *didn't* make the "right choice," it seems clear at the end of *Civil War II: Amazing Spider-Man* that whatever he plans to do, Cole isn't on his way to becoming a supervillain.

Gazing into the Palantir

Cole's story returns us to the problem of what we can know and what we can foretell about the future. What Ulysses *sees* in his vision about Cole turns out to be true: he does put on the Clash suit again, and he does fight Spider-Man. But Ulysses' *interpretation* of that vision turns out to be false. Cole doesn't "go bad" in the sense that he returns to life as a supervillain.

And his prediction that Cole will take up the Clash identity isn't the only time one of Ulysses' visions gets misinterpreted. In *Civil War II* #5, Ulysses shows a group of superheroes perhaps his most disturbing vision: Spider-Man[23] stands next to Captain America, who has been impaled on what looks like a piece of jagged metal, and behind them stands the ruins

20. *Civil War II: Amazing Spider-Man* #4.

21. Ibid.

22. *Civil War II: Amazing Spider-Man* #3.

23. The black-and-red-suited Miles Morales version, not the original Peter Parker Spider-Man.

of the U.S. capitol building. The vision leads everyone to believe that Miles is going to murder Steve Rogers, but as readers of *Captain America: Steve Rogers* know, there is much more to the story. Steve Rogers' identity has been magically altered by the Red Skull using a cosmic cube, transforming him from America's super-soldier and the Sentinel of Liberty into a Hydra sleeper agent.[24] What we readers know, but the heroes in *Civil War II* do not, is that the vision is badly misleading. It probably shows the aftermath of a fight between Miles and Steve after Miles learns of Steve's "true" identity and allegiance.

In this way, Ulysses' visions are much like the Palantiri of J. R. R. Tolkien's Middle Earth mythos. The visions might often reveal "true" things to those who see them, but even the facts can mislead us if they're taken out of context.[25]

A Warning

As we move further into a future where facts and data become currency and where various institutions and organizations become more and more interested in using that data to predict human behavior, we ought to heed Tony Stark's warnings in *Civil War II*. There seems to be no way to escape the coming world of data and information—indeed, it's already here. But while we might not be able to turn back the clock on the increasing sophistication of surveillance, intelligence, and data analytics, we can think more deeply about the consequences of that new world, about our place in it, and about the way in which it makes us see ourselves.

24. I discuss this part of Captain America's story in Chapter 1.

25. Perhaps ironically, one of America's largest intelligence software companies is called "Palantir."

5

THE DARK KNIGHT RETURNS

Why No Single Principle Is Sufficient

Opposing the State

From the moment Captain America punched Adolf Hitler in 1941 down to the questions of identity raised in the most recent X-Men comics, super-hero comics have been inherently political, even when they aren't overtly so. In fact, the very existence of superheroes is itself a political statement. You can't write stories about people who dress up in fancy costumes and fight crime outside the sanction of the state without raising questions of politics. And, with some exceptions, superhero comics seem to inherently lean a certain direction when it comes to questions of power and individu-alism. Though early on heroes were often supported and sanctioned by government officials, they began to frequently run afoul of the government as comics matured. After all, their use of force in order to achieve justice and safety is a direct challenge to the power of the state.

The term "state" can be difficult to define. Scholars don't always agree on its precise meaning. But in modern politics, most people agree that one essential feature of the state is that it has a monopoly on the legitimate use of force. In his essay "Politics as a Vocation," for example, Max Weber writes,

> Force is certainly not the normal or the only means of the state—
> nobody says that—but force is a means specific to the state. Today
> the relation between the state and violence is an especially intimate
> one. In the past, the most varied institutions—beginning with the
> sib[1]—have known the use of physical force as quite normal. Today,
> however, we have to say that a state is a human community that
> (successfully) claims the monopoly of the legitimate use of physi-
> cal force within a given territory.[2]

In other words, within the territory controlled by a state, only the government may authorize the use of violence for the purposes of coercion. Usually this means that only the state itself may use such force, but it does
sometimes authorize the use of violence by private individuals to protect
their property or land. In any case, though, the defining feature of a state is
what Weber describes as a "monopoly" on the use of force.

So what does this mean for superheroes, who by definition use force
in order to secure peace, protect victims, and to coerce criminals into obeying the law—all of which can only be done legitimately by the state? In
some cases, superheroes work as agents of the state and therefore exercise
violence legitimately. For example, Alpha Flight, the Canadian answer to
the Avengers, works under the authority of Department H, a branch of the
Canadian government. The fact that the group answers to a government
body essentially makes its members government agents (though instead of
wearing black ties they wear colorful costumes).

There are several other examples of state-sanctioned superheroes. In
the beginning of his career, Captain America operated as a soldier in the
U.S. Army. When he fought Nazis and punched Hitler in the face, people
could cheer him on without feeling guilty because he did those things with
the approval of his country. And in the Marvel Cinematic Universe, War
Machine (or "Iron Patriot" in *Iron Man 3*) is a Lieutenant Colonel in the Air
Force and acts directly under the authority of the U.S. president.

Sometimes the legitimacy of a hero's actions is unclear, as is often the
case with Batman in the mainstream DC universe. For much of his career,
Batman has worked in cooperation with the Gotham police force. At first,
they try to stop him, and then they barely tolerate him. But before long, the
police (or, at least, Jim Gordon) begin to rely on him as an enforcer of the
peace. Jim Gordon has not only the Bat Signal, but a direct telephone line

1. A family group.
2. Weber, *From Max Weber*, 78

to the Batcave. His cooperation with Batman implicitly means that he, as a representative of the government, sanctions Batman's actions. Even though what Batman does is in violation of the law, the fact that representatives of the state tolerate him gives Batman a *kind* of legitimacy.

In most cases, however, superheroes necessarily operate outside of state authority, therefore challenging the state's monopoly on violence. This is not a challenge that the representatives of the state can take lightly: after all, the fundamental characteristic of a state is that only it can authorize the legitimate use of force. Only the state can use violence to coerce its citizens to behave in a certain way. So even though Daredevil thinks that he is helping his city when he prowls the streets at night beating up criminals and leaving them for the police to find, New York City officials have to see his actions as a challenge to their authority. They have to treat him not as a hero, but as a threat.

This problem has perhaps never been better dramatized than in Frank Miller's game-changing series *The Dark Knight Returns*, which not only marked a major evolution in the tone of Batman stories, making the Caped Crusader darker and more brutal than the Batman of the 1950s, 60s, and 70s; it also forced readers to confront the major issue at the heart of the very idea of superheroics: the use of violence for coercion and justice. Who gets to decide when a person can use force? In *TDKR,* Batman's decision to take the law into his own hands brings him up against the most powerful opponent he's ever had to face: Superman.

Superman and Batman have fought several times over the course of their histories, but the fight that Miller presents us with in *The Dark Knight Returns* is altogether different than most. For example, when Supes and Bats fight in *Hush,* it's because Superman has been drugged by Poison Ivy; he isn't in his right mind, and he wouldn't otherwise be fighting Batman. And when Supes comes to blows with Bats (along with the Green Lantern) in the first issue of the New 52 *Justice League* title, they fight over a simple misunderstanding. But in *The Dark Knight Returns*, no mind-controlling poisons or misunderstandings bring the two heroes into conflict. This fight won't be resolved as easily as it is in other battles because it is an ideological one. In this dark future, Superman now works as an enforcer for the state— a state which cannot tolerate the existence of an outsider like Batman who doesn't answer to the government. Yet because the state has become ineffective in protecting its citizens (at least in Gotham), Batman *has* to fight criminals. And though he doesn't believe that his actions are technically "legitimate," he does believe that he has a *right* and an *obligation* to do what he does. In the event that the state ceases to uphold its obligations, does the individual have the right to act?[3]

Since the question is a moral one—having to do both with *rights* and what is truly good—we might be able to answer it by appealing to some of the most important theories of morality: deontology, utilitarianism, and virtue ethics.

The School(s) of Morals

Superheroes can often be models of virtue and moral principles. For example, Captain America exemplifies honor, courage, perseverance, patriotism, devotion to justice, and other important virtues.[4] He also stands for some very strong moral principles. In his famous speech to Spider-Man during the superhuman Civil War, for example, he admonishes Spidey to stand by his convictions, even when others oppose those convictions. Superman famously embodies the principles of "truth, justice, and the American way." Batman gives us an example of patience and endurance, Wonder Woman of love, and Spider-Man of self-sacrifice. In a way, we could see comics from the Golden Age down to the present day as a school for the various forms of ethical theory.

For example, many heroes appeal to absolute moral truths that everyone ought to know. This is an ethical theory called *natural law* that comes to us from sources as ancient as the Bible and the ancient Greek play *Antigone* and was perhaps most systematically explained by great Christian philosophers like Saint Thomas Aquinas. Natural law ethics emphasizes obedience to a set of moral rules that are built into the nature of the world and into human nature itself. In order to be a good person, I must follow those rules, and I can know them as long as I have a well-formed conscience and appeal to the right authorities—for example, Scripture or the great philosophers.

Other heroes appeal to a system of ethics called *deontology*. In deontology, the ethical theory whose most famous exponent was perhaps the German philosopher Immanuel Kant, I can be a good person by applying my reason to the discovery of moral behavior. Kant argues that I determine whether or not a behavior is good by asking whether or not it could be

---

3. For more on this question, see Tony Spanakos' essay "Governing Gotham," collected in *Batman and Philosophy*, edited by Mark D. White and Robert Arp.

4. For more on this, see Mark D. White's book *The Virtues of Captain America*.

universalized: "Act only according to that maxim whereby you can at the same time will that it should become a universal law."[5] If I tell a lie in a given situation, would that be morally acceptable? I answer by asking another question: "Would lying as a universal rule be acceptable?" If I say no, then I must conclude that I can't tell the lie right now, either. Deontology is like natural law theory in that it emphasizes rules that govern behavior.

In another ethical theory called *utilitarianism*, I determine whether an action is just or unjust by taking into consideration whether or not it will bring about more good than bad. In other words, utilitarianism is a form of *consequentialism*, an ethical theory that judges the rightness of an action by looking at its consequences. If I am faced with choices A, B, and C, I should ask myself which of these options will produce the greatest good for the greatest number of people. Utilitarians call this the principle of *utility*. Whatever produces the most good has utility.

At the end of Sam Raimi's first *Spider-Man* film, for example, the Green Goblin tries to make Spidey choose between saving his beloved Mary Jane Watson or a tram car full of children. Utilitarianism would say that someone faced with such a choice ought to save the children, since doing so would lead to more good for a greater number of people than saving MJ. (Of course, Spidey being Spidey, he manages to save everybody.)

Unlike the previous ethical theories, *virtue ethics* doesn't begin with a decision about my actions. Rather, it begins with my character. It asks what kind of person I am or what kind of person I want to be. In other words, what kinds of virtues do I have? Am I a courageous person? Am I humble? Generous? Temperate? Honest? If I possess those virtues, then I will act virtuously. But the first thing is to *have* the virtues, and good actions will proceed from my having them. If I am a courageous and self-sacrificing person, I will act for the good of others even when I have to risk my life, health, or well-being to do so. If I have a sense of righteous indignation at injustice, then I will work to right wrongs. If I am a humble person, I will put the happiness of others before my own happiness.

While each of these ethical theories is helpful in its own way for thinking about what it means to live a moral life, each can also lead us astray because of a temptation that often arises the temptation to set up some single virtue or moral principle as an absolute at the expense of other virtues or principles.

---

5. Kant, *Ethical Philosophy*, 30.

For example, while possessing the virtues will generally help me to be a good person, no single virtue can steer me in the right direction all the time. If I have a virtue without also possessing at least some of the others, then I am almost certainly going to become what most of us would call a bad person. For example, imagine that I am courageous, but I do not have any humility or righteous indignation. Because my courage is not tempered and guided by a healthy disregard of my own interests and a desire for justice, it will lead me to become a bully or an irrationally violent person.[6]

Or imagine that I possess a strong sense of righteous indignation, but I do not also possess good judgment or humility. Good judgment allows me to recognize true injustices and to distinguish between which actions are appropriate or helpful in a given situation and which ones are not. Humility teaches me that I am not always right, that I should take other people's opinions into consideration, and that I should regard the needs of others as more important than my own. If I have a strong desire to see justice done, but I lack good judgment and the understanding that I can make mistakes, then my desire for justice will lead me to act in ways that turn out to be unjust. Think, for example, of rioters protesting the results of the 2016 presidential election. They certainly have the right to be dissatisfied with their new president, and they certainly have the right to protest his more outrageous statements and actions, but if their desire for justice leads them to destroy people's property or to hurt people who voted in a way that they don't like, then their indignation has not led them to act morally.

The same problem arises for any of the other virtues in isolation, as well. For example, tolerance is one of the most important virtues of a free and open society because it allows for people with different beliefs and practices to live in the same place without conflict. But a society that is tolerant without also having good judgment and righteous indignation would be a terrible place to live. It is good that the United States is a place of religious toleration, a place where Muslims, Jews, Christians, Sikhs, and others can exist and practice their religions without public or government interference. But no society can tolerate *all* religions. For example, we couldn't tolerate the version of Islam practiced by ISIS; nor could we tolerate the human sacrifice practiced by certain ancient South American religions.

---

6. If you are familiar with the ancient poem *The Epic of Gilgamesh*, for example, think of Gilgamesh at the beginning of his story: he's strong and courageous, but he has no humility, so he mistreats his people.

Almost everyone recognizes that people in a democracy should be tolerant, but we also recognize that we should not tolerate *everything*. But the virtue of tolerance itself cannot tell us what we should tolerate and what we shouldn't. We need other virtues like honesty, righteous indignation, and most importantly the good judgment that comes with the intellectual virtues in order to decide what we should tolerate.[7]

And lest this should seem only a problem for virtue ethics, the other ethical systems do not fare any better if they set up a single rule or principle as an absolute or as the most important. For example, if I am a proponent of natural law or deontology, but I insist that the only really important rule is being nice to people, then I'm going to end up treating some people unfairly. It is not truly just—nor is it really possible—to be nice to everybody. To jump right to the most dramatic example possible, being nice to Hitler at the height of his power would have meant participating in unspeakable evil committed against Jews and others under his rule. Almost everyone would agree—even those who insist that kindness is the pinnacle of good behavior—that morality demands that we act *unkindly* to a person like Hitler.

Even utilitarianism isn't exempt from the problem; in fact, it might suffer most from it because utilitarianism by definition sets up a single principle as its moral standard. If the principle of utility is absolute, then that might allow (or even require) me to do some real evil to a minority of people if doing so provides enough benefit to the majority.[8]

An understanding of this problem can help us to make sense of the political implications and ideas inherent in any superhero comic, and in particular the problems raised in *The Dark Knight Returns*.

A Dark Future

The Dark Knight Returns reinterprets the 1980s as a dystopian near-future in which there is a profound disconnect between the state and the mass culture on the one hand and the citizens on the other. The book opens with a depressed Bruce Wayne, ten years retired from crime fighting, trying to escape his depression through alcohol and through almost suicidal drag racing. Miller juxtaposes the darkness surrounding Bruce with the

7. For more on the problem of emphasizing one virtue over all others, see Chapter 4 of C. S. Lewis' book *The Problem of Pain*.

8. To their credit, most utilitarians do not seem to consistently follow their own philosophy on this point.

light-hearted tone of the Gotham news network. The anchor attributes the rise in crime to a heat wave—as if a temperature of 97 degrees alone is enough to drive people to brutality and murder—and then cheerfully remarks on the long absence of the Batman.

The heat wave itself—which climbs from 97 to 112 within the first few pages of *TDKR* #1—suggests the oppressive atmosphere of this future. The public is stifled by the rise of the Mutant gang, by a government that is deeply out of touch with its citizenry, and by a mass media that seems to be perhaps more delusional than the criminals in Arkham Asylum. Even Bruce Wayne is oppressed by this environment (not to mention the crushing weight of guilt that rests on his shoulders after the death of Jason Todd).

It isn't an accident that Batman returns from his ten-year retirement the same night that a storm front comes through Gotham. Just as the storm marks a change in the oppressive atmosphere that has hung over Gotham (literally), so does Batman's return mark a change in the political situation. Because the government has been failing at its job and allowing Gotham to become a city of crime, Batman has returned like a storm to relieve social and political oppression.[9]

But while Batman wages his war on the Mutant gang, his actions increasingly attract the attention of the state, especially the U.S. president. When Batman becomes an embarrassment to the ineffectual state that he can no longer ignore, the president decides to send Supes to stop him:

> I like to think I learned everything I know about running this country on my ranch . . . and, well, it's all well and good . . . on a *ranch,* I mean . . . for the horses to be all different colors and sizes . . . as long as they stay inside the fence. . . . It's even okay to have a *crazy bronco* now and then, . . . does the *hands* some good to *break him in,* . . . but if that bronco up and kicks the *fence* and gets the other *horses* crazy . . . well, it's bad for business. . . . Now, son, I'm not asking you to drag him kicking and screaming into the stable. Just *settle* him *down,* . . . ride him around the yard a few times if you have to.[10]

The problem is that while Superman works as a legitimate agent of the U.S. government, Batman has always been a clandestine enforcer who operates outside the bounds of the law. As Ellen Yindel, the incoming police

---

9. The cover to the first issue of *TDKR* features the now-famous image of Batman's silhouette against a dark sky, a bolt of lightning piercing the night behind him.

10. *The Dark Knight Returns* #2.

commissioner, puts it, "His actions are categorically *criminal.*"[11] But the *criminality* of Batman's actions is only secondary to the real problem: what he does challenges the authority of the state, indeed, calls its very existence into question.

Both Batman and Superman believe that they're doing what is right, or at least what is *best*. Superman believes that he is keeping the peace. Batman believes that he is enforcing the justice that the state can't or won't enforce itself. Who is right? While one could make a strong argument either in favor of Batman or of Superman, it seems to me that in *TDKR*, both heroes are guilty of setting up a single principle or virtue as an absolute value at the expense of other important moral values.

Superman's Obedience to Authority

For most of his history, the Man of Steel has been the quintessential American hero. Even before his catchphrase became "truth, justice, and the American way," his role as "champion of the helpless and oppressed in [an] unceasing battle against evil and injustice"[12] has always made him a personification of American ideals. Like Captain America, Superman has stood not for the American government, but for American *values*, the ideals that make America good even when her leaders aren't good. In *TDRK*, however, we find this champion of the oppressed reduced to a mere weapon to be used at the behest of the U.S. government. Until now he has been an independent agent who serves American ideals—ideals that are represented by the state but also transcend the state. But now in this dystopian future America, he has willingly become a pawn of those who happen to have power.

How could this happen? It happens because the Superman of Miller's Dark Knight Universe values legitimacy more than anything else. What's most important to him is that he operates within the clear bounds of the law: "Sooner or later, somebody's going to order me to bring you in. Somebody with *authority*."[13] What he means is that his first and most important moral obligation is to obey the legitimate authorities, those people and institutions who have the right to command and coerce. No moral obligation or responsibility—the pursuit of justice, the loyalty required by his friend-

11. Ibid.
12. *Action Comics* #14 (1938).
13. *The Dark Knight Returns* #3.

ship with Bruce, or anything else—can supersede his obligation to obey those invested with legitimate authority.

Of course obedience to the people who rightfully hold power is undoubtedly a good thing. That's what allows for a functioning government, police force, and military—all of which are necessary for democracy. But unless such obedience is balanced by good judgment and a clear understanding of right and wrong, it will leave us being obedient out of fear to institutions that commit injustice and evil. In fact, Superman cites fear as one of his motivations for supporting the government:

> They'll kill us if they can, Bruce. Every year they grow *smaller*. Every year they hate us more. We must not remind them that giants walk the earth. . . . I gave them my obedience and my invisibility. They gave me a license and let us live. . . . But now the storm is growing again. They'll hunt us *down* again—because of *you*.[14]

In the past of this alternate universe, the public and the government turned against superheroes, and those heroes very nearly lost their lives. One could argue, then, that Superman's obedience in *TDKR* isn't so much a moral choice as it is merely a means of survival in a world that increasingly hates superheroes, and fear certainly plays a part in what he does. But while fear is a part of his moral reasoning, Superman's willingness to work as an attack dog for the U.S. government can't entirely account for his obedience. As Bruce tells him, "Nobody can make you do anything you don't want to do, Clark."[15] Indeed, only moral obligation can explain Superman's obedience to the state in *TDKR* because the state has no real means of threatening or coercing him. In fact, Superman survives the most powerful weapon that the state possesses—a nuclear missile—in the very pages of *TDKR*.

Deep down, Superman has to believe in his duty to serve, so like a good soldier, he obeys his orders. But doing so leads him to ignore the fact that the government is clearly failing to live up to its own obligations, which include defending the lives of its citizens. Batman himself takes a dim view of Superman's obedience: "'Yes'—you always say *yes*—to anyone with a badge—or a flag."[16] What Bruce doesn't say—what is implied in his word "always"—is that Superman will obey even when doing so is clearly in conflict with other moral obligations.

14. Ibid.
15. Ibid.
16. *The Dark Knight Returns* #4.

Batman's "One Rule"

Though he strikes fear into the hearts of criminals with his brutality and terrifying persona, Batman is famous for his one rule—the rule not to kill. He might spend his nights spying on people and beating criminals to a pulp, but the one line that he won't cross is that he won't kill.

The Dark Knight hasn't always had a strong prohibition of killing, of course. For example, in *Detective Comics* #27, Batman knocks a criminal to his death in a vat of acid, and in issue #30, he kicks a man's head hard enough to break his neck. More recently, Batman tallies up a fairly large kill count in *Batman v Superman: Dawn of Justice* (to the consternation of many fans).

Some exceptions aside, though, the no-killing rule has been an essential part of his character for most of his history. In fact, his unwillingness to kill has been the subject of many of his greatest stories. For example, in *Batman* #614, Batman, overwhelmed with the memories of the Joker crippling Batgirl and brutally killing Jason Todd, nearly strangles the Clown Prince: "I cannot . . . I will not . . . accept any responsibility . . . for The Joker. . . . Except that I should have killed him long ago." Only Catwoman and Jim Gordon stop him from strangling the Joker in an alley. And when Bruce comes to his senses, he thinks of his parents: "I made a promise on the grave of my parents that I would rid this city of the evil that took their lives. Tonight . . . I nearly became a part of that evil."

But did he? Would Batman killing the Joker be equal to the murders that the Joker has committed? Obviously not, but Batman believes that crossing that line would somehow make him into the evil that he fights. "Your compassion is a weakness your enemies will not share," Henri Ducard tells Bruce in *Batman Begins*. "That's why it's so important," Bruce replies. "It's what separates us from them."

Though he never spells it out in a philosophically precise way, Batman's rule against killing is an example of Kantian moral reasoning. Kant distinguished between the "right" and the "good." While killing the Joker might bring about good results, it can never be *right* to kill him because killing can't be universalized. It would be a very bad thing if all heroes took it upon themselves to kill bad guys.

There is a lot to be said for Batman's refusal to kill. He could have saved himself a lot of trouble and pain if he had killed the Joker (and for that matter, several of his most murderous villains), but he is willing to suffer for his devotion to justice and righteousness. But many others have paid for that devotion, as well. In *The Dark Knight Returns*, for example, the Joker appears on a television talk show and murders over three hundred people in the audience with his poison gas. Then he escapes to a county fair, where he murders over twenty people, including sixteen Cub Scouts. When Batman finally catches him in the fair's Tunnel of Love, he breaks the Clown's neck, but stops short of killing him: ". . . voices calling me a killer," Batman thinks. "I wish I were."[17] The Joker collapses and wonders why Batman won't kill him. "I'm really . . . very disappointed with you, my sweet. . . . The moment was . . . perfect . . . and you . . . didn't have the *nerve*. Paralysis . . . *really* . . . . Just an ounce or two more pressure and . . . ."[18] And with a maniacal laugh, the Clown contorts his body until he finishes severing his spine, killing himself.

In a sense, the Joker's suicide in *TDRK* is his final triumph over the Dark Knight. When Batman wishes that he *were* a killer, it might be an admission that there's something morally problematic about his refusal to kill the Joker for all those years. That's not to say that his rule against killing is a bad thing—it definitely isn't. (Though the Punisher is a fan-favorite character, few people would argue that he is morally superior to Batman because he's more than willing to kill his enemies.) But the fact that Batman has set up his no-killing rule as a moral absolute without balancing it with other rules and virtues means that just in the pages of *TDKR*, well over three hundred people are dead who would have been alive had somebody taken the Joker out of the picture a long time ago. When the Joker kills himself, he's laughing because he's seen the truth: Batman won't kill him simply because he doesn't have the nerve, and his lack of nerve is at least indirectly responsible for the deaths of hundreds.

So to Answer Your Question . . .

So how does all this help to answer my original question? Is Batman right for stepping outside of legitimate authority? When the institutions of justice and law fail to do their job, is it right for individuals to act outside of the system? There are a lot of ways to answer that question, but one essential part of any answer is that in order to be justified in making himself above the law, Batman must have an adequate ethical system. That is, if he steps outside the system in order to achieve justice, he must have a moral code

17. *The Dark Knight Returns* #3.
18. Ibid.

that is adequate to the pursuit of justice. Unfortunately (and as a big fan of Batman, it pains me to write this), he doesn't.

In *TDKR*, the ethical systems that both Superman and Batman follow are inadequate because they're too simple. That might strike some people as odd, given that Miller set out to complicate and deconstruct the superhero genre when he wrote the book. But what makes things so dark in the Dark Knight Universe is the fact that its heroes have ethical systems that are too simple to deal with the complexity of their world. It isn't enough to simply obey orders, and it isn't enough to do whatever it takes as long as you don't kill. Sometimes it's necessary to disobey orders, and sometimes it's necessary to kill.

In our own world, many of us are equally guilty of setting up a single virtue or principle as the only thing that truly matters. For some people, it's tolerance. For others, it's environmentalism. For still others, it's opposition (or support for) abortion rights, LGBT rights, or a host of other rights and privileges. For some people, the only real moral imperative is the equitable distribution of wealth. But while there is much to say in support of each of these views, none of them is adequate to the challenge of building a society that is truly good and just.

6

Avengers vs X-Men

Bigotry and the Problem of Power

The Legacy of Hatred

Perhaps at no other time in history have people been as sensitive to bigotry and prejudice as we are in the early part of the twenty-first century. Nearly everyone living in the U.S. today has grown up in the shadow of the giants who gave us the civil rights movement. We admire the example of the civil rights leaders of the past and rightly abhor the racism and other forms of bigotry that they opposed. Many of us grew up reading *To Kill a Mockingbird* and saw Atticus Finch as a hero. We want to be like him. We want to have the courage of Martin Luther King Jr., Muhammed Ali, James Meredith, Rosa Parks, Ghandi, and others. We want to be righteous like they were.

I remember the awe and reverence with which I read the words of "Letter from Birmingham Jail" for the first time, and the swell of pride I felt as a child when my father told me about his father, who was the only man in his neighborhood who didn't make black people go to the back door when they came to his house. Because he was a Cajun and a Catholic living in the deep south, my grandfather understood how much prejudice and bigotry could hurt and refused to participate in it.

In just the last several years, we have seen many examples of the evils of hatred: ISIS killing Christians and Yazidis in the Middle East; Dylann Roof killing members of Emanuel A.M.E. Church in Charleston, SC; the terrorist attacks in Paris; the killing of Christina Grimmie, who was apparently targeted because of her Christianity;[1] the language of some political candidates regarding immigrants and Muslims; bigotry against the disabled, not only by trolls on the internet, but also by certain distinguished faculty members at Princeton and Oxford.

One of the most dramatic recent examples of hatred has been the attack on the Orlando night club Pulse, when an ISIS sympathizer killed or critically injured more than a hundred people. His crime was undoubtedly motivated at least in part by hatred of homosexuals.

Just as dismaying as the Orlando massacre itself was the response of the general public to the incident, though. Politicians, activists, and average citizens all joined the fray in order to score political points following the Orlando shooting. Some used the opportunity to blame guns; others used it to renew calls for anti-Islamic immigration policies and for the U.S. to take a more aggressive role in combating ISIS; secularists used the attack as evidence of bigotry and hatred at the heart of religion—not any particular religion, just "religion"; still others—like Chase Strangio, an ACLU attorney—blamed the attack on the "Christian right."[2]

Like similar events, the Orlando attack highlighted the problem of prejudice and racism, and yet it also underscored the deep political and philosophical divisions in our culture. It revealed, for those who are honest enough to look, problems that often escape our notice: our readiness to blame our political opponents for acts of violence committed by disturbed people; our readiness to think the worst of anyone who disagrees with our political and social orthodoxies; our unwillingness to acknowledge threats to our way of life because to do so would contradict our preferred political and social narratives. Bigotry of any kind is undoubtedly wrong, but simply blaming "hatred" or "bigotry" or "homophobia" or "racism" for an evil act sometimes obscures rather than illuminates a problem, and politicizing crimes like the Orlando massacre (in the service of the right or the left side of the political spectrum) often only serves to make the underlying problems worse.

---

1. Greene, "Kevin Loibl Shot & Killed Christina Grimmie Because She Was A Christian."

2. Gehrke, "ACLU Lawyers Blame 'Christian Right.'"

The Hatred of Mutants

Since their creation in 1963, the X-Men have been seen as Marvel's answer to all kinds of prejudice. In an interview with *The Guardian* after the release of Brian Singer's first *X-Men* film, Stan Lee said that

> it occurred to me that instead of them just being heroes that everybody admired, what if I made other people fear and suspect and actually hate them because they were different? I loved that idea; it not only made them different, but it was a good metaphor for what was happening with the civil rights movement in the country at that time.[3]

Writers, artists, and filmmakers have taken that "good metaphor" and applied it in a number of ways. From their beginning, the X-Men have labored under the weight of a deeply-held hatred against mutants, and that hatred has taken on new significance in every decade of their history. In 1963 people could see the mutants as analogues for African Americans, even identifying Charles Xavier with Martin Luther King and Magneto with Malcolm X. Throughout the years, X-Men stories were used to explore prejudice against a number of groups—religious, national, and cultural— and in recent years, mutants have come to be identified with the LGBT community.

Though mutants were originally conceived as an analogue for minority races, their association with homosexuality has become especially apparent in recent years. In Brian Singer's film *X2*, for example, Iceman "comes out" to his parents as a mutant, and his mother asks, "Have you ever tried *not* being a mutant?" In *X-Men: The Last Stand*, Worthington Labs announces a "cure" for the X-gene—a thinly veiled metaphor for Exodus International and other ex-gay groups. In *X-Men: First Class*, when Hank McCoy's boss finds out that Hank is a mutant, Hank says, "You didn't ask, so I didn't tell." And in *X-Men: Days of Future Past*, Magneto commandeers the television airwaves of the 1960s and tells his mutant brethren to "come out."

Similarly, the comics have sometimes been a little on-the-nose with the mutants-as-gays metaphor, occasionally devolving into outright cartoonish and offensive depictions of those who hate mutants. For example, in *New Avengers* #30 and in *All-New X-Men* #19, we see heroes battling the Purifyers, a group of fundamentalist Christian, anti-mutant terrorists who quote Scripture and pray the Lord's Prayer even as they attack innocents

---

3. Strauss, "Generator X."

and declare that "God doesn't want mutants. He gave the garden of Eden to humans." In the twenty-first century, it's impossible to read a story like this one and not see Christians on the one side and people of the LGBT community on the other, but instead of having the (presumably) intended effect, the comparison highlights a problem with the mutants-as-gays metaphor—indeed, a problem that hinders an allegorical reading of the X-Men that closely identifies them with real-world groups.

To begin with, there are no real-world counterparts to the Purifiers— at least, not among Christians. Their closest analogue among Christian groups is perhaps Westboro Baptist Church, but even that comparison barely works. The Westboro folks say and do reprehensible things—including picketing the funerals of dead soldiers and the people massacred in Orlando—but they're hardly super villains or terrorists.

More importantly, however, there is a real problem with reading mutants as an analogue to African Americans or to gays. In the Marvel Universe, mutants are not *homo sapiens*; they're *homo superior,* the next step in human evolution. They aren't baseline humans with added abilities like Spider-Man or Daredevil; they are an entirely *different species*. It would be insulting to any group—African American, homosexual, or otherwise—to say that they are a different species of human. Moreover, whatever one's opinions about sexual morality, it seems very odd to say that a group of people who by definition cannot reproduce naturally are the next step in human evolution.

So much for an allegorical reading of mutants, then. And yet no one can deny that the *X-Men* books are concerned with the human fear of difference. Mutants like Toad, Beast, Mystique, and others are rejected for their physical differences. "Normal" people are repulsed by Nightcrawler's blue skin, prehensile tail, and demonic overall appearance. *X-Men: Days of Future Past* captures this theme perfectly when Beast and Mystique find themselves in a crowd at the Paris Peace Accords, surrounded by people who stare at them like freaks.

But more than the fear of difference, *X-Men* stories explore another, more difficult theme: power and the fear that it excites. After all, what makes mutants *different* is not primarily their appearance (although some *homo superior* do look quite different from *homo sapiens*), but what they can *do*. Nightcrawler's appearance might be frightening, but his ability is scarier: he can teleport virtually anywhere as long as he can see his destination or picture it in his head. In other words, locks can't deter him. Mutants like the Blob, Colossus, and Beast have greater strength and durability than the average human is capable of. Magneto can move, bend, twist, and levitate any metal object. Mystique can make herself look and sound like anyone. Perhaps most frightening of all, telepaths like Charles Xavier, Rachel Summers, and Emma Frost can not only read people's minds, but also control them. If powers like these existed in the real world, people would find them unsettling at best, even if we thought that the people who possessed them were good.

Though there are people—like the Purifiers—who hate and fear mutants purely out of bigotry, most people's fear of mutants is "rational." They're more afraid of what mutants can *do* than of what they *are*. That doesn't necessarily make those people better or more admirable than the Purifiers or members of the KKK, but it does make their fear more understandable. Someone might object that mutants are subjected to fears and prejudices that other powered beings in the Marvel Universe do not have to endure. For example, the members of the Fantastic Four would be indistinguishable from mutants were it not for the fact that Reed Richards, Sue Storm, Johnny Storm, and Ben Grimm were not born with their powers. If anti-mutant feelings are more about power than about difference, why don't people hate the FF the way they hate the X-Men?

The answer to that question is no doubt as complicated as the answers to questions about real-world bigotry, but the ancient Greeks might be able to supply an explanation. Because mutants are supposed to be the next step in human evolution, they are a threat not just to the *status quo,* but to the very existence of humanity. Theoretically, anyone could be an Iron Man, a Mister Fantastic, or a Captain Marvel as long as the conditions were right, but mutant powers are different. They're a signal to *homo sapiens* that their time is coming to an end. As Phil Sheldon says in *Marvels* #2,

> There was something *about* the mutants. They were the dark side of the Marvels. Where Captain America and Mister Fantastic spoke to us about the greatness within us all . . . the mutants were *death*. They'd didn't even have to *do* anything. They were our replacements, scientists said. The next evolutionary step. We—homo sapiens—were obsolete. And *they* were the future. They were going to kick the dirt onto our graves.

To "normal" humans, the X-Men are what Kronos is to Ouranos and what Zeus is to Kronos: a reminder that one day, they will be powerless. Their existence points to our demise.

Rather than reading the X-Men only as a parable about irrational hatred, then, I want to suggest another, more complex reading, one that doesn't depend upon seeing a one-to-one relationship between mutants and real-world minorities. The story of the Marvel mutants has been an exploration between the relationship between fear and power. And perhaps at no other time have the themes of prejudice, fear, and power come together so explosively and (philosophically speaking) fruitfully than in the period leading up to 2012's crossover event, *Avengers vs X-Men*.

The Beginning of the Storm

The major conflict in *AvX* has roots that reach into the deep past of the Marvel universe. Since they first appeared in 1963, the X-Men have pursued the dream of Charles Xavier, who sought to end the hatred of mutants by showing the world that they could be a force for good. This means that the X-Men often work to protect the very people who hate and fear them. Xavier's philosophy amounts to a program of bringing about peace and justice in the world by loving one's enemies—a teaching that no one has ever pretended was easy. And throughout their history, the members of the X-Men have often suffered terribly for their commitment to that philosophy of love. Storylines like *Days of Future Past* and *God Loves, Man Kills* in particular challenge the X-Men's resolve to fight for the people who reject them. As one would expect, by the first decade of the twenty-first century, some of the X-Men harbor resentment over the Sisyphean task that Xavier has set for them.

Between 2004 and 2011, a number of events occur in the Marvel universe that bring mutant-related tensions to the crisis-level that we see when *AvX* begins. Many of these events involve the Scarlet Witch (Wanda Maximoff), a member of both the X-Men and the Avengers and the mutant daughter of Magneto.[4] Wanda has a history of mental instability and possesses the ability to alter reality—a power that has been used to disastrous effect on a number of occasions.

---

4. Sometimes things change as suddenly and dramatically in comic books as they do in soap operas. In *Uncanny Avengers* #4, Wanda's parentage and origin (and those of her twin brother, Pietro) were retconned. As of now, Wanda and Pietro are not mutants, and Magneto is not their father. For the sake of simplicity, however, this book will treat the origin that they had from 1963 to 2014 as canonical.

In 2004's *Avengers Disassembled*, Doctor Doom and a possessed Scarlet Witch devastate the Avengers and sow seeds that will affect the Marvel Universe for over a decade, contributing to major events like *House of M*, *Civil War*, and *Avengers vs X-Men*. *Disassembled* results in the deaths of two Avengers and in the entire superhero community fearing Wanda. Even though she was possessed at the time and acting under the influence of Doctor Doom, Wanda's actions in *Disassembled* call into question her sanity and cause many people to distrust and hate her. And because Wanda is a mutant, people often identify the entire mutant population with her.

After *Disassembled*, Pietro (Quicksilver) is afraid that the Avengers and the X-Men are conspiring to kill Wanda, so he convinces her to use her powers to create a world in which everyone's heart's desire is fulfilled, believing that in such a utopia, he and his sister will be safe. The result is a dramatically altered society in which mutants are the powerful majority. *Homo sapiens* are now a quiet minority living under the rule of *homo superior*, and Magneto stands at the top as an absolute ruler. At the end of the story, Magneto kills Quicksilver in a fit of rage, causing Wanda to have a nervous breakdown. After she defeats Magneto, Wanda resurrects her brother and utters three words: "No more mutants." In one flash of light, she de-powers nearly all of the millions of mutants in the world—an event that would later become known as "M-Day."

With only around 200 powered mutants left across the globe[5] and mutant-human relations suffering a devastating setback after *House of M*, the mutant population finds itself in a desperate situation. Their only hope for salvation comes in the form of a baby born in a small Alaskan town in 2007's *Messiah Complex*.

By a complicated backstory involving time-travel and an alternate future, Hope Summers is the granddaughter of Cyclops. The X-Men regard her as a messiah for the mutant race, and indeed her story mirrors the story of Christ's in a number of ways. For example, like Christ, she has a "miraculous" birth: she is the first and only mutant birth after *House of M* and the Scarlet Witch's "no more mutants." The circumstances around her birth also mirror those of Christ: intent on wiping Hope out, the Purifiers invade the Alaskan town where she is born and kill all of the young children there. Hope survives because her father, Cable, escapes with her in a kind of parallel to Christ's sojourn in Egypt.

---

5. *Schism* #1; *X-Men: The 198*.

By the time *Avengers vs X-Men* begins, Hope has come to live with the X-Men in the present. She spends her time training for combat and for the day when she will save the mutant race, but she's a reluctant savior. Resentful at being confined to Utopia, she sneaks away every night against the wishes of Cyclops:

> Hope: Protecting a world that hates and fears us. Isn't that our job?
>
> Cyclops: Not when it means needlessly putting yourself in danger.
>
> Hope: And here I thought this place was called Utopia. Funny name for a prison.
>
> Cyclops: You've never been a prisoner here. . . . But you also know how dangerous it is for you to be out there on your own. You're too big a target. You're too important to everyone here.[6]

Longing for a normal life, Hope doesn't see herself as a messiah, and she doesn't desire power; she just wants to help people in the best way that she can. Though she says that she sneaks out in order to "clear her head," she engages in superheroics on her outings, even taking down the Serpent Society on her own. The momentous circumstances of her birth and the burden of being "too important" weigh heavily on her, and beneath her petulant teenage exterior, we can see the humility of someone who doesn't think of herself as worthy of the great power and responsibility that have been given to her. Though no one understands this until the end, Hope's reluctance to accept the title "messiah" is precisely what makes her messianic.

X-Men Divided

At the beginning of *Schism*, most of the world's remaining mutants have gathered to live on an island called Utopia off the coast of San Francisco. Cyclops (Scott Summers) and Wolverine travel to the U.N. in Switzerland, where Cyclops will address the nations of the world who have gathered for an international arms control conference. The conference's topic is the proliferation of Sentinels, giant robotic weapons designed to hunt and kill mutants.

While Cyclops argues for the dismantling of all Sentinels, the Hellfire Club orchestrates a coordinated attack on the U.N. A mutant named Quentin Quire interrupts him and telepathically forces all of the delegates

6. *Avengers vs X-Men: Prologue.*

present to reveal their darkest secrets ("I would like to take this opportunity to list the various ethnic minorities I despise," says one delegate; "I beat my children," says another. "I do it quite often, in fact. I . . . I do it . . . because I enjoy it").[7] Meanwhile, a group of Sentinels enters the building and attacks Cyclops and Wolverine, and Quire makes terrorist threats on international television, taking credit for the attack at the U.N. "in the name of us all" (mutants).[8]

The incident at the U.N. sparks a global crisis for mutants, and most of the X-Men spread out across the world to hunt down Sentinels. With Utopia left practically undefended, the Hellfire Club launches a huge Sentinel toward the island to wipe out the young mutants who are gathered there. Cyclops and Wolverine find themselves at odds over how to respond to the attack. Cyclops wants the young mutants to join in the fight, while Wolverine wants to keep them out of it.

Schism leaves the world's mutants divided ideologically. Though they defeat the Sentinels, Cyclops and Wolverine can no longer work together. Scott remains in Utopia with a more radical group, while Wolverine and those who side with him return to upstate New York to rebuild Charles Xavier's old school there, renaming it the Jean Grey School for Higher Learning.

During the following months, tensions increase between the two groups, with Scott's group becoming more radical. Meanwhile, Wolverine and his school continue to work toward the goal set by Professor X when he originally founded the Xavier Institute for Higher Learning.

The Return of the Phoenix

The Phoenix Force is one of the most powerful and most dangerous entities in the Marvel Universe. As its name suggests, the Phoenix appears as a huge, fiery bird as it travels across the universe and endows those it possesses with the symbol of the phoenix on their chests. Not evil in the way that characters like Thanos or the Red Skull are evil, the Phoenix is a force of nature, the manifestation of all of the creative energy in the universe. Its cosmic role is somewhat like that of a wildfire to a forest: it destroys, but through that destruction often brings about new life.

7. *Schism* #1.
8. Ibid.

In *Avengers vs X-Men*, when the Avengers realize that the Phoenix is on its way to Earth with the intent of bonding with Hope Summers, they go to Utopia in force to take her into their custody, hoping to stop the Phoenix from possessing her. Scott, seeing the return of the Phoenix and its choice of Hope for its host as a sign that Hope is a true messiah to mutants, resists and starts a fight on the beach of Utopia between the Avengers and the X-Men.

When Iron Man and Hank Pym devise a way of disrupting the Phoenix Force before it possesses Hope, they inadvertently split it and cause the fragments to possess five other mutants: Cyclops, Namor, Emma Frost, Colossus, and Magik.

Endowed with enormous power, these Phoenix-possessed mutants—now called the Phoenix Five—take Hope back to Utopia and begin reshaping the world to their liking. The fight between them and the rest of the world's heroes is massive in scope. It spans continents and even spills over onto the Blue Area of the moon,[9] kills and resurrects Hawkeye, destroys major cities, devastates an important marriage between an Avenger and an X-Man, ends in the (so far) permanent death of Charles Xavier, and cements the split between the branches of X-Men led by Wolverine and Scott Summers. The main book had twelve issues, and nearly every title that Marvel published in 2012 carried the *AvX* branding.

The reason the fight proves to be so massive, so lengthy, and so bitter is that both sides are fighting for the most fundamental cause: survival. The Phoenix Five and those mutants who follow them believe that they have a moral obligation to protect and restore their race. They believe that after decades of anti-mutant bigotry and the decimation of mutants following *House of M*, the only way for the mutant race to have a future is through the power of the Phoenix Force.

Most of the rest of the world, on the other hand, believes that the Phoenix is too dangerous to be wielded by anyone—and with good reason: when she was possessed by the Phoenix, Jean Grey (Marvel Girl/Phoenix/Dark Phoenix) had wiped out an entire alien civilization and nearly destroyed the X-Men; and at the beginning of *AvX*, the Phoenix wipes out all life on an alien planet in a matter of minutes as it crosses the universe on its way to Earth.

---

9. An ancient inhabitable area on the dark side of the moon created by the Kree, an alien race that has for years interfered with Earth's history and biology.

Building a Perfect World

After the battle on the moon, the Phoenix Five begin using their powers to create a new world: Magik transforms the Horn of Africa into fertile farmland; Colossus builds huge glass domes in northeast Russia and turns the permafrost beneath them into wheat fields; Namor harvests fresh water from beneath the ocean floor in the Aleutian Trench; and Emma Frost builds a fusion reactor and a miniature sun in the Gobi Desert to generate cheap power. Refugees begin to leave Wakanda and return to previously impoverished countries like Ethiopia and Sudan. When the Avengers battle and are nearly defeated by Zzzax, a monster made up of electrical energy, Colossus arrives and saves them. But as Iron Fist tells Captain America, instead of fighting, Colossus and Zzzax "just talked it out,"[10] and Colossus goes on to utilize Zzzax as the "new, cheapest energy source on the planet."[11] Mutants turn a S.H.I.E.L.D. installation into a school. Cyclops and Magneto turn Utopia into a perfect haven for mutants. Magik, Emma Frost, Namor, and Colossus collect and destroy the world's weapons of war.

Indeed, the Phoenix-possessed mutants appear to have created a perfect society across the globe, but the Avengers and world governments don't trust them. As the U.S. president tells Captain America, "When the world works it is because there has always been some outlying culture of accountability. Right now, these X-Men do not have that."[12] The power of the Phoenix—even divided among five hosts—is so great that not even the mightiest of Earth's heroes can keep it in check. So Cyclops appears at the United Nations to assure the world of the Phoenix Five's peaceful intentions:

> We have given you water to drink and food to eat. We have given you energy—the very key to modernity. . . . From this day forward, we give you peace and freedom from the aggression that has marked the darkest days of mankind. Go. Build great things, greater than have ever been seen before, . . . but no more weapons. . . . From this day forward, we will no longer tolerate violence towards mutant or man. . . . Pax Utopia.[13]

Scott's speech bears an underlying threat, but no one can deny that his intentions are honorable. Indeed, he and the rest of the Phoenix Five have

10. *Avengers vs X-Men #6.*
11. Ibid.
12. Ibid.
13. Ibid.

given the world what every society has longed for. Without scarcity of land or resources, people have nothing for which to compete with each other, and without competition, people have no reason to fight. "What a magnificent thing they have built," Magneto tells Charles Xavier. "Great deeds by the greatest of men."[14] And these "great deeds" are truly for everyone; the Phoenix Five (at least at first) make no distinctions between mutant and normal human. As Hank McCoy tells Captain America, "My friends— *people I have known my entire life*—are remaking this planet into a place that is finally tolerable. A world we can *all* live in."[15]

The problem isn't with Cyclops's intentions or his personality. He took a radical turn after *Schism*, but he has always wanted peace between mutants and humans. Though he loses himself by the end of the conflict, at the outset he realizes that he has to leave room for people who disagree with his actions: "We finally have the power to remake the world in our image. We have to get along to do it . . . and *not kill* people that disagree with us. . . . This isn't a war. It's a *rescue mission*. Conduct yourselves accordingly."[16]

And yet for all Cyclops's insistence that they are working selflessly for the good of all, the Phoenix Five can't remake the world without losing their humanity and becoming totalitarians. Indeed, all people who try to reshape our imperfect world into something perfect *must* become totalitarians. History is strewn with blood and misery caused by men who tried to use power to create a perfect world: Robespierre, Napoleon, Lenin, Stalin, Hitler, Mao, Pol Pot—these men weren't cackling supervillains out to destroy the world. Each of them had a picture in his mind of what the perfect world looked like, and each set out to make that world a reality.[17]

But they were bad men, someone might object. When good people set out to change the world, they don't do things like create gulags and concentration camps. Satin Teresa of Calcutta, Martin Luther King, Jr., Ghandi,

14. Ibid.

15. Ibid.

16. *Avengers vs. X-Men* #7.

17. Many people have noted the totalitarian and repressive nature of the society that Plato describes in *The Republic*. But as Karl Popper notes in *The Open Society and Its Enemies,* "it is Plato's ideal to arrest social change," since following Heraclitus he believes that change leads to discord (102). In other words, Plato doesn't set out to create a repressive society; he merely has an idea in his mind about what the perfect society would look like. That society would be perfectly stable because it would be free of change, but since it is "probably quite true that social change can be arrested only by a rigid caste system," Plato's ideal republic looks very much to us like a totalitarian state (102).

and any number of unnamed and anonymous people have made the world better by what they did. But unlike men like Robespierre and Stalin, these people have changed the world by standing up to power, by *serving*. And in most cases, they did it by *giving up* some measure of their own power. They *never* did it by seeking power in order to use it over other people. They recognized that in spite of the best intentions, people cannot be made moral or good by the use of power.

Cyclops begins by using the Phoenix only to help others, but his "singular vision"[18] fails because it does not take into account human nature or the corrupting effect of power. At first he only uses his power to shape the physical environment: he provides food, water, and energy for the world, and he destroys machines and weapons of war. But he fails to see the truth about human nature. No matter how much we improve our environment, we ourselves are not perfectible. No amount of moral exhortation, social engineering, or evolution will make people morally perfect. And as soon as someone begins to use power in the effort to *make* people good, that person becomes a totalitarian.

Cyclops seems aware of the problem from the beginning. In the one-shot issue *Avengers vs. X-Men: . . . In A Handful of Dust*, Scott travels to the Blue Area of the moon so that he can escape the noise of other people's thoughts. There he "resurrects" the ghost of Jean Grey out of moon dust and talks to "her" (he's really only talking to himself using the image of Jean) about what he has done on earth. She tells him, "You've used the Phoenix Force very *well* and very *logically* . . . so far."[19] But she warns him that in wielding the power of the Phoenix, he will lose himself and become the Dark Phoenix just as she did before she died. But Scott thinks that the problem is a matter of strength:

> Cyclops: That was *your* experience. But I've always been more controlled than you, than just about anyone. You used to say that I invented repression. If anyone can hold the Phoenix Force in—
>
> Jean (interrupting): It's not about losing *control*. It's about losing *yourself*.[20]

At first, Scott seems to have understood what Jean tries to tell him. He realizes that the most profoundly good act he has ever witnessed—Jean

18. *Avengers vs. X-Men: . . . In A Handfull of Dust.*
19. Ibid.
20. Ibid.

willingly giving up her life to save the X-Men from being destroyed by the Phoenix Force—"feels petty" now that he has remade the world in his own image—a realization that gives him pause. "Don't I still have my humanity?" he asks the moon-dust Jean, and in the Carlo Barberi and Marte Gracia artwork it's clear that the question anguishes him. But just when it seems that he has recognized the problem at the heart of his whole project of reshaping the world, Scott returns to earth, resolved to remain a good man sheerly by the force of his will:

> I know that I have to be *vigilant*. I *cannot*—I *will* not—let the Phoenix change me. Inside all this power, I have to preserve the man I've always been. I have to remember *why* I fight. Because if I lose sight of *that* . . . what's it all been for?[21]

Honorable though his intentions are, he's missed the whole point of his encounter with the dust-Jean. The problem isn't that there is a danger in using power to create a perfect world, a danger that can be avoided by a particularly strong person who remains "vigilant." The problem is that *anyone* who uses power in that way *will* inevitably become a tyrant. The very idea of a perfect world is totalitarian—even when the idea is conceived by decent people with the best possible intentions.

The first crack in Scott's ability to maintain control of both himself and of the other Phoenix-possessed mutants comes when Magik and Emma Frost attack the Avengers in *AvX #7*. Magik opens a portal into the Avengers' hideout, but the Scarlet Witch injures her. Emma arrives through the portal and finds Magik lying on the ground. "Wanda Maximoff," she says, "murderer of the mutant race,"[22] and she begins to blaze with the flames of the Phoenix Force. When she is about to attack Wanda, Clint Barton (Hawkeye) fires an arrow, distracting her and allowing Wanda to escape. But Emma turns her attention on Hawkeye: "How dare you! We're trying to save the world!" she says, and lights him on fire just as Doctor Strange teleports the rest of the Avengers away.

When Cyclops chastises Emma for trying to kill Hawkeye—she was, after all, never in any danger from the archer's arrows—she responds, "I didn't kill him and I wasn't trying to kill him. I got mad and the power—look Hawkeye's still alive, and we can heal him."[23] Never mind that she caused

21. *Avengers vs. X-Men: . . . In A Handful of Dust.*

22. *Avengers vs. X-Men #7.*

23. Ibid.

Clint immense suffering, and never mind that she and Magik attacked the Avengers without provocation—she didn't kill him, so that makes her actions all right. The all-excusing motivation of "saving the world" means that she can do whatever it takes as long as her end goals are righteous.

Moreover, Magik says that she doesn't believe the "fairy tale" that the Avengers "are trying to sell us" about Wanda—that she is stable and repentant for what she did on M-Day: "I looked at Wanda Maximoff and I saw . . . I saw evil, Scott. I saw evil that can hurt us all. I think the Phoenix came to us so we could purge that evil from Earth forever."[24] One of the most dangerous aspects of the Phoenix Force is that it doesn't tell its host what its purpose is. To those who possess it (or, rather, are possessed by it), the Phoenix is a raw power that merely amplifies everything about them.[25] Cyclops' desire to see justice, Namor's fiery temper, Emma's underhandedness—the Phoenix Five don't become something qualitatively different as Phoenix-hosts; they merely become amplified versions of themselves. So for Emma Frost and Magik, their resentment of Wanda over M-Day becomes distorted into blind outrage. Wanda didn't kill mutants with her "no more mutants"—she just took away their powers. But to the Phoenix-possessed Emma, she is the "murderer of the mutant race," and to Magik, she is "evil that can hurt us all." Wanda can't be excused for the decimation of mutants, but her crime isn't genocide.

But to those who have power, anyone else who has power becomes an enemy. Moreover, the Wanda-Hawkeye incident exposes the conflict and dysfunction at the heart of the Phoenix Five. Cyclops fights to maintain control over himself and the other four, constantly reminding them of the righteousness of their purpose. But Magik becomes increasingly paranoid, Namor's temper increasingly brings him into conflict with Scott and becomes dangerously impulsive, and Emma starts to feed the division between Namor and Cyclops.

To make matters worse, when Namor launches an assault on Wakanda and when the Avengers defeat him, his portion of the Phoenix abandons him and distributes itself among the remaining Phoenix Five. The implication is not lost on them. Adam Kubert's artwork nicely captures the realization: Magik closes her eyes with pleasure as she receives her increased portion of the Phoenix, while over her shoulder, Colossus asks, "Is that

24. Ibid.

25. See what the moon-dust Jean Grey says about the Phoenix in *Avengers vs X-Men: . . . In A Handful of Dust*.

what happens when one of us falls?"[26] The next panel shows a close up of Cyclops's red visor, and then the POV pulls back to show his entire face. Namor's fall, which might have increased their resolve to work together and end the conflict, instead deepens the mistrust and division between them.

After Namor's fall, it doesn't take long for the Phoenix Four to turn on one another. In issue #9, Doctor Strange teleports the Avengers to a Siberian volcano where Magik has created a portal to Limbo. There she and Colossus have been holding captured Avengers prisoner. They manage to recover all of the captives and narrowly escape, but Spider-Man stays behind to hold off Colossus and Magik. Unable to defeat them in a physical fight, he encourages the bickering already happening between them: "You both know what would happen to all that power if one of you was to *fall*, right? I'm sure neither of you wants to see *that*."[27] The art focuses on Piotr's and Illyana's faces, and then the next panel zooms out to show a massive explosion of energy over the Siberian landscape and the Phoenix erupting from the crater of the volcano.

Meanwhile, Scott finds Emma meditating in the Danakil Desert in Ethiopia. She confesses to him that the Phoenix is corrupting her will:

> Since Namor fell, since we received his portion of the power, I've been reaching out, touching every mind on the face of the earth, including the Avengers. I could reach inside their heads right now and simply turn them off, just like flicking a switch. I think . . . I think part of me *wants* to do it.[28]

She tells Scott that she has found out where the Avengers are keeping Hope—the mystical city of K'un Lun, which no one should be able to enter without permission—and Scott immediately flies away to retrieve her. Emma tries to stop him—"I'm worried about what I might do next. Please, stop me"[29]—but there's no stopping him. Later, she goes to the home of a Gulf War veteran who, while he was on a flight in the Middle East, accidentally hit a mutant who was flying for the first time. Emma tortures him psychically and kills him right in front of his family. "You thought it was your little secret. No one has secrets anymore. Not from me."[30]

---

26. *Avengers vs X-Men* #7.
27. *Avengers vs. X-Men* #9.
28. Ibid.
29. Ibid.
30. Ibid.

When Scott breaks through K'un Lun's dimensional barrier and tries to take Hope, she absorbs and harnesses the power of the dragon, Shao Lao, and knocks Scott through the dimensional barrier and all the way out of Earth's atmosphere. He lands on the moon and lies there for an hour before he can even get up. Astonished that Hope has the strength to hurt him, he decides that he "needs more power. He needs Emma."[31] Still fighting to hold on to his integrity, Scott doesn't yet try to take Emma's power; he only wants her to join him in fighting Hope. But when the combined forces of the Avengers and the rest of the X-Men come to Utopia to confront him and Emma, he wrests her half of the Phoenix from her and uses its full power to kill Charles Xavier.

Hope Summers, Spider-Man, and the Good of Power

When the Avengers first recover Hope from the Phoenix Five, they take her to K'un Lun where they hope to train her to fight the Phoenix using the same mystic arts that empower Iron Fist. According to legend, Shao Lao, the dragon that inhabits K'un Lun, once defeated the Phoenix. But when Yu Ti sees the image of the Phoenix and of a Spider in the scrying vessel of Bo-Ling, he concludes that Spider-Man should be the one to train Hope.

The choice surprises everyone, including Spider-Man himself. His self-deprecating and joking personality makes him seem like the most unlikely candidate. "I wonder if you are to teach her self-loathing,"[32] Yu-Ti says when Spider-Man objects to his new job. Both Hope and Spidey think that the webslinger can teach little to the Mutant Messiah about how to handle the Phoenix when the time comes for her to be tested against it.

But by the end of the *AvX* conflict, the reason that Spider-Man must be the one to train Hope becomes clear. Though Yu-Ti and Hope express their doubts about him, Spidey's apparent self-loathing isn't just a personality quirk that conceals some secret knowledge that he can impart to Hope; it's precisely the point. Only a person who doesn't take himself seriously can crack the kind of self-deprecating jokes that Spidey does, and only a person who doesn't take himself seriously knows what to do with power. Hope spent years training under Scott Summers, who drilled her constantly about her importance as the Mutant Messiah and indoctrinated her with his radical ideas about mutants and humans. That training resulted

31. Ibid.
32. *New Avengers* #27 (2005).

only in her discontent and resentment. But her very first conversation with Spider-Man changes Hope. Spidey tells her about his Uncle Ben and about the mantra that he told Peter before he died—*With great power comes great responsibility*—and Hope changes from an angry teenager who insults Spidey's suit to an eager disciple: "What *else* did [Uncle Ben] say? Did he say anything else? Should I get a new costume? Maybe I should."[33] But even when he gives inspiring speeches and wise words to his new student, Spidey doesn't take himself too seriously. He gives her inspiring talks, but he continues to crack jokes—not just to ease the tension, but to tear himself down, to remind not only Hope but himself that she shouldn't take him too seriously.

This self-deprecation doesn't undermine the lesson that the wall-crawler tries to teach. Instead, it reinforces the lesson—because the lesson is *humility*. The reason that the Phoenix Five ultimately prove unworthy of power is precisely their lack of humility, their inability to see that even though they have the power to reshape society into a perfect one, they might not be the perfect architects of that society. Setting aside Namor's arrogance and Emma's scheming, even Scott's perfect desire for justice and the superhuman lengths to which he goes to build a fair society proves to be only pride at work. Only a tremendously prideful person can believe that he knows just what the world needs in order to make it perfect.

Spidey proves the depth of his humility when the Avengers rescue the prisoners from the volcano prison in Siberia. In the middle of a fight with Colossus and Magik, he realizes that short of some miracle, none of them are going to escape: "But then I remembered something I'd once heard a very wise man say: . . . Once you're an Avenger, sooner or later the time comes when it's your turn to step up to the plate."[34] That "very wise man" was Spidey himself speaking to Hope, and of course the self-compliment is meant ironically. The fact that he cracks his self-deprecating jokes even privately to himself is a sign of their sincerity, and he proves his humility and selflessness by staying behind to distract Colossus and Magik while his fellow Avengers escape. He isn't stupid or arrogant enough to think that he can fight the Phoenix-empowered Rasputin siblings and win. He knows that he will probably die or become a prisoner in Limbo forever, but he also knows that his job as an Avenger is more important than he is, that the lives of his friends are more important than his own life. *With great power comes*

33. Ibid.
34. *Avengers vs X-Men* #9.

great responsibility. That is another way of saying that power is only good when it is used with humility in the service of others.

Thankfully, Piotr and Illyana take each other down in their bickering over power before they kill the web-slinger. Their fall strengthens the last two Phoenix hosts—Cyclops and Emma—which looks to everyone like a disaster. When Cyclops "tears [his] way through dimensions"[35] and arrives in K'un L'un, Iron Fist tells Hope, "I am sorry we will never get to finish your training."[36] But what he doesn't realize is that Hope's training is already finished: "I don't want to change the world," she tells Captain America in K'un Lun when he asks her why he should trust her with the power of the Phoenix. "I wouldn't even know where to begin. And if the Phoenix kills me, so be it. I'll gladly take that bullet if it means the end of all this fighting."[37]

Hope and the Ultimate Sacrifice

For those who know the story of Jean Grey's possession by the Phoenix, it's easy to expect that Hope will die at the end of *AvX*. In order to save her friends from the Phoenix, Jean had to willingly sacrifice her own life. Hope's title of "Mutant Messiah" and the biblical circumstances of her birth strongly suggest that the solution to the problem in *AvX* is for Hope to become possessed by the Phoenix and then to willingly die.

But there is more than one way to make the ultimate sacrifice. Death is a sacrifice because it is the ultimate loss of power: we are powerless against it, and in it we lose every bit of power that we might have. Hope doesn't pay the price of death at the end of *AvX*, but she does something like it: she willingly gives up an immense power.

When Scott takes away Emma's portion of the Phoenix Force and kills Charles Xavier, he believes that there is no one left to do what must be done: "This world will burn, and from its ashes, a new world will rise. A brave new paradise forged in fire."[38] But when the combined powers of Hope Summers and the Scarlet Witch bring him to the brink of defeat, he realizes that something has gone wrong—not with the world, but with him and his use of power:

35. Ibid.
36. Ibid.
37. *Avengers vs. X-Men* #12.
38. Ibid.

94

> All I wanted to do was change the world. To see my children grow up to be something other than time-traveling freedom fighters. To see mutants able to use their powers for more than just fighting killer robots. To usher in an era of peace. And I did. I made miracles. But somewhere along the way . . . I went off track.

But the realization lasts only for a moment, and the power of the Dark Phoenix flares up inside him. He lashes out at his attackers, but he falls in a last push that involves the Avengers and the X-men backing up Hope and Wanda. The Phoenix abandons him and joins with its originally intended host: Hope.

While the rest of the heroes look on in fear, Hope uses her power to repair the damage done by Scott in his rage as the Dark Phoenix. She traverses the world in a blinding flash of light and rebuilds bridges, puts out fires, and closes the volcano prisons that the Phoenix Five created in Siberia. When she returns to San Francisco and appears before the gathered Avengers and X-Men, all looks lost: "All this power . . . this is how it was meant to be. This is my destiny. I see where the others went wrong. Where they faltered, I will not fail. I will be the White Phoenix. I will be the savior of all."[39] And if not for the support of the Scarlet Witch, Hope might have become a Dark Phoenix like all the other hosts of the Phoenix Force. "You were *born* to be the Phoenix," Wanda tells her, "but *not* so you could wield this power. It's because you're the only one with the strength to let it go. . . . Please, no more playing God." And when she joins hands with Hope, the two of them speak in unison—"No more Phoenix"[40]—and the Phoenix leaves Hope's body and disappears into space.

Power in the Service of Justice?

There can be no doubt that mutants have suffered persecution and bigotry for their entire history, and at times the persecution has been vicious. But if the conflicts that have followed in the wake of the X-Men, X-Force, and other mutant groups are any indication, power is never the answer to hatred. It might be the only way to protect those who are threatened by violence, but when power—be it political, social, religious, or the Phoenix Force itself—is used to combat bigotry, the result will only be more hatred and, in the end, totalitarianism.

39. Ibid.
40. Ibid.

When Psylocke nearly captures Daredevil (Matt Murdock) in New York, Matt stops her primarily by speaking the truth to her. As both a lawyer and a vigilante who has spent both sides of his life fighting against New York's criminal underworld, Matt has seen power used in the worst possible ways, and his words have a powerful effect on Psylocke:

> Daredevil: You're angry. . . . You feel *persecuted.* . . . Maybe you're right. With all that power, I guess we'll see how differently you X-Men do things. If this ambush is any indicator, you'll have us on an island of our own before this is all over.
>
> Psylocke: I . . . I . . .
>
> Daredevil: Have a lot to think about, it seems. Before you get up and chase me you might want to ask yourself one question: What do you really want?[41]

Even though Daredevil's words have a powerful effect on Psylocke—in the art she looks deeply troubled, and though she can still catch Daredevil, she lets him go—she continues to work with the X-Men and the Phoenix Five out of loyalty to her fellow mutants. This kind of loyalty (we might even call it *tribalism*) is at the heart of the whole conflict of *AvX,* and it is only when the X-Men begin to commit real atrocities that they begin to realize that loyalty to their kind and a real desire for justice are not enough to keep power in check. Psylocke finally joins the Avengers in *AvX* #12 As they watch Colossus and Magik put Thor in their Limbo prison, Storm, Pixie, Gambit, and Armor look on in horror, and Pixie and Gambit says what they are all thinking:

> Pixie: Dear God, they're all being *corrupted* by the Phoenix, aren't they?
>
> Gambit: Damn it, this time we were in the *right*, we were actually gonna remake the world. And now we're throwing Avengers into volcanoes. Damn it!

What they all fail to see is that there was no way for it to be otherwise. Power of the kind that the Phoenix bestows (or maybe the better word is *inflicts*) will always result in the kinds of evils that it opposes in the first place—if not worse evils.

Does that mean that there *are* no solutions to the problems faced by the mutants? If power won't put an end to hatred and persecution, are

---

41. *Avengers vs. X-Men: Versus #4.*

we left with no options short of outright warfare that only leads to peace through catharsis and sacrifices?[42] The only answer that Marvel has to offer comes in the form of the Uncanny Avengers.

When Captain America first comes to Utopia to take Hope into custody before the arrival of the Phoenix, Scott accuses him of not doing enough to help mutants against their persecutors, and his words haunt Cap for the entire conflict. When he questions Cyclops after he has been captured, Cap acknowledges his own role in the treatment of mutants over the years:

> I'll take my share of responsibility for all of this as well. Back on Utopia, you were right about one thing: the Avengers should've done more to help mutants. I should have done more. I allowed the world to hate and fear them for far too long. I won't make that same mistake again.[43]

What makes Cap's answer to the problem different from Scott's is that instead of using his strength to enforce a solution, he forms a voluntary association—the Avengers Unity Squad—that brings together classic Avengers and X-Men, "working together, setting an example of cooperation. With Xavier gone, and Cyclops locked up, someone has to stand up and represent the mutants."[44]

The idea of a Unity Squad might sound like a feeble gesture against the complicated problem of anti-mutant bigotry. And to some it might seem like more of the same: it's the philosophy of Charles Xavier—mutants "protectin' those who hated and feared us 'til they didn't," as Wolverine puts it in his eulogy for Xavier[45]—tried in a different context. People like Cyclops call it a failed philosophy, and in a sense, they're right. But it is precisely that philosophy's weakness, the unlikelihood of its success, that makes it good, protects it from becoming something evil. There's a reason why preachers of peace from Jesus down to Ghandi have warned against the dangers of power. And in the Marvel universe, there's a reason why the approaches of Professor X and the mutant terrorist Magneto have yielded such different results, a reason why the conflict of *AvX* only ends when Hope Summers willingly gives up the power to reshape the world into what she wants it to be.

42. See the discussion of René Girard's theory of mimetic violence and scapegoating in Chapter 2.

43. *Avengers vs X-Men* #12.

44. *Uncanny Avengers* (2012) #1.

45. Ibid.

Part II

Heroes on the Screen

by Corey Latta

Let me be reverent in the ways of right,
Lowly the paths I journey on;
Let all my words and actions keep
The laws of the pure universe
From highest Heaven handed down.
For heaven is their bright nurse,
Those generations of the realms of light;
Ah, never of mortal kind were they begot,
Nor are they slaves of memory, lost in sleep:
Their Father is greater than Time, and ages not.

—Sophocles
Oedipus Rex

7

DAREDEVIL

The Prodigal Son, Retold

There are some superhero stories that cannot be understood apart from a keen appreciation of religion. Eastern ideas of spiritual transcendence in *Doctor Strange*, Nightcrawler's Catholicism and mysticism, and Thor's Norse mythology are a few examples of the central role religion can play in a superhero's saga. Far from serving as mere trope to make the story more interesting, religion, if present in a superhero myth, should serve as an interpretive key for unlocking the secret doors of the hero's identity.

Daredevil proves to be just this kind of character—a door, opened widest by those who use the key of Matt Murdock's relationship to his Catholicism. The inner tension between a sinner's rage and a saint's redemption, between brutal justice and tender mercy, between tormented exile and peaceful rest—these things are essential to understanding who Daredevil is.

Some might downplay the role of religion in a character like Daredevil as a kind of creative color. Perhaps someone not personally interested in religious themes and allusions might dismiss Daredevil's religious devotion. But it simply won't do to say that religion is unimportant to the story of the Man Without Fear.

Matt Murdock's religion is distinctly Catholic, and his relationship with Catholicism has been a consistent theme in both print and screen iterations. One need only read Frank Miller's 1986 seminal *Born Again* storyline[1] as a supreme example of how deeply ingrained Catholic Christianity is in Daredevil's mythos.

Born Again patterns Matt Murdock's battered story after the passion and resurrection of Christ. In fact, several specific symbols situate Matt within a larger Christian narrative. For example, the splash pages in the first three chapters—titled respectively "Apocalypse," "Purgatory," and "Pariah"—depict Matt lying down. In "Purgatory" and "Pariah," he's in the fetal position. The posture is one of defeat and death. In the fourth chapter, "Born Again," an injured Matt lies in a cruciform posture in a Catholic mission, caressed and cared for by Sister Maggie, a nun[2] who assumes the role of Mary holding the crucified body of Jesus. Matt finds himself in a recreated Pietà. In the fifth chapter, "Saved," we find Matt combatively posed in a stance of strength and ferocity, a posture of resurrection. Miller's story clings to these Catholic symbols because they're vital to who Daredevil is. They're as fundamental to his persona as they are representative of his larger story.

Return and Redemption

At its heart, Daredevil is a story of return and redemption. In Scripture and in Christian thought, *return* is closely tied to the idea of *redemption*. It means coming back to God after exile and separation from Him. Redemption is salvific recovery from guilt and sin, pain and violence, hate and vengeance. Redemption traditionally means being saved from damnation or condemnation.

The Old Testament prophets are especially concerned with return and redemption. Though each of the prophets wrote in different times and different historical circumstances, the situations that they addressed were predictably similar: Israel, the chosen people of God, found themselves estranged from God due to their own waywardness. God allowed them to be scattered among the pagan nations of the earth, consigned to a purgatorial existence in a hostile world until they decided to return to God, who always faithfully accepted them back. Jeremiah and Ezekiel are only two of the many biblical authors who preach this message of return:

---

1. *Daredevil* #227–#233 (1964).

2. Who also turns out to be Matt's mother.

> Behold, I will gather them out of all the lands to which I have driven them in my anger, in my wrath and in great indignation; and I will bring them back to this place and make them dwell in safety. (Jer 32:37)

> I will bring you out from the peoples and gather you from the lands where you are scattered, with a mighty hand and with an outstretched arm and with wrath poured out. (Ezek 20:34)

Both prophets speak of God's restoring Israel to the land he promised them, a place of forgiveness. It was in this land that Israel was meant to find peace with their God.[3] To the exiled Jewish communities that comprised the prophet's original audiences, return to the promised land meant restoration to an intimate relationship with God, a return to God's presence.[4] Return meant, in the most practical sense, redemption. To reenter God's presence after displacement signified salvation. Indeed, these two concepts, redemption and return, often appear together in Scripture. The Psalmist speaks of a saving path, a redeeming return, to God:

> You make your saving help my shield,
> and your right hand sustains me;
> your help has made me great.
> You provide a broad path for my feet,
> so that my ankles do not give way. (Ps 18:35–36)

And the prophet Isaiah wrote that the ransomed—a common synonym for "redeemed"—people of God would return to a redemptive estate of eternal rest:

> The ransomed of the LORD shall return and come to Zion with singing; everlasting joy shall be upon their heads; they shall obtain gladness and joy, and sorrow and sighing shall flee away. (Isa 35:10)

In other words, the ideas of return and redemption were inextricably bound up with the idea of a return to the place reserved by God for His people.

While these biblical motifs of return and redemption are important for the Christian faith as practiced across denominational lines, they are especially important in Catholic Christianity. Inherent to Catholic practice—and important to Daredevil—is the act of confession of sin to a priest.

---

3. See Gen 12:7; 13:5; 15: 7, 18; Lev 20:24; Josh 5:6.

4. Exod 40:34.

Theologically, symbolically, and practically, the penitent returns to God in the act of confession. Sin has separated sinner from Savior, so repentance is necessary. And repentance requires a return to the place where the penitent can receive redemption. On these two points, the priest serves dual functions. In regards to return, the confessional becomes the place of gathering, the sacred point to which the sinner can return for mercy and belonging. In relation to redemption, the priest makes known, over and against the sinner's derelict life, God's welcoming love.

The ideas of return and redemption are important to understanding an essential aspect of Matt's character—his lost relationship with his father. Matt Murdock's story begins before he lost his sight and gained a super alter ego. It begins with his father, Jack, who raises Matt alone in the crime-ridden New York neighborhood Hell's Kitchen. Jack is brawny and tough, protective and fierce. Matt's relationship with his father is the single most influential force in his life, and he grows up with a love and awe made more intense by his father's death. When Jack, a boxer with a reputation in Hell's Kitchen for his in-ring resilience and brutality, is killed by gangsters for refusing to throw a fight, Matt is left alone, bitter, and angry. He enters into a fatherless exile, and his life becomes a revenge quest, an exilic separation from peace. After years of intense training, a blind, fatherless Matt with heightened senses and extraordinary combat abilities dons the horns to fight organized crime as Daredevil.

Matt's lost relationship to his father opens up the space in which return and redemption are meant to fit. This idea is perhaps most effectively explored in Netflix's *Daredevil* television series. Among the ways the show remains true to Daredevil's long comic history is through a focus on Matt's lost relationship with his father and on his relationship to his Catholic faith. Herein, between literal fatherlessness and priestly fatherhood, lies a tension the show devotes significant time exploring. Driven by his separation from his father and his devotion to his faith, Matt finds himself drawn toward spiritual paternity in the person of Father Lantom.

Matt's relationship with the priest highlights the tension between his fatherlessness and his search for a spiritual father. The show dramatizes this tension in Matt's visits to Father Lantom for confession. In one of the earliest moments with Father Lantom, one in which we first encounter return and redemption, Matt begins his confession with,

> Bless me Father, for I have sinned. It's been . . . too long since my last confession. My dad, he used to come to this church back when

> I was a kid. He was a fighter. Old school. Boxer. Lost more than he
> won. Had a 24–31 record before he, uh . . . . But he could take a
> punch. Jesus, he could take a punch.

Matt is a son in emotional exile, living in a state of unresolved separation
from his deceased father and from the God his father once worshipped.
Matt reaches back to an irretrievable, more innocent, time when he was
with his father and right with God. The way Matt describes his father
speaks to how secure he felt from the hostile world of Hell's Kitchen under
the care and guidance of Jack Murdock. The scene gives us a distinct sense
of how his father's memory helps Matt connect to God. He chooses his
father's church for confession, and to return to his father's church becomes
the means by which he can return to God. The confession itself becomes a
testimony to his father's role in his life.

It really can't be overstated how important it is that Matt opens up
about his late father to his Priest. Father Lantom is the one person occupying the one place to which Matt can return to receive redemption. Matt's
confession here isn't merely about sin. In fact, the point of the scene isn't
confession at all, not in a traditional sense. Instead, it's connection, a return
to the place where Matt can be fathered. After bloody nights fighting crime
in the outer dark[5] of Hell's Kitchen, the confessional booth serves as a place
where Matt can be gathered to grace again. By returning to Father Lantom,
Matt returns to his father and to redemption.

The presence of Father Lantom reveals why Catholicism is so essential to *Daredevil* as a narrative. Catholicism contains Matt's personal arc. A
traumatic event separates Matt from his father, and he spends his life there-
after unsettled and wandering through the unwelcoming world of grief and
anger. Matt's great need is to be received in his sins and forgiven for them.
He goes about setting wrongs to right through brutality. He's a vigilante.
He spends his days practicing law in a perpetual struggle to subsidize his
nights breaking the law. Though his purpose is peace for the greater good,
his methods require unlawful violence. Father Lantom is the man who can
receive Matt in his fatherlessness and grant forgiveness for the life to which
he's turned to redeem his loss. For Matt, Hell's kitchen is a wilderness, a
cruel place from which he longs to escape, though he reenters it nightly.
In this hellish space, between father lost and father sought, Matt reenacts a
prodigal story.

---

5. See Matt 8:12; 22:13; and 25:30.

The Prodigal Story, Retold

The Prodigal Son parable in Luke 15 is one of the New Testament's clearest expressions of return and redemption, and it is on this story that *Daredevil* is theologically grounded. But in addition to what the prodigal story means for the character of Matt Murdock, the parable grants insight to *Daredevil's* political commentary. In fact, Jesus originally meant the parable to be a theological *and* a political statement on how return and redemption could restore a community—as Daredevil believes, even a community as destitute as Hell's Kitchen.

The Parable of the Prodigal Son describes a son who asks his father for his share of his father's estate and then goes away and wastes that inheritance on sinful living. After he has run out of money, he lives in poverty until hunger and desperation bring him to his senses. He returns to his father, confesses his sin, and asks for mercy. The father, overjoyed at the return of his lost son, welcomes him and celebrates with a feast. The prodigal son's older brother, however, is not happy about his return, and refuses to join the feast. Having been a dutiful son his entire life, he resents the favor and grace that the father shows to the ungrateful younger son.

The parable about the prodigal contains three crucial elements: the wandering younger son, the welcoming father, and the eldest son. The youngest son, the prodigal, is often seen as the story's touchstone, the character Jesus's hearers would have most related to. He's fallible, human, a sinner. His actions toward the father are reprehensible. In Jesus's day, to ask for one's birthright was to wish the father dead. And to receive the birthright was to live as if the father had indeed died. In the absence of the father, the Jewish son wanders into pagan lands, dirtying himself by a reprobate lifestyle until realizing that even a servant's life in his father's house would be better than exile. So he returns to the father.

The father stands at the head of the story. In the patriarchal society of the ancient Near East, Jesus's audience would have focused on him more than his two sons. Hearers would have paid closest attention to what he said and did, particularly in response to the younger son. Indeed, his response is what makes him exceptional. Instead of exercising his patriarchal right to reject his soiled son, he accepts him by running toward the wayward while he was still very far off. Jesus's hearers would have understood the father's welcome as an absolutely radical act. Older Jewish males did not run; doing so would have been beneath their dignity. And they certainly didn't demean themselves by going out to dishonorable sons, as this father does.

He goes out to his reprobate son when he sees him far off, and he leaves the feast to go out and beg the eldest son to return.

Lest the connection between Daredevil's story and the prodigal parable seem strictly theological or individual, we must see the parable as Jesus's original audience would have. New Testament scholar N. T. Wright argues that Jesus's parable was far more sociopolitical than personal. Jesus's Jewish audience would have associated the prodigal son with the nation of Israel with their father, Yahweh. As Wright says about the parable, "This is the story of Israel, in particular of exile and restoration."[6] In other words, the Parable of the Prodigal Son isn't merely the story of one man's forgiveness; it's the story of an entire community's redemption. The son stands for a community. His need for forgiveness is a people's need for return. The forgiveness the father offers the returning son is a welcome to a fatherless nation—"Forgiveness of sins is another way of saying 'return from exile.'"[7] Jesus's hearers would have taken the parable to mean hope for a separated people and not just for one sinful person. The prodigal son's very existence in the parable was meant to announce that "Israel's history is turning its long-awaited corner."[8] The father's forgiveness is actually the promise of communal reconciliation, and his proclamation that the lost son has been found is the climactic moment of reconciliation in a story that "demands a last scene, preferably a reconciliation."[9]

For *Daredevil*, the demand for reconciliation can only be met with Matt's redemption from a vigilante life, his return to the father where that redemption is found, and with his return the return of Hell's Kitchen from its exilic, blighted state. What lies behind Jesus's parable and *Daredevil's* use of the parable is the sense that the son's return represents something larger and more communal. The return and redemption spoken of in the Old Testament prophets is the return and redemption of the parable's wandering son. God saw his people as a son and longed that they be renewed by returning to him. This is why the prophet Hosea, describing the scattered people of Israel, writes, "Out of Egypt I have called my son" (Hos 11:1). The nation described as a son in Hosea is the son to return in the prodigal story.

6. Wright, *Jesus and the Victory of God* 126.

7. Ibid., 268.

8. Ibid., 127.

9. Ibid., 129.

The Ill Intent

It is important to understand that not everyone gets to make the return that the prodigal son makes. Matt isn't the only character in *Daredevil* whose fatherlessness is his primary motivation. Like Matt, Wilson Fisk, Daredevil's primary antagonist, lost his father early in life. Unlike Matt, though, Fisk didn't lose his father to a tragedy—he killed him. Fisk's father was brutally abusive, and in a moment of desperation, Fisk killed his father with a hammer in order to protect his mother from him.

And a more important difference is that Matt's and Fisk's fatherlessness drives the two of them to lead very different lives. Matt lives his in pursuit of revenge and justice, while Fisk grows up to become the Kingpin, an organized crime boss who is intent on taking control of Hell's Kitchen.

When he is apprehended by the police at the end of the season, Fisk tells his captors the biblical Parable of the Good Samaritan. In that parable, a man is walking from Jerusalem to Jericho, and he is attacked by robbers and left to die on the side of the road. Three travelers pass him: a priest and a Levite, both of whom refuse to help him; and a Samaritan, who has compassion on him, takes him to an inn, and pays for his care:

> Fisk: It's funny, isn't it? How even the best of men can be deceived by their true nature.
>
> FBI Agent: What the hell does that mean?
>
> Fisk: It means that I'm not the Samaritan. That I'm not the priest, or the Levite. That I am the ill intent who set upon the traveler on a road that he should not have been on.

Fisk's choice of this parable is particularly interesting given Fisk's relationship to Hell's Kitchen and his antagonism toward Daredevil. Fisk is the "ill intent" because of his exploitation of his community. Every move Fisk makes, though seemingly in his community's best interest, leads to the community's further corruption and degradation. If society were the Samaritan in the parable, then as Fisk admits, he's the passerby who robs it. Fisk's relationship to the city is made more interesting by his lack of a father figure. His troubled childhood is marked by the absence of approval by a father figure and the presence of peer acceptance by organized gangs. So it is that Fisk's fatherlessness translates into a politic of oppression over a society of criminality. As the show plays out, it becomes more clear that Fisk is wandering in a land from which he'll never return.

Daredevil's Return

Unlike Fisk, however, Matt *does* return from the isolation of his fatherlessness by forming a relationship with Father Lantom. His visits to Father Lantom are his return journey, which stretches itself out throughout the entire series. Matt, who desires connection with this lost father, Jack, lives his prodigal return with Father Lantom. Like the prodigal, Matt is guilt-ridden and troubled. The occasion for his return is often merely to relieve that guilt, if only for a moment. Once, in opening up about a man whose life he couldn't save, Matt says, "He was a good man. And he's gone because I haven't stopped what's happening to this city." Ever the figure of grace, Father Lantom replies, "Can't put that on yourself, Matthew. You've done everything you can. A lot you probably shouldn't have." The scenes of Matt's confessions all portray Father Lantom's faithful presence. Like the father of the parable, Father Lantom remains resolutely in place, awaiting the son's arrival. The conversations change, but at the heart of each remains the relationship between Matt and Father Lantom, who is well aware of Matt's spiritual needs:

> Lantom: Father Lantom: How you holding up?
>
> Matt: Like a good Catholic boy.
>
> Father Lantom: That bad, huh?

It's Matt's need, the need of a prodigal son, that perpetuates his return. Caught in the sins of vigilante justice and fully aware of his actions, Matt both moves away from and draws nearer to Father Lantom: "I'm not seeking penance for what I've done, Father. I'm asking for forgiveness . . . for what I'm about to do." This confession is not unlike the prodigal's: "Father, I have sinned against heaven and against you. I am no longer worthy to be called your son."[10] Matt's penance for the sins he has yet to commit is the unmasked confession of a shameless son. The power of the confessions is in their transparent honesty, which reveals the Father's welcome as well as the confessor's need for that welcome. Father Lantom receives Matt willingly, like the prodigal's father, always ready to meet Matt wherever he is in his return from the mire of Hell's Kitchen. And instead of passively listening to a suppliant's plea, Father Lantom actively creates a home to which Matt can

---

10. Luke 15:18.

return. Father Lantom's willingness to meet Matt in his struggle is akin to the prodigal's father running to meet the iniquitous son.

As conversations between Matt and Father Lantom unfold, the confessional booth becomes the shoulder of a concerned father. In one of Matt's earliest visits, Father Lantom tends to Matt on personal and theological levels. Like a faithful father, the Priest is willing to walk with Matt from painful experience to doubt-filled belief:

> Lantom: I have a pretty good idea of who you are and what you do. How you do it . . . , that's something else entirely.
>
> Matt: Accident when I was a kid. Used to think it was God's will.
>
> Lantom: Used to?
>
> Matt: Yeah, he made each and every one of us with a purpose, didn't he? A reason for being.
>
> Lantom: I believe so, yes.
>
> Matt: Then why did he put the Devil in me? Why do I feel it in my heart and my soul clawing to be let out if that's not all part of God's plan?
>
> Lantom: Maybe you're being called to summon the better angels of your nature. Maybe that's the struggle you're feeling deep within you.
>
> Matt: And how do you know the angels and the Devil inside me aren't the same thing?
>
> Lantom: I don't, but nothing drives people to the church faster than the thought of the Devil snapping at their heels. Maybe that was God's plan all along. Why he created him, allowed him to fall from grace to become a symbol to be feared, a warning to us all, to tread the path of the righteous.

We might note how the conversation begins with Matt's childhood then moves to talk of a salvific path as an adult. Father Lantom's counsel recalls the Psalmist's words, "You provide a broad path for my feet."[11] In this confessional scene, the two men make a creative attempt to address Matt's most formative childhood moment. And it's at that formative moment that Lantom meets Matt. The exact reason for Matt's visit is intentionally unclear, as the point of the scene isn't what Matt came to confess, but what Father Lantom could say in turn. The scene belongs to the Father, and the viewer's attention is on his response to Matt. This transfer of importance from Matt

11. Ps 18:36.

to Father Lantom is common in the confessional scenes. True to the prodigal story that these scenes appropriate, the emphasis is on the father/Father. It's to the Father that the son returns and by whom he knows redemption.

The soul-clawing angst Matt brings to Father Lantom comes from the exilic nature of both his fatherlessness and from the exilic state of Hell's Kitchen. The prodigal's inner turmoil has as much to do with where he is as it does with what he's done. Like the prodigal who has to hire himself out after he squanders his inheritance, Matt has to live among the unclean things of the world. There can be no redemption for the son or the place in which he wanders unless he return from it.

The Elder Brother

In the parable, the prodigal's humble return is contrasted with his eldest brother's obstinate refusal to enter the father's house. The brother, disdainful of the prodigal's return after his disgraceful behavior, becomes angry and rejects his father's welcome. Where the youngest is characterized by a desire for mercy, a harsh insistence on justice drives the eldest. He would see his prodigal brother punished, left in a fatherless exile. In *Daredevil*, that eldest son is Frank Castle, the Punisher.

Frank is a hard, embittered man. Like Daredevil, Frank, deals in vigilante justice. Unlike Daredevil, however, the Punisher's form of justice is deliberately lethal—as his alias suggests. If Daredevil wants to redeem his community, the Punisher wants to reprove it. Like Matt, whose vagabond life is tied to his fatherlessness, Frank sets out on a bloody path due to his own form of fatherlessness. Unlike Matt, Frank was a father and a husband. The deaths of his wife and child drive him to vigilante isolation, and he devotes his life to exacting revenge on New York's criminal underworld. The loss of his paternity has pushed Frank to the extreme measures of capital justice.

The contrast between the two men couldn't be more stark. In his loss, Matt realizes his need for regained relationship, while viewers witness Frank's painful refusal to reconnect to the redemptive relationship. He holds Daredevil in contempt because Matt's morality and mercy prevent him from killing even the worst criminals: "I think you're a half-measure. I think you're a man who can't finish the job. I think that you're a coward." The same resentment that causes the elder brother to reject his father's pleas drive's the Punisher's attitude toward Matt. Daredevil is one who has been forgiven much, so there is mercy in his non-lethal vigilantism. The Punisher, on the other hand, has much to forgive, so his methods are exacting.

Like the prodigal whose return is rooted in a longing for merciful redemption, Matt must simply move closer to the Father. And like the elder brother, the Punisher, who lives in bitter self-exile and acts from the pain of the loss of his child, holds others to the unmerciful standard of his individual and unspoken justice.

The Political Implications

The contrast between Matt and Frank highlights the sociopolitical theme of the show. While Frank's crusade for justice would leave the city in his own sorrow, Matt would bring it out of its reprobation by his own return to the Father.

Indeed, in *Daredevil*, Matt brings the pigsty with him when he returns from his exile—a return that means not only the reconciliation of the prodigal to the father, but also the return of Hell's Kitchen. A final line from Frank Miller's *Born Again* captures the nuanced way Netflix's *Daredevil* acts as a religious work—"I live in Hell's Kitchen and do my best to keep it clean."[12] For Matt, keeping Hell's Kitchen clean means returning Hell's Kitchen back to the same faithful Father to which he's drawn.

Of the communal meaning behind the Parable of the Prodigal Son, Wright says, "Israel could be allowed to sin, to follow pagan idolatry, even to end up feeding the pigs for a pagan master, but Israel could not fall out of the covenant purposes of her god."[13] There is a similar inevitably in Matt's return. Even though he has to fight hard for it, the redemption that Matt seeks—the redemption of Hell's Kitchen—is as sure as his faithfulness to Father Lantom and as resilient as Daredevil's battle against all that hasn't known the peace his faith offers. Thus, the sociopolitical point of *Daredevil* is that through his relentless spiritual return, Matt stands to bring all of Hell's Kitchen to the very redemptive purposes he so vigilantly seeks.

Wright argues that the purpose of the parable is not strictly didactic; rather, it's mimetic: "The parable does not 'teach', in the sense of teaching abstracts of timeless truth; it acts. It creates a new world."[14] By following the prodigal path, Matt as Daredevil enacts a communal mission. It's a new

12. *Daredevil* #233 (1964).

13. Wright, *Jesus and the Victory of God*, 129.

14. Ibid., 130.

world that Daredevil wants to usher in. His return to a place of fatherly redemption is more than the individual soul's search for salvation.

The prodigal story's purpose is shared by—though unknown to—his community. When Matt returns to Father Lantom, he brings his hopes for Hell's Kitchen with him. Politically and socially, he enacts the restoration of his community not just through vigilante activism but by returning to his "Father" for redemption. The destination for Matt and Hell's Kitchen is always the Father, the center and telos of the story. The centrality of the father has always been at the heart of Matt's, and therefore, Hell's Kitchen's, journey.

In one of the show's early scenes, Jack Murdock decides not to throw his next fight even though he's been told that he has to. He says, "Just once, I want Matty to hear people cheer for his old man. Just once." Jack's desire is for his son to know him and to be reconciled to a community who has yet to know him. The Hell's Kitchen that took Matt's father from him is the same community that Matt is fighting to bring closer to what Father Lantom represents. His fight against the crime in Hell's Kitchen embodies a political and social upheaval, the return of the new fatherless world back to old fathered peace. If he has to, he'll drag Hell's Kitchen to the Father with him kicking and screaming.

I said before that we can't ignore the religious details of a story like Matt's. The devil lives in the details. To rightly see *Daredevil* is to trace the threads of return, redemption, and the catholicity of fatherly belonging to the knot that ties those threads together. The story of Matt Murdock calls on Catholicism and biblical narrative to create a character that acts on behalf of society by returning to sacred peace in order to redeem his community. The son's return to his father is arduous, but "like a good Catholic boy," he'll get there.

8

BATMAN V SUPERMAN

Mythology, Theodicy, and the Dawn of Justice

The Generative Power of Myth

Among the many functions that myths perform, depicting the creation of civilization is the one of the most important. Myths narrate how reality first came into being and how that reality causes change in culture as well as in the natural world. For example, Hades's kidnapping of Persephone causes winter; the divinely endowed strength of Samson, the Hebrew Judge, solidifies Israel as a warrior state at his death; and the Titan Prometheus brings fire to humanity, sparking an industrious new age in human history. In myth, reality is the province of the supernatural, and humanity exists within that reality, responding to divine impetus in ways that create history. As myth scholar Mercea Eliade has written, "Myth tells how, through the deeds of Supernatural beings, a reality came into existence, be it the whole of reality, the Cosmos, or only a fragment of reality—an island, a species of plant, a particular kind of human behavior, an institution."[1] It's precisely this quality of showing how something came to exist that Zack Snyder's 2016 *Batman v Superman: Dawn of Justice* calls on the mythic. There are two unique ways in which the film summons the mythic—both found in

---

1. Eliade, *Myth and Reality*, 5–6.

the title, *Batman v Superman: Dawn of Justice*—the conflict between god and man and the power of that conflict to create political reality.

The Messianic and the Mortal

In the contest between Batman and Superman—the *v* of the title—we find the film's first mythic convention: the clash between god and man. Director Zack Synder establishes the conflict early and clearly in the film. To Batman, Superman stands for all that man is not, and therefore, threatens all that man is. To Superman, Batman stands for all that man shouldn't be, unlawful and unjust. Conflict is inevitable. Superman's seemingly divine power exposes mankind's vulnerability, creating a sense of anxiety about the superhuman, leaving a lingering suspicion among politicians, pundits, and Bruce Wayne that the "gods" might, as Alfred puts it, "hurl thunderbolts." This age-old idea of the divine-human contest—which goes back to the rage of Achilles and the frightening power of Ares—operates on a mythic level to reveal something about the nature of both god and man, who stand opposed to one another. This clash between supernatural and natural eventually leads to what Eliade calls the production of a reality.

Now, Snyder's cinematic vision summons the mythic in its enactment of the contest between the immortal and the mortal. It's important to stop here and note that Superman is not divine. The Son of Krypton is a humanoid alien. But Superman's presence on earth—an incarnational presence of the ontologically *other* and displayed as something far beyond mortal limitation—creates a binary of being, the supernatural and the mortal. Astrophysicist and cosmologist Neil deGrasse Tyson has a cameo appearance in which he explains the significance of Superman's presence in the world:

> We're talking about a being whose very existence challenges our own sense of priority in the universe. And you go back to Copernicus where he restored the sun in the center of the known universe, displacing Earth. And you get to Darwinian evolution and you find out we're not special on this earth. We're just one among other lifeforms. And now we learn that we're not even special in the entire universe because there is Superman. There he is, an alien among us. We're not alone.

Snyder includes these lines about Superman's alien nature in order to emphasize the hero's *otherness*, but the director moves beyond Tyson's merely scientific explanation in order to portray Superman as something more.

For Snyder, Superman's myth depends on the ways in which his existence highlights human limitations. Superman confronts us with a mythic binary between the human and superhuman. In fact, Snyder has been building on this binary between human and wholly other since 2013's *Man of Steel*.

In *Man of Steel*, one of Snyder's primary interests is to present the otherness of Kryptonian culture compared to the ordinariness of human existence. General Zod, the chief antagonist in *Man of Steel*, despises humanity for its finitude and its weakness. Superman, who is raised by a pair of loving human parents, has taken on human morality, sentiment, and a sanctified view of life. Though he is something far more than mortal, Superman sees human flourishing as his life's purpose. He fights for truth, justice, and a distinctly American sense of freedom and happiness with transcendent—indeed mythic—abilities. Both Superman and Zod hover above human weakness in a contest of champions that threatens human existence.

The gap between the human and superhuman only widens as Snyder's vision unfolds. Superman's *otherness* doesn't just come from his ability to fly above Metropolis's skyscrapers; in his very being he is galaxies removed from humanity. DC's deity figure has taken up permanent residence among the mortals.

The supernatural portrayal of Superman that Snyder begins in *Man of Steel* and continues in *Batman v Superman* has a rich source history. Given how god-like he would become, it's interesting that Superman began as a more humanist character. Jerry Siegel and Joe Shuster, young Jewish-American writers and cartoonists, first introduced Superman in the 1933 short story "The Reign of Superman." In his debut, Superman was a malicious vagrant with psychic powers, a character who more closely resembled Nietzsche's Übermensch than later versions. This unpopular first attempt was followed by the more heroic iteration that we are all familiar with. For the new version, Siegel and Shuster drew from composite sources—works of science fiction, charismatic popular culture figures, hero stories, strongmen, and biblical figures like Moses and Christ. Siegel and Shuster's Judaism had a powerful influence on the character, and their ultimate vision for Superman, first appearing in 1938's *Action Comics* #1, was more Christ than Übermensch.

Since his debut, stories about Superman have frequently dealt with his messianic origin. Director Brian Singer, commenting on his 2006 *Superman Returns*, says that the Son of Krypton is "the Jesus Christ of Superheroes."[2]

2. Quoted in "The Spiritual Side of *Superman Returns*," SuperheroHype.com,

Superman's mythic messianism begins on Krypton, where scientist Jor-El sends his son, Kal-El, away to save him from imminent death. Kal-El's[3] exilic story is similar to that of Moses, the miracle-working prophet of Exodus, and that of Jesus, God's Son and spoken Word—especially in Matthew 2 when Jesus and his family have to flee death so that he can fulfill a divinely appointed purpose. Like Moses and Jesus, whose most formative years were spent in obscurity, Kal undergoes a quiet development in which he grows in "wisdom and in stature."[4]

Superman's public life also resembles Christ's. Both Superman and Jesus retreat from the public for solace—Superman to his Fortress of Solitude and Jesus to the wilderness.[5] Both are known by their public miracles. Both understand that people's perception of them hinges on the works that they perform. (As Jesus says, "Unless you people see signs and wonders, you will never believe."[6]) For example, in *Batman v Superman*'s Day of the Dead scene, Vikram Ghandi, a documentarian with a cameo in the film, says about the public's reaction to Superman: "We, as a population on this planet, have been looking for a savior. Ninety percent of people believe in a higher power, and every religion believes in some sort of messianic figure." Ghandi's comments are the voiceover to a scene in which Superman's rescues a young girl during a *Día de Muertos* festival. Hundreds surround him with outstretched arms, each eager to touch the hem of his cape. Not unlike the way Judeans who witnessed Jesus's deeds were astonished and left to admit the reality of who Jesus was, the people of Metropolis and the world at large are awed by Superman's abilities and have to grapple with his apparent divinity.[7]

Ironically, in Snyder's vision, it's precisely Superman's seemingly divine powers—his "signs and wonders"—that threaten Batman. If Superman is a type of Christ, then Batman plays the part of zealot and reluctant convert: a Thomas slow to reconcile himself to the evidence of who Superman

available at http://www.superherohype.com/features/92345-the-spiritual-side-of-superman-returns.

3. It's important to note that El in Hebrew means "god," and "Kal-El" is similar to the Semitic phrase "voice of God."

4. Luke 2:52.

5. Luke 5:16.

6. John 4:48.

7. Cf. Heb 2:4; Luke 9:43.

is.[8] Indeed, Batman's doubt in Superman's apparent deity precipitates the film's conflict. Batman's suspicion is one of the many ways he enacts the mortal aspect of mythology. Whereas Superman began as a representation of the Übermensch and then moved to a more Judeo-Christian messianic figure, Batman began and remains more like Nietzsche's Übermensch, an extraordinary man who achieves excellence and fights evil sheerly by his indomitable will.

Batman wants to bring Superman down to human level, to close the mythic gap between god and man. In the middle of his epic fight with Superman, Batman bitterly says,

> I bet your parents taught you that you mean something, that you're here for a reason. My parents taught me a different lesson, dying in the gutter for no reason at all. . . . They taught me the world only makes sense if you force it to.

Batman assumes the voice of humanity. Resilient and self-willed, he has learned through futility and desperate force of will lessons that he thinks Superman in his divinity has yet to learn. He says to a battered Superman, "You're not brave. Men are brave." In other words, *You say that you want to help people, but you can't feel their pain, . . . their mortality. . . . It's time you learn what it means to be a man.* While the world stands in awe of the Man of Steel, Batman jeers at him.

Batman's contempt for Superman's otherness is partly rooted in Snyder's interpretation of the Dark Knight. Moviegoers have never before seen a Batman as brutally primal—or, in many regards, *human*—as Snyder's. Batman might be a kind Übermensch, but he remains profoundly mortal.

One way that Snyder creates a Batman so viscerally human is to book-end the movie with death. The opening scene begins with Bruce narrating a funeral, and the first line of that narration sounds like it could come from the Book of Ecclesiastes: "There was a time above, a time before. . . . But things fall—things on earth." And by movie's end, viewers find Bruce again at a graveside, this time mourning the slain Superman. These bookend scenes emphasize Bruce's mortality by reminding him and the audience of human frailty and finitude.

Bruce's humanity, further demonstrated by bouts of rage, manic dreams, and visceral grief, can't be covered by a mask or cowl. Unlike former, sleeker incarnations, Snyder's Batman is palpably physical, a veiny

---

8. See John 10:10–11 and John 20:27–28.

hulking figure susceptible to injury and given to brutality. Batman's vulnerability lies in contrast with Superman's bare invincibility. The asymmetry between beings leaves Bruce with a decision to make about Superman. In myth, mortals are often faced with a choice as to whether they'll trust the gods. Often that trust will determine some aspect of mortal existence. If man decides he can trust the gods, there's a chance for peace; but if man opposes the gods, there's conflict. And in *BvS*, Batman cannot bring himself to trust Superman.

Near the beginning of the film, Bruce Wayne gets a close-up view of Superman's fight with Zod and is infuriated by the Kryptonian's abilities. While Superman's power is overwhelmingly evident to Batman, his ethics remain suspiciously unclear. Since in Snyder's version of the story, Metropolis and Gotham City neighbor one another, Bruce is witness to an overwhelming display of violent power as Superman and General Zod battle in the staggeringly destructive set piece at the end of *Man of Steel*. Witnessing that devastation ruins any chance that Bruce has of trusting Superman. In an early conversation in *Batman v Superman*, Alfred, alarmed by Bruce's plan to confront Superman, asks, "You're gonna go to war?" Bruce answers,

> That son of a bitch brought the war to us two years ago. Jesus, Alfred, count the dead . . . thousands of people. What's next? Millions? He has the power to wipe out the entire human race, and if we believe there's even a 1 percent chance that he is our enemy we have to take it as an absolute certainty . . . and we have to destroy him.

To Batman, Superman is an atomically powerful threat, an unpredictable presence in an already unstable world. And he isn't alone in his doubts. For example, Senator Finch—a principled politician determined to bring Superman under the control of the U.S. government—says, "the world has been so caught up with what Superman can do that no one has asked what he *should* do."

The Problem of Evil

The major conflict of the film—"God versus man," as Luthor puts it—highlights the problem of evil, which asks why a good God would permit evil and suffering. There are two principal problems with reconciling the existence of evil with the existence God. The first is that if God were all-good, he wouldn't allow evil or suffering. Assuming God's goodness, evil exists because God isn't powerful enough to stop it. The second is that if God were all-powerful, then he could prevent evil and eliminate suffering. Assuming God's omnipotence, evil must exist because God is either morally indifferent or malevolent. It's this question of supernatural goodness and omnipotence that makes up the very bedrock of the conflict between Batman and Superman.

The clearest articulation of the film's concern with the problem of evil comes from its main villain, Lex Luthor. Toward the end of the film, Lex describes the problem of evil in a vindictive rant:

> What we call God depends upon our tribe, Clark Jo, because God is tribal. God takes sides. No man in the sky intervened when I was a boy to deliver me from Daddy's fist and abominations. Mm-mm. I figured it out way back: if God is all powerful, He cannot be all good. And if He's all good then He cannot be all powerful. And neither can you be. They need to see the fraud you are.

Here Lex says more overtly what Batman has been thinking all along. If Superman is so powerful, why is there still so much evil and suffering in the world? Can we really trust a savior who has not only allowed but caused suffering and destruction?

Just as Batman's doubts about Superman lead to the film's titular battle, Lex's hatred of Superman moves him toward an inevitable conflict with the Man of Steel. But while they start in similar places, Bruce and Lex have different ultimate goals: In the first meeting of the Dark Knight and the Man of Steel, Batman asks, "Tell me: do you bleed? You will." He wants to humanize the god in order to show that Superman isn't really superior to humanity. Lex, on the other hand, maliciously seeks to topple the divine order, desiring to take the place of the divine. As he says to Superman on the roof of LexCorp Tower, "And now God bends to my will." Lex attempts to answer the problem of evil by manufacturing a god of his own making, an anti-Christ figure known as Doomsday. "If man won't kill God, the Devil will do it!" he says at Doomsday's birth.

Batman eventually comes to believe in Superman, even following him into battle. Two things bring about this conversion, this Damascus road experience. First, the realization that Bruce and Clark's mothers share a name humanizes Superman for Batman. This humanization reconciles the "god" and the man in much the same way as the Incarnation reconciles God and humanity. Second, Superman's self-sacrificial death at the end of the film proves his love for humanity and shows that Batman has been wrong about him this whole time. "I failed him in life," he says at Clark Kent's funeral. "I won't fail him in death." Batman's conversion amounts to the film's *theodicy*, its answer to the problem of evil.

From Theodicy to Polity

I began by saying that the two primary ways Snyder's film called on the mythic could be found in the title. *"Batman v Superman"* highlights the film's concern with the conflict between the divine and the mortal and with the problem of evil. It's in *"Dawn of Justice"* that we find myth's second operation, which is to show how the conflict between gods and men gives rise to political reality. As Eliade writes, myths

> narrate not only the origins of the World, of animals, of plants, and of man, but also all the primordial events in consequence of which man became what he is today—mortal, sexed, organized in a society, obliged to work in order to live, and working in accordance with certain rules. If the World exists, if man exists, it is because Supernatural Beings exercised creative powers in the "beginning."[9]

Every organizing principle that comprises the social and political order of public life originates from the generative contact between the supernatural the natural. The conflict between the gods and man turns out to be a creative force, indeed, a dawn of some new form of public reality—namely, justice.

In *Batman v Superman*, justice is birthed from the mythic conflict between god and man, which has its fullest expression in the problem of evil. Is God good? Is he all-powerful? If he's both, why does evil exist? While Luthor never finds a satisfactory answer to the problem of evil, Batman recognizes Superman's goodness, resulting in his conversion to Superman's side and inspiring him to form the Justice League. Lex, on the other hand, can't hold the ideas of omnipotence and goodness in harmony, and this misalignment leads him to acts of injustice.

By the end of the film, Batman and Lex have moved from occupying starkly different positions on the same side of the theodicial problem to starkly different positions on radically opposed sides of the problem of evil. Theodicy moves Batman toward justice. Left unsettled, the problem of evil

9. Ibid., 11.

moves Lex farther away from justice. For both Batman and Lex, theodicy produces polity.

In Snyder's myth, a person is just—in right relationship with the good, the right, and the lawful—when he has reconciled himself to divine goodness and power by siding with deity, in this case, with Superman. It's this kind of reconciliation that Batman comes to by the end of the film. And it's due to that reconciliation with the deity figure in the myth that Batman will undergo a change in how he exists politically, that is, in how he lives as a member of the polis. In Batman's story, the v produces a *dawn*. The generative nature of the film's mythic conflict creates new political realities that cohere with Superman's personal principles—truth, goodness, and justice. Batman's existence in the polis will now find meaning through this new community—a community whose existence is inspired by Superman's self-sacrifice. Through this community's relationship with the Man of Steel, there will dawn a new society of justice.

But while Superman's death reconciles the divine and the mortal to one another and inspires the formation of the Justice League, it leaves Luthor in a much different place within the new political reality. By the end of the film, we find Lex enclosed, both literally and metaphorically, by what the Greeks called *agōn* (ἀγών), which means "strife," "struggle," or "contest." English words like "antagonism" and "agony" derive from *agōn*—and both are the unfortunate results of strife and contest. In the Greco-Roman world, that contest might be with a god, and the agony experienced is the result of losing. Given his relationship to Superman, Lex's self-enclosure and agony prove inevitable. In this myth, he has engaged in a struggle with divinity, and he has lost. He began the film as a quirky, crafty, and self-serving figure, but by film's end, he has become diabolical—a figure in utter opposition to the good. It's predictable—actually, necessary—then, that Lex's life in the polis will now spiral into evil. And it is fitting, in light of their individual contests with Superman, that Batman and Lex share a final antagonistic scene together, in which Lex cryptically hints at some coming threat that will disrupt the new age of justice. Batman, a reborn icon of justice, and Lex, the incarnation of *agōn*, stand in opposition to one another, both transformed by the deeds of the supernatural, both born into new relationships with justice. Batman, now a believer in Superman, promises swift justice on Lex's future transgressions.

One of Lex's last statements is, "Now God is good as dead." For Lex in Snyder's myth, no ungraced epitaph could be more fitting. Superman does indeed die. But not unlike the death of Christ, Superman's death proves to be a birth because it dawns a new movement. Eliade writes, "Myths describe the various and sometimes dramatic breakthroughs of the sacred (or the 'supernatural') into the World."[10] Thus, the death of Superman serves as the final act of *Batman v Superman*'s mythic generation, the final breakthrough of the divine into the mortal, and the catalyst for a new political vision. Bruce's "I failed him in life. I won't fail him in death" becomes the mission statement for a new age of justice. At one moment in the movie, a commentator speaking on the implications of Superman's intervention in human affairs, says, "on this earth, every act is a political act." Every act, indeed—even death.

10. Eliade, *Myth and Reality*, 6.

AFTERWORD
Where Do We Go from Here?

ARMOND BOUDREAUX

What It Means to Be Reasonable

If nothing else, this book is a plea for reason and fairness. One of the great values of superhero stories like *Civil War*, *Avengers vs. X-Men*, and others is that they force readers to see the social, spiritual, and intellectual consequences of political conflicts and disagreements. And being made to see those consequences is a good thing for a number of reasons, not least because it might encourage us to treat each other with more civility. I hesitate to use the word *tolerance* because it is one of the most abused words in the English language right now, but I suppose that in the end that's what Corey and I have been arguing for.

Our society suffers from a species of intolerance that is quite different from forms that we've seen in the past. Ours is an intolerance that preaches tolerance even as it persecutes and rejects people who hold views different from our own. Ours is an intolerance that forces people out of jobs for not holding to our own intellectual or moral orthodoxies. In other words, ours is an intolerance that punishes people for believing the wrong things. The American experiment—and indeed one of the goals of Western culture—was to bring people with different beliefs and practices together in a way that would allow them to share certain fundamental rights without infringing on the rights of the others. We were supposed to be able to follow the dictates of our own consciences while allowing others to do the same. In the first decades of the twenty-first century, that goal seems to be slipping further and further from our reach.

But it doesn't have to be that way. We can do better by being more truly rational than we have been recently. Karl Popper defines "rationalism" in this way:

> We could then say that rationalism is an attitude of readiness to listen to critical arguments and to learn from experience. It is fundamentally an attitude of admitting that *"I may be wrong and you may be right, and by an effort, we may get nearer to the truth."* It is an attitude which does not lightly give up hope that by such means as argument and careful observation, people may reach some kind of agreement on most problems of importance. In short, the rationalist attitude, or as, I may perhaps label it, the "attitude of reasonableness," is very similar to the scientific attitude, to the belief that in the search for truth we need co-operation, and that, with the help of argument, we can attain something like objectivity.[1]

Liberal republicanism—by which I mean a society that allows individual liberty and in which the people and their elected representatives have political power—cannot function if its citizens do not at the very least share something like Popper's understanding of "rationalism" or "reasonableness." Since republics lack a centralized authority like a monarch, reasonableness itself must become the supreme ruler—that is, what must rule society is the habit of rational people deliberating about how to best order their lives together.

What this looks like in practice is that when I interact with another member of society about some policy or rights issue, by default I adopt a certain attitude: before I have good reason to believe otherwise, I assume that the other person is well-meaning and has the best interests of society at heart; I assume that she is willing to consider evidence and arguments presented by others; I assume that she is willing to present evidence in support of her own arguments; I assume that she is willing to revise or change her own position if the evidence demands it; and I place the same expectations upon myself.

Another way of saying this is that I must approach any disagreement about the ordering of society with the assumption that the people I'm talking to are not minions of evil bent on global domination. Unless I am

---

1. Popper, *The Open Society and Its Enemies*, 442.

presented with compelling evidence to the contrary, I have to assume that they are good people who mean well, want what's best for everyone, and are willing to accept the truth when it's presented to them. I also have to recognize that just as they might be wrong, I might also be wrong—but that working together, we all might come closer to the truth.

Intellectual humility is the key ingredient to this kind of reasonableness. It is important for people to have convictions and to live by them, but it is equally important that we remind ourselves constantly that we could be mistaken about any number of things. In addition, we must always be honest with ourselves about the reasons that we believe certain things, and we must be willing to modify or outright change our beliefs if there is good reason to do so.

Now all this might sound so commonsensical that it isn't even worth saying, but for at least the last few decades, Western society has been slowly rejecting Popper's definition of reasonableness. We pay lip-service to it, certainly, but we rarely practice it any more. Our politics consists of various factions competing for power, mostly by means of sophistry and *ad hominem* attacks on people who think differently than we do. In other words, we use cleverness to make whatever we want sound reasonable (regardless of whether or not it actually *is* reasonable), and we demonize the people who disagree with us. This can be seen at every level of public discourse from public events at universities all the way down to internet memes passed around on social media.

One of the best examples of this is what happened to Peter Tatchell, a British LGBT advocate, at Canterbury Christ Church University in 2016. Tatchell was invited to speak at an event on "re-radicalizing queers," but Fran Cowling, the LGBT representative for the National Union of Students, sent a letter to the University saying that she wouldn't share a stage with Tatchell because she believes that he is "transphobic." Her reason? Tatchell signed an open letter that supported free speech and opposed the growing trend of universities refusing to provide a platform to people with whom they disagree (in particular on sexual issues).[2] In other words, because Tatchell supports the right of people who disagree with him to speak and argue for their views, those who disagree with him tried to deny him the right to speak.

This incident perfectly illustrates how problematic terms that purport to describe various forms of bigotry have become and how damaging they

2. McVeigh, "Peter Tatchell: Snubbed by Students for Free Speech Stance."

can be to rational discourse. It is now the habit of many people to use terms like "transphobe" (as well as the plethora of various other phobias that seem to afflict every level of society) to describe anyone who disagrees with them. The effect that this produces is that instead of engaging with each other rationally, we simply resort to name-calling. Instead of reasonable discussion and persuasion when we encounter disagreement, we try to discredit one another with labels. Thus, we end up with the absolutely absurd claim that a man like Peter Tatchell (one of the founders of OutRage!, for crying out loud) is "transphobic."

And though it might seem to be primarily those on the left who deploy terms for various kinds of phobia in order to shut down their political opponents, people on the political right have been just as guilty of name-calling as their leftist counterparts. The terms "communist" and "socialist," for example, often get used as political weapons instead of terms of description. To some people, anyone who believes that government should place some limits on capitalism is a "socialist." Even the term "liberal," which in its proper usage refers to a person who believes in a high degree of civil, political, and economic freedom, is now frequently used as a term of attack that connotes a person who wants the government to control everything.

In the U.S., the 2016 election brought the problem that I've just been describing to the forefront in a dramatic way. As it became clear that Donald Trump and Hillary Clinton were going to be the nominees for the major parties, public discourse about the election increasingly became an irrational display of *ad hominem* attacks. Those who supported Donald Trump were automatically racists or xenophobes. Those who supported Clinton were called fools, "feminazis," or worse. It didn't matter that many people supported Trump or Clinton because they thought that one was the lesser of two evils. Support of either candidate automatically made you evil. Meanwhile, Republicans who refused to support their party's nominee were labeled as disloyal or divisive and guilty of "moral preening."[3]

On social media, internet memes told us that those who supported one candidate or the other were a "special kind of stupid."[4] They reminded us that whenever we feel like we aren't smart enough, we should remember that there was somebody out there voting for Trump (or Clinton). Fake news did everything that it could to prove that anyone who disagrees with

---

3. Grim, "Establishment Republicans Tired of 'Slick Moral Preening' by GOP Trump Opponents."

4. Here I refer to a popular meme that features the actor Sam Elliot.

us is an evil bigot bent on white supremacy or a dastardly communist determined to subjugate us all.

In addition to name-calling and *ad hominem* attacks, we now use language to hijack reasonable discourse in other ways, as well. For example, consider a phrase like "opponents of marriage equality." Those who employ such language are not using it to make a rational defense of their position. The term "marriage equality" is usually used in order to avoid making a rational defense of same-sex marriage or some other marriage configuration and instead jump right to demonizing anyone who takes a different position. Meanwhile, some who oppose same-sex marriage often call themselves "pro-marriage," a term which also side-steps the need to rationally defend their position.

We've also abused language in other ways—ways that ultimately damage our ability to be reasonable or rational with one another. For example, we've misused the word "fact" for so long that we accept as a "fact" any claim that happens to confirm what we already believe. We rely on "fact-checkers" who are often just as biased and manipulative as the people they claim to monitor. And to paraphrase Juvenal, who fact-checks the fact-checkers, anyway?[5]

Meanwhile, various groups of people across the country work hard to shut up or shut down anyone who dares to disagree with them. Ironically, the places where this kind of behavior occurs most often is at colleges and universities, institutions that exist precisely for the purpose of pursuing truth through rational inquiry. Even more ironically, students, professors, and administrators frequently try to shut down people who disagree with them in the name of tolerance and freedom of speech. For example, there is a U.S.-based conservative political group for students that maintains a "watchlist" of college professors who "advance a radical agenda in lecture halls." The web page for the "watchlist" says that the group will defend free speech and the right of college professors to teach whatever they think is best, but maintaining a "watchlist" at all belies that claim. And at various colleges around the country, a number of professors have come under fire for failing to live up to approved progressive orthodoxies either in the classroom or in some other venue. In almost all cases, students have demanded censure or firing for the offenders.

---

5. In his *Satires*, the Roman poet Juvenal famously quipped, *Quis custodiet ipsos custodes?* ("Who watches the watchmen?") The same line inspired the title of Alan Moore's graphic novel *Watchmen*, which deconstructs the idea of superheroes.

A republic cannot function if we continue to engage with each other in this way. Our political system depends on our ability to respect those who disagree with us and to resolve differences by rational persuasion, not by *ad hominem* attacks or Orwellian monitoring of people's opinions and statements. It also depends on our ability to be rational, to acknowledge that we will never be right about everything, and to accept evidence when it is presented to us. What is frightening about the current state of politics, particularly in the West, is that we are increasingly losing our ability to be rational with one another. In other words, we are rapidly forgetting what used to be common wisdom, wisdom that Peter Tatchell expressed perfectly when he responded to the students who wanted him disinvited from speaking at Canterbury Christ Church: "Bad ideas are best and most effectively defeated by good ideas."[6]

Politics = Power?

At this point, it shouldn't be surprising that we can turn to superheroes for help in seeing the consequences of the irrational course that we have set for ourselves. At the end of *Civil War*, Captain America and the superheroes who have joined him in opposing the Superhuman Registration Act[7] are winning the fight against Iron Man and the pro-registration forces. The Vision has disabled Iron Man's armor, and Cap himself is ready to deal the final blow against Tony. But then he looks around at the damage that the fight has caused and drops his shield on the ground.

Though many people sympathize with Cap's side in the superhuman Civil War, in the end it doesn't really matter whether or not Cap is right, because the politics of the Marvel Universe, much like the politics of the real world, is not about the pursuit of truth: instead, it's about power, and there was no way for the anti-registration side to win in terms of power. They can win the fight against the pro-registration side, but victory means nothing if they can't persuade the world. So Cap surrenders himself to the authorities, and at first, no one understands what he's doing:

> Spider-Man: We were beating them, man. We were winning back there.

6. Tatchell, "Free Speech is Under Attack in UK Universities."

7. See Chapter 3.

Captain America: Everything except the argument. And they're not arresting Captain America. . . . They're arresting Steve Rogers. That's a very different thing.[8]

You might say that Cap's surrender is the only truly good act of the entire story because it gives the lie to the politics of his world: the SRA was never really about what is right; it was always about power. And there was never a real conversation about the SRA; it was simply passed by Congress and forced upon heroes who had acted responsibly their entire careers, people who had risked their lives over and over again to protect the public without any thanks or reward. In the world of *Civil War* (and, I'm afraid, in our own world), the only thing that matters is power. When Cap surrenders, it's not an admission that his side is wrong; it's an admission that when politics stops being the rational pursuit of truth and becomes a struggle for power, the only moral thing to do is to refuse to participate in the struggle. Doing so often has dire consequences, but it might also be the only way to expose the inherent dysfunction of a political system that is based entirely on power and not on the rational pursuit of truth.

In 2015, Marvel revisited *Civil War* and told a story that imagined what would have happened if Cap had not surrendered to the pro-registration forces. The picture is not pretty. In this world, the U.S. no longer exists; instead, two nations have formed in the wake of the conflict: the Iron (with Tony Stark as its president), which encompasses the eastern U.S., and the Blue (led by Steve Rogers), which includes the central U.S. and the western states. The two sides are in a perpetual state of conflict, and each side holds an advantage over the other: the Iron, as an internationally recognized state, has trade privileges that the Blue does not have; but the Blue has the majority of the territory. Each has something that the other wants—in other words, each has power over the other, and each tries to use that power to exert its will over the other.

When Tony and Steve come together to try and find a peaceful solution to the conflict between the two states, it becomes clear that there can be no compromise when all that matters is power. And as it turns out, while the two sides fight each other for a greater share of power, they both fail to see that they're both being manipulated by a third party who has been orchestrating the conflict between the Iron and the Blue from the beginning.

The lesson of the 2015 reimagining of *Civil War* isn't that what divides us is merely a distraction from the "real" issues. Most of the things that

8. *Civil War* #7 (2006).

divide us *do* matter—some of them quite a lot. But as long as we refuse to engage in real, honest deliberation about our political differences and instead simply fight (not necessarily with superpowers or with violence, but with our slogans, picket signs, Tweets, sound bytes, and lawsuits), then either our civilization will destroy itself from within, or it will be brought low by a hidden enemy that we fail to see until it's too late.

We have to reason with one another and remember that everyone— even that person whose views and behavior we find so intolerable—is made in *imago Dei*. We have to remind ourselves constantly that despite what internet memes and the talking heads on television tell us, our political opponents have reasons for believing what they believe. That doesn't necessarily mean that we have to abandon our own views, but it does mean that instead of thinking of people across the political aisle as enemies, we have to think of them as fellow citizens and partners in the ordering of society. The sooner we do so, the sooner we'll be able to begin the process of reconciling ourselves to one another. Until then, we'll continue down the road that our superheroes have been warning us in books like *The Dark Knight Returns, Kingdom Come,* and *Civil War.*

BIBLIOGRAPHY

Eliade, Mircea. *Myth and Reality*. New York: Harper & Row, 1963.

Englehart, Steve. "Captain America II." http://www.steveenglehart.com/Comics/Captain%20America%20169–176.html.

Gehrke, Joel. "ACLU Lawyers Blame 'Christian Right,' GOP for Orlando Terrorist Attack." http://www.washingtonexaminer.com/aclu-lawyers-blame-christian-right-gop-for-orlando-terrorist-attack/article/2593679.

Gorman, Siobhan, and Jennifer Valentino-Devries. "New Details Show Broader NSU Surveillance Reach." http://www.wsj.com/articles/SB10001424127887324108204579022874091732470.

Greene, Stan. "Kevin Loibl Shot & Killed Christina Grimmie Because She Was a Christian." http://www.smobserved.com/story/2016/06/11/news/kevin-james-loibl-shot-and-killed-christina-grimmie-because-she-was-a-christian/1425.html.

Grim, Ryan. "Establishment Republicans Tired of 'Slick Moral Preening' by GOP Trump opponents." http://www.huffingtonpost.com/entry/establishment-republicans-never-trump_us_57bc8d91e4b00d9c3a1a4dbc.

Kant, Immanuel. *Ethical Philosophy*. Translated by James W. Ellington. Indianapolis: Hackett, 1981.

Lewis, C. S. *On Stories and Other Essays on Literature*. New York: Harcourt, 1982.

———. *The Problem of Pain*. New York: Harper Collins, 1996.

McVeigh, Tracy. "Peter Tatchell: Snubbed by Students for Free Speech Stance." *The Guardian*. 13 February 2016. https://www.theguardian.com/uk-news/2016/feb/13/peter-tatchell-snubbed-students-free-speech-veteran-gay-rights-activist.

Miller, Frank, and Klaus Janson. *The Dark Knight Returns*. New York: DC Comics, 2002.

Perry, Walter L., et al. "Predictive Policing: The Role of Crime Forecasting in Law Enforcement Operations." https://www.rand.org/pubs/research_reports/RR233.html.

Popper, Karl. *The Open Society and Its Enemies*. Princeton: Princeton University Press, 1994.

Skelton, Stephen. "The Spiritual Side of *Superman Returns*." http://www.superherohype.com/features/92345-the-spiritual-side-of-superman-returns

Strauss, Bob. "Generator X." https://www.theguardian.com/film/2000/aug/12/features

Tatchell, Peter. "Free Speech is Under Attack in UK Universities." http://www.petertatchell.net/free_speech/free-speech-is-under-attack-in-uk-universities.htm.

de Tocqueville, Alexis. *Democracy in America,* vol. 2. Edited by Eduardo Nolla. Translated by James T. Schleifer. Indianapolis: Liberty Fund, 2012.

Tolkien, J. R. R. *The Monsters and the Critics and Other Essays.* London: Harper Collins, 1983.

Waid, Mark, and Alex Ross. *Kingdom Come.* New York: DC Comics, 1996.

Weber, Max. *From Max Weber: Essays in Sociology.* Translated and edited by H. H. Gerth and C. Wright Mills. London: Routledge, 1970.

White, Mark D. "Why Doesn't Batman Kill the Joker?" In *Batman and Philosophy: The Dark Knight of the Soul,* edited by Mark D. White and Robert Arp, 5–15 Hoboken, NJ: Wiley & Sons, 2008.

———. "*Civil War II*: How the Comics Sausage is Made . . . ." http://www.comicsprofessor. com/2016/01/how-the-comcs-sausage-is-made-civil-war-ii-new-york-daily-post. html

———, ed. *Superman and Philosophy: What Would the Man of Steel Do?* Hoboken, NJ: Wiley & Sons, 2013.

Wright, N. T. *Jesus and the Victory of God.* Minneapolis: Fortress, 1996.

In addition to these sources, we have also quoted from a number of individual issues of comic books published by Marvel Comics. These include issues from the following volumes:

Avengers vs. X-Men (2012)
Daredevil (1964)
Civil War II (2016)
Civil War II: Amazing Spider-Man (2016)
Civil War (2006)
Civil War (2015)
Captain America (1968)
Captain America: Sam Wilson (2015)
Captain America: Steve Rogers (2016)
Iron Man (2005)
House of M (2005)
Marvels (1994)
New Avengers (2005)
X-Men: Schism (2011)
Uncanny Avengers (2012)

Printed in Germany
by Amazon Distribution
GmbH, Leipzig